400 LOSERS

Delinquent Boys in High School

Winton M. Ahlstrom

and

Robert J. Havighurst

400 LOSERS

Jossey-Bass Inc., Publishers
615 Montgomery Street · San Francisco · 1971

400 LOSERS
Delinquent Boys in High School
              Winton M. Ahlstrom and Robert J. Havighurst

Copyright © 1971 by Jossey-Bass, Inc., Publishers

Jossey-Bass, Inc., Publishers
615 Montgomery Street
San Francisco, California 94111

Library of Congress Catalog Card Number 74-149914

International Standard Book Number ISBN 0-87589-084-9

Manufactured in the United States of America
              Composed and printed by York Composition Company, Inc.
              Bound by Chas. H. Bohn & Co., Inc.

JACKET DESIGN BY WILLI BAUM, SAN FRANCISCO

FIRST EDITION

Code 7103

The Jossey-Bass
Behavioral Science Series

General Editors

WILLIAM E. HENRY, *University of Chicago*

NEVITT SANFORD, *Wright Institute, Berkeley*

Preface

The report of a study of socially maladjusted boys in Kansas City, Missouri, *Four Hundred Losers* grew out of a series of discussions among James A. Hazlett, superintendent of schools in Kansas City; Homer C. Wadsworth, school board member and director of the Kansas City Association of Trusts and Foundations; staff members of the Ford Foundation; and Robert J. Havighurst of the University of Chicago, who had just completed a longitudinal study of adolescent youth in a typical midwestern community. The decision to operate a work-study program for socially maladjusted boys was a result of these conversations. The program was a joint project of the Kansas City Public Schools and the Kansas City Association of Trusts and Foundations, with the aid of funds from the Ford Foundation and the cooperation of the Institute for Community Studies of Kansas City.

The project was a carefully designed control group experiment with boys, starting at the eighth grade and continued through the high school age period. The experiment featured a work-experience program combined with a modified academic program. It was expected that the boys in the experimental work-study group would show better social adjustment and early adult competence than those in the control group, who remained in the regular high school program. The experiment showed that the work-experience program was related to improved social adjustment in some but not all of the boys in the experimental group. Clearly the problem of growing up to a competent early adulthood is so complex for these rather severely maladjusted boys that a work-experience program will not solve the problem for all such boys.

Four Hundred Losers reports the growing-up experience of these boys, carefully comparing the boys in the experimental group with the boys in the control group. Such close relations developed between the boys and the men and women engaged in the research project that the study was able to record intimate details of the lives of those boys, details which would never have been discovered in a more superficial study with the ordinary research instruments of social surveys. The principal value of the study is the insights obtained into the lives and experiences of boys—white and black—who seem destined to be losers in the game of growing up in a modern big city. *Four Hundred Losers* is addressed to people who want to understand better the experience of problem youth—educators, concerned citizens, social workers, counselors, and group workers.

The study required the active interest and support of the Kansas City Public Schools. It was essentially a project of these schools, with a research component for which funds were provided by the Kansas City Association of Trusts and Foundations and the Ford Foundation. The scientific direction was a responsibility of the Institute for Community Studies of Kansas City. A steering committee operated throughout the eight-year period of the study and consisted of the administrators named below, together with James A. Hazlett, superintendent of schools: Homer C. Wadsworth, executive director, Kansas City Association of Trusts and Foundations; Paul H. Bowman, director, Institute for Community Studies; Clyde J. Baer, director of research, Kansas City Public Schools; Robert J. Havighurst, professor of education and human development at the University of Chicago and research consultant for the project.

At the administrative level two directors—Bernard Greene for the first two and one-half years, followed by Ralph Berry, who remained until the program terminated—both brought to their roles as directors of the work-study project many years of background experience in working with high school youth in career development programs. Greene's commitment to the concept of meaningful educational and school experience for all youth was clearly expressed in his untiring efforts to find appropriate staff for the work-study program and to guide its implementation and direction toward program objectives. Berry, carrying on Greene's work, focused his energies on upgrading the quality and training aspects of work placement of boys in full-time jobs as they moved out of school into the world of work. He kept full records of the work experiences of the boys and wrote the major part of the chapter on work experience.

Needless to say the major contributions came from the teachers, work supervisors, and employment coordinators who worked directly with study group youth on a day-to-day basis. These school personnel —without additional compensation—were involved daily in the tough and often frustrating problem of finding ways of helping alienated urban adolescents grow up more satisfactorily. These men and women gave time and energy in face to face working with maladjusted boys. They also maintained a number of different records for the research staff, collected various kinds of data, and attended work-study staff meetings apart from their own regular duties and obligations (including hall, cafeteria, and playground monitoring and other extracurricular activities). We acknowledge with appreciation and respect the contributions of the following school personnel who participated in the work-study program. Teachers: Guy Burton, Margaret Cato, Kyle Conway, Joseph Grant, Maxine Grayson, Ellen McGinnis, Ruth Moore, Ray Naudet (served also as work supervisor), Grace Williams, Jerome Winegar, William H. Young. Work supervisors: Robert Beers, Lyle Forshee, Lewis Livingston, Luther Strickland. Employment coordinators: Clarence Stephenson (served also as work supervisor), Roger Moore, Jack Peter (served also as work supervisor). The academic program for this group of boys was created by Gordon Wesner, director for secondary curriculum, in summer workshops with classroom teachers.

Contributing to the efficiency of the operation of the program and to the research evaluation were the many special skills of the project secretary, Hazel Veering, who was with the program at the beginning and continued for the first three years. She organized the process of recording and storing multiple and cumulative data from various sources over the years, and she maintained current case-study folders on the four hundred study group boys. In addition to many other duties, she edited and typed interviews, manuscripts, and progress reports. To her we extend our most sincere appreciation.

In the program of research which began with the screening of seventh grade boys for the work-study program in 1960–1961, each of three junior research associates employed at different times in the program made special contributions. Thomas Moorefield, who was with the program at its inception, left after two years to continue his work toward a doctorate. His documentation of the screening process and other information relevant to the process of implementing a new program for disadvantaged youth in the public schools has been most helpful in delineating the dimensions of the problem. His careful supervision of the sampling for the second experimental group provided the base for a valid comparison of the experimental and control groups. Donald Joslin, the second junior research associate, made a most significant contribution through his skills in interviewing boys and their families. His interview data provide rich descriptions of the study group boys and are used frequently throughout this book. Joseph Herdler, the third junior research associate, focused upon the delinquency patterns of study group boys. The data he collected in this area provide the base for much of the arrest data used in the chapter on delinquency.

General direction of the research program was assumed by a senior research associate, of whom there were three at different times. For the first year the senior associate was Alvin W. Rose of the department of sociology at Wayne State University. When Rose departed on a Fulbright appointment for work in Africa, the senior position was assumed by Frederick Trost, from the faculty of the Western Oregon College of Education. Trost worked particularly with the interviewers. When he returned to his post in Oregon, the senior research associate post was filled by Winton M. Ahlstrom, who has been in charge of the research program since 1962.

Lastly, we recognize the contribution of those school administrators who accepted a new, untried school program for maladjusted youth in their schools and cooperated in attempting to make the program work. These principals were James F. Boyd of Central Senior, A. Leedy Campbell of Lincoln Junior, Jay Danielson of Northeast Junior, L. Clayton Dickson of East High School, Edward Fields of Central Junior, Harry I. Harwell of Lincoln Senior, M. W. McKenna of Northeast Senior, John Perry of West Junior, and C. O. Williams of East High School.

Kansas City, Missouri
Chicago
September 1970

WINTON M. AHLSTROM
ROBERT J. HAVIGHURST

Contents

400 LOSERS

Delinquent Boys in High School

PROLOGUE

An Approach to Delinquency

The two major groups of problem youth in American society today are from opposite ends of society. There are upper-middle-class youths who have been favored materially and who rebel at the way adults run society. There is also a perilously large group of socially disadvantaged youths whose difficulties are manifested in delinquency and in aimless search for excitement. The problems of ghetto and slum youth, while not as dramatic as those presented by the affluent young who preach and practice a way of life alien to the adult society which nurtured them, are chronic and pervasive signs that much is wrong in the way many urban disadvantaged children grow up.

The end of World War II marked the beginning of a great increase in juvenile delinquency. At the same time there began to be great emphasis on young people's staying in school, completing high school, and getting post–high school training to meet the challenges and opportunities of the new technological age. Vast amounts of money have been spent on studying the problems of delinquents and high school dropouts, and many experimental attempts to reduce both groups have been initiated. Yet in 1961, when the present study began, rates of delinquency were higher than ever before and were still increasing, and about one-third of those who began high school did not graduate.

1

During the 1960s the effort to combat this increasing tide of delinquency and to stem the dropout rate continued with even greater urgency. Large amounts of money were appropriated for programs and experiments which tried to provide meaningful experience for socially disadvantaged youths in school and in work in order to produce more satisfactory growth and thus less need to resort to delinquency or to dropping out of school. Work experience and remedial education programs were initiated in high schools to keep the delinquent or potential delinquent in school or to give him opportunities for work experience outside school where he could meet with success not experienced in school. Other programs provided counseling, guidance, and social work assistance to young people in trouble and to their families.

By 1969 it was apparent that all these efforts and expenditures of money had remarkably little effect. Rates of delinquency have risen and new forms have appeared. Some of these, such as disruptive and destructive protest movements, occur almost exclusively among middle-class and upper-middle-class youth. Vandalism and drug use are on the increase and are found among all segments of youth. The incidence of burglary, robbery, larceny, and other activities clearly defined as juvenile crime continues to be much higher among urban inner-city youth, as is the incidence of early school-leaving. It is in urban areas that the greatest efforts have been made to reduce delinquency and dropping out and that failure to accomplish these aims has been most clearly evident.

That the task is difficult, complex, and discouraging is indicated by a recent study in Washington, D.C. This fairly costly project was financed partly by the Public Welfare Foundation of Washington, and mainly by the United States Office of Education.[1] It extended for three years, from June 1964 to June 1967. The purpose of the project was to work with delinquent dropouts to prepare them for passing the high school equivalency test, getting meaningful employment, and earning a living through legitimate means. The subjects were Negro youths between sixteen and twenty-one from the slum areas of Washington, D.C. Ten subjects were brought into the project in June, 1964,

---

[1] C. R. Jeffery and I. A. Jeffery, "Dropouts and Delinquents: An Experimental Program in Behavior Change," *Education and Urban Society*, 1969, *1*, 325–336.

and an additional forty subjects were admitted after September, 1965, under the Office of Education grant.

The boys and girls were paid twenty to forty dollars a week for coming to the center, studying, passing tests, and working at jobs in connection with the center. During the three years, the project made contact with 167 youths, of whom 25 per cent remained to the end, 43 per cent dropped out, and 32 per cent remained only one day. At the end of the project twenty-two students took the high school equivalency test given by the board of education and thirteen passed. There was no relation between passing the test and number of weeks in the program or units of programed study completed. Students generally cheated on the teaching machines; they abused staff members verbally but not physically. They broke into the center at night and stole clocks, tables, clothing, purses, cameras, and a television set. The longer a student stayed in the project, the higher were his chances of being arrested for delinquency. This study, like many others which show negative results, attempted to work with older adolescent hard-core delinquents, already high school dropouts. Failure to recognize the significance of the delinquent role for these youths and the developmental characteristics associated with it has led to much frustration in attempting to provide experience which will allow such youths to grow up in more acceptable ways.

Careful observers and students of the delinquency problem see the delinquency of many disadvantaged youths as a more or less natural aspect of growing up in the modern postindustrial society which does not provide functional roles for them. Most early high school dropouts, including the most seriously socially maladjusted ones, are found among out-of-school and unemployed youths living in slum areas. It is estimated that of the approximately 30 per cent of youth who drop out, about one-half manifest serious social maladjustment. This 15 per cent of the total high school age group contributes disproportionately to the rising rate of delinquency and social deviancy. It is this group of boys who are most seriously limited in fitting into the social and occupational structure of today's world. They cannot use the school to achieve adulthood. They do not develop attitudes and work habits essential to successful work careers. Unable to grow up in the way society approves, they become misfits in school and in the larger community. Such youths deal with their frustrations and tensions in ways which do not offend their values or the values of the subculture in which they develop. This is a natural outcome of these boys' circumstances and of the way they experience life.

Although efforts to help such youths grow up more satisfactorily have largely been unsuccessful, experiences during the fifties and sixties have taught us that there are no simple solutions to the problem, just as there are no simple explanations of it. For example, the broken family in an urban slum area may bear a strong statistical relationship to delinquency, but one good parent is better for a child than two bad parents. The general consensus now, after years of study, is that the problem of juvenile delinquency and social maladjustment must be approached from several different but related directions. We must work on those social situations which seem to give impetus to the development of delinquent behavior and social maladjustment. The total socioeconomic setting of the low-income and racially segregated ghetto family is the focus of concern at one level; so are family relationships. The school situation and the neighborhood or street-corner environment are other areas.

Another area, the work and employment situation, became the focus of much interest and concern during the 1960s. There were several reasons for this. Many more youths in urban centers became old enough to drop out of school during this period, while at the same time there were fewer jobs for unskilled high school dropouts, particularly those from minority groups. Out-of-school, unemployed young people in ghetto communities were the "social dynamite" Conant[2] had identified at the beginning of the 1960s. Additionally, there was increasing emphasis on the need for society to provide a social role for the non-academically-oriented young person. The concept of the juvenile work role was being discussed, and some were proposing that this role, which had been an integral part of the social-occupational structure in the early 1900s, be recreated today.

However, the published results of work experience experiments with the socially maladjusted during the 1960s have not been promising. A few, like the Jeffery study, have indicated complete failure. It must be noted that most studies of this kind have involved hard-core problem youths who at age sixteen or older had already dropped out of school and had long histories of juvenile delinquency. Published

[2] J. B. Conant, "Social Dynamite in Our Large Cities." Speech before the Conference on Unemployed, Out-of-School Youth in Urban Areas, Washington, D.C., May 1961.

reports show few programs which appear to have made any inroads on the delinquency and social maladjustment of these youths.

The study reported in this book also focused on work experience as an experimental variable. The target group was thirteen- and fourteen-year-old boys screened in 1961 and 1962 as socially and educationally maladjusted from among all seventh grade inner-city classrooms in Kansas City, Missouri public schools. The ratio of Negro to white youths was three to two. The boys were divided into experimental and control groups. Experimental boys, beginning in the eighth grade, received special attention through half days of classroom work geared to their abilities and their assumed needs, interests, and personal orientations and half days of supervised work experience; these boys had their own teachers and work supervisors. Control group boys were enrolled in regular school programs and their progress was followed. The study was longitudinal and complete records were maintained on the school, work, community, and family adjustment of the boys, both while they were in school and up to the age of eighteen or nineteen. Work experience, as the independent variable, included three different developmental stages involving different kinds of work experience, supervision-guidance, and rewards.

The findings, reported in detail in this book, indicate that only about one-fourth of the boys profited from the Work-Study Program. Thus, this study, using work experience as a variable in an experimental design involving predelinquent thirteen and fourteen year old boys at the beginning, failed to demonstrate that supervised work experience, even under relatively controlled conditions, could be useful in materially reducing delinquency among youth so disposed. However, because of its longitudinal design, the study permitted us to do more than merely identify successful or unsuccessful adolescents among the study group. Following the boys into their eighteenth and nineteenth years made it possible to identify five different types of late adolescent adjustments. Our accumulated information about these boys over the six years of their early and middle adolescence made it possible to study the life circumstances and conditions associated with these five patterns. This book, then, while reporting specific experimental findings, is mostly concerned with describing the life context within which successful and unsuccessful adaptations emerge in late adolescence. It is hoped the study helped us to better understand the problems inner-city youths face as they attempt to find their way through adolescence into manhood.

1

Identity Achievement for Maladjusted Boys

Adolescence is a search for adult identity. Often it is not as much a self-conscious, systematic exploration as it is a blind groping for something the adolescent boy cannot clearly define. But the dominant motive of adolescent behavior is the desire to grow up and be a man. In simpler societies, including our own society before 1930, the boy in search of identity learned to do the work of a man and to grow up sexually as a man. There was plenty of work for a boy to do. He could quit school at fourteen or sixteen and graduate through a series of jobs to a man's estate by the age of eighteen or twenty.

That has all been changed. Society has become urban; technology has become automated and cybernated; knowledge of the kind learned in school and college has become the foremost qualification for the worker's role. We live in a knowledge-transacting society. Knowledge, more than anything else, gives the growing youth access to his goal of identity achievement. The knowledge level signified by a high school diploma is coming more and more to be a requirement for an adult job. This puts the high school dropout at a serious disadvantage. As late as the 1920s he could get a variety of jobs and, through juvenile work experience, obtain the skills necessary for moving into an adult work role. In the early 1960s, however, one in four high school dropouts aged sixteen to twenty-four was unemployed, in contrast to one in eight high school graduates of the same age.

Some dropouts make good. There is still unskilled work to do, and much of this work is available to juveniles. On the basis of several community studies of young men and on the basis of unemployment data, it appears that roughly half the boys who drop out of high school make a fairly satisfactory work adjustment. The problem, however, is intensified in large cities where ethnic minorities are crowded into slums. A survey in the early 1960s of eighteen major American cities revealed a large labor surplus in three-quarters of them. A study of the employment status of a sample of youths sixteen to twenty-four years old residing in several slum areas found the number of unemployed to range from 40 per cent to a high of 70 per cent in a Negro slum. Such youths are handicapped by lack of social and mental skills enabling them to use school as an avenue toward adulthood and by lack of basic positive attitudes toward work and the work role stemming from their subcultural pattern of life with its limited opportunities for achieving identity as a worker.

The handicap is significant and pervasive for the disadvantaged when work-role identity is viewed as a developmental process dependent first on early childhood experiences in the primary family and then later on experiences in school and the community. Three stages of vocational development are important and probably necessary in the achievement of the adult worker role: The first is identifying with a worker, who may be the father, mother, or other significant person. In this stage the concept of working becomes an essential part of the ego ideal. The second stage is acquiring the basic habits of industry, learning to organize time and energy to complete tasks—school work or chores—and learning to put work ahead of play in appropriate situations. The third stage, acquiring identity as a worker, includes choosing and preparing for an occupation and getting work experience as a basis for occupational choice and for assurance of economic independence.

These stages are significantly limited for many disadvantaged youths. In the Kansas City study the focus was on inner-city seventh grade boys who showed signs of major lacks in the first two stages and thus appeared headed for difficulty in achieving masculine identity. This target group was representative of the 10 or 15 per cent of boys from working-class families in low-income urban areas who begin showing signs of serious maladjustment to school and society by thirteen or fourteen years of age.

The Work-Study Program we developed for these boys was based on four simple—overly simple, as it turned out—propositions. First, in the eighth grade there is a visible subgroup of boys who are maladjusted to school and will almost certainly drop out when they reach the end of compulsory schooling. Second, these boys would do better in school if they had a program that helped them achieve worker identities. Third, with such a program they would make better adjustments to school and would show less delinquency. Fourth, with such a program they would be better workers at the age of sixteen or eighteen and would be able to fill the adult worker role successfully.

The Kansas City program was a sequel to one begun a decade earlier in a midwestern city, which involved one thousand school children.[1] In that study it was found that about 15 per cent of the high school age population, or about one-third to one-fourth of boys from working-class families, composed about half the high school dropouts and about 90 per cent of juvenile delinquents. It was discovered in following these boys through adolescence into young adulthood that many could not use regular school in growing up and that society offered no alternative pathways to growth. Failing in school, most of these youths dropped out before completing the tenth grade and before they had met even the minimal educational requirements for entering the labor market. Aimless and drifting, many of these youths got into trouble with the police, and most appeared to be heading for marginal social and economic status as adults. It was for boys such as these that the Kansas City Work-Study Program was specifically developed.

Essentially the program was designed to hold boys in school longer and to reduce the incidence of social maladjustment among them by providing, through the eighth, ninth, and tenth grades, half days of supervised and graduated work experience and half days of academic work geared to ability, interests, and needs. The intent was to provide opportunities for the kinds of experiences believed important for work-role identity, particularly those in the last two stages of the vocational development process. These kinds of opportunities were known to be seriously limited for target group boys.

[1] R. J. Havighurst and others, *Growing Up in River City* (New York: Wiley, 1962).

In the half day of classroom study, small classes were instituted to permit more individualized instruction in a less competitive setting than regular school programs. The focus was on improving language and other mental skills and on learning about the world of work and the larger society. In the half day of work experience, the focus was on improving work habits and work attitudes, developing self-reliance, and, in general, preparing boys for adult work roles through supervised juvenile work experience.

The Work-Study Program included three stages. In Stage One, beginning in the eighth grade when boys were thirteen or fourteen years old, they worked half of each school day in group work under the supervision of work supervisors, men who knew how to use tools, could manage difficult boys, and could serve as models for the boys.

They attended a special study class the other half day. This first stage included various group work projects around the schools and in the community, for which the boys received token pay of a dollar a week. The focus was on learning to work with others, following instructions, using and caring for tools, and developing good work habits and attitudes. In short, Stage One was designed to develop a work orientation which would permit boys about fifteen years of age to move into Stage Two, part-time paid employment with private employers, while continuing the half day of classroom study. In Stage Two, a full-time employment coordinator sought out and developed job openings in the community, assisted boys in finding suitable work, helped them with adjustment problems, and observed and recorded their progress. The boys continued to spend half days in school.

In Stage Three, boys moved out of school completely, into full-time work in the community. This stage extended through the seventeenth and eighteenth years or even longer, during which time the employment coordinator worked closely with the boys, observing and recording progress and problems as entry was made into the adult world of work. At the termination of Stage Three, boys who remained in the program received high school certificates, authorized by the board of education, certifying that they had successfully participated in a program of supervised and graded work experience sponsored by the Kansas City, Missouri public schools.

A unique feature of the Kansas City Work-Study Program was its experimental research design. This included multiple criteria and a validated procedure for identifying the target group, a procedure adapted with slight modifications from one developed in the "River City" study.[2] It also included the use of control and experimental groups for assessing, over several adolescent years, the effects of the Work-Study Program on behavior and attitudes of participating boys. The two major hypotheses were that boys vulnerable to delinquency will become less delinquent if they have a systematic work experience, commencing as early as age thirteen or fourteen and continuing until they reach seventeen or eighteen, and that such boys will remain longer in the organized school setting if such a program is part of the curriculum than will similar boys in the regular high school curriculum.

Screening for the program began in the spring of 1961 for Group One and in the spring of 1962 for Group Two. Seventh grade boys in low-income areas in Kansas City were studied through examination of their cumulative record folders, through a rating scale (Behavior Description Chart) filled out by their teachers, and through a sociometric instrument (Who Are They) administered to their classmates. (See Appendix A for screening measures.)

Four hundred boys[3] were selected from the seventh grades of inner-city schools, approximately half in the spring of 1961 and half in the spring of 1962. Each youth selected had to meet the multiple criteria of average or below average (but not retarded) intelligence, above average aggressive maladjustment scores on peers' and teachers' ratings, and below average classroom achievement in the sixth and seventh grades. The first group was 60 per cent Negro and 40 per cent white; in the second group a more equal racial balance was obtained. The boys were divided into control and experimental groups. Control boys were placed in regular junior high school programs and their progress was followed without intervention. The experimental group beginning the program in September 1961 contained four inner-city school subgroups. The second experimental group, beginning a year later, contained five. At the time the boys entered the eighth grade the median age was thirteen and one half.

The screening of the first group in 1961 and experiences during

---

[2] Havighurst and others, *op. cit.*

[3] Four hundred twenty-two boys were initially screened, but there was an initial attrition rate which reduced the study group to four hundred boys. Not all data were available in each assessment area for the total group screened, hence numbers of subjects in tables vary somewhat.

the first year provided the basis for modifying screening and operational procedures for Group Two a year later. In Group One, experimental and control groups were formed by a matching procedure. Additional information collected during the first year indicated that the experimental group included more seriously maladjusted boys than did the controls. Additionally, an upper age limit was not established for Group One, so that a number of boys already age fifteen were included. It was apparent the first year that these older, more sophisticated boys were the source of much disruption in experimental groups. The screening of Group Two boys included an upper age cut-off point and the formation of experimental and control groups based on a random sampling procedure which resulted in much more comparable groups.

There was one difference in the selection of both experimental groups that we felt might have some effect on later comparison studies. This was that all experimental boys had been given permission by their parents to enroll in a work experience program which did not include a high school diploma. Thus, these parents, in a sense, agreed with the screening information that their boys were having difficulty in school and would probably drop out of high school. However, not all parents asked for consent agreed that this was the situation, and some refused permission. Of 235 parents asked, 47 (28 and 19 in Groups One and Two) refused permission. Their sons were designated control nonconsent subgroups and enrolled in regular high school to be studied independently of the larger control group. However, since parents of the larger control group were not informed of the Work-Study Program and were not asked to make a decision concerning a high school program not leading to graduation, it was considered likely that within this larger control group there was also a nonconsent subgroup. It was assumed that its size would correspond to that among parents whose consents were requested. Such a subgroup was considered statistically in comparison studies of experimental and control groups.

The Kansas City, Missouri School District served about 30 per cent of the school children in a metropolitan area with a 1963 population of about 1,200,000. Enrollment in the school district in 1963 was 73,000. This included about 75 per cent of the low-income population of the metropolitan area and was 36 per cent Negro. The junior and senior high schools reflected the socioeconomic and racial composition of the areas they served. In the ten senior high schools in 1959 the proportion of the senior class going on to college varied from 18 to 83 per cent.

The experimental and control groups were selected from the five lowest status junior high schools. Two of them were almost entirely Negro; one was all white; one was almost entirely white, with a Mexican-American minority and a small Negro group; the fifth was about 95 per cent white. During the years of the experiment, 1961–67, the high schools became more and more overcrowded. Classroom space was at a premium, although none of the schools was on a double shift. Only one school had enough space to provide the Work-Study group with a classroom that was not overcrowded. The problem of space was so acute in three of the senior high schools that it had a major effect on the attitude of the school principals toward the project.

The four hundred boys in the control and experimental groups constituted 12 to 14 per cent of the boys in the eighth grades of the schools where the survey took place. These, in turn, constituted roughly the lower half, in socioeconomic status, of the eighth grade enrollment in the district. It is safe to say that the total Work-Study experiment, both experimental and control groups, involved 6 or 7 per cent of the boys in the eighth grade, and that these came from the 7 or 8 per cent most maladjusted boys in the school system. The schools which were not served were of higher socioeconomic status and had much less school maladjustment of the kind we studied.

The research program had a longitudinal design including collection of various kinds of social-psychological data over a six-year period. These data fell into two major classes, community-based data from institutions serving or involved with children and their families, including the school, the police, the juvenile court, and welfare agencies, and individual-based data from the boys and members of their families, particularly their parents. (See Appendix B for detailed description of community sources of information, measures employed, and records and descriptive materials maintained on each boy.) While the testing of experimental hypotheses employing such data was one concern, our major attention was given to setting up a system for collecting and evaluating a wide variety of information relevant to better understanding the world of school, work, family, and community life experienced by socially maladjusted boys during adolescence.

Much information about the boys and their families came from the boys and parents themselves in four sets of interviews extending over the six years of the study. The first series, in 1961 and 1962 for Groups One and Two respectively, were during the summers after the youths were identified as the target group. (See Appendix B.) This initial interview with the parents of all boys took place in the homes and included both structured and semistructured sections. One section included questions about family structure and organization, type of home, and the neighborhood. Another section was designed to obtain the information necessary for developing delinquency prediction and family cohesiveness scores based on Glueck and Glueck parent-child and family relationship factors.[4] The interviewers were home-school coordinators with experience with inner-city youth and their families. Prior to interviewing they attended a workshop where the nature of the interview desired, interview techniques, and recording procedures were reviewed and discussed.

Another interview with the parents of both experimental and control youth was made when most of the boys were about sixteen years old. One purpose of this interview was to obtain information about any changes in family structure and organization, living conditions, and other circumstances since the initial interview. Another purpose was to provide information about family relationships, parents' attitudes and feelings toward their children and their future, and parents' attitudes toward the school and toward their children's education. In substance, this second interview was to identify the social-psychological conditions and circumstances which characterized the boys' family lives and relationships just prior to the time they would be legally able to drop out of school.

Two sets of adolescent interviews with experimental and control boys were obtained, the first when they were about sixteen years of age, the second in late adolescence when most were about eighteen years of age. These interviews were to obtain information concerning boys' attitudes toward parents, work, school, police, society, the future, girls, peers, and, for experimental youth, the Work-Study Program. In the first adolescent interview, when most boys were still in school, they were asked about their immediate school situations, their reasons for considering dropping out or staying in school, and any contingency factors which they saw as likely to influence their decisions. In the sec-

---

[4] S. Glueck and E. Gueck, *Unraveling Juvenile Delinquency* (Cambridge, Massachusetts: Harvard University Press, 1950), pp. 260–262.

ond interview, similar questions were asked of boys still in school. Those who had dropped out were asked why they had left school, how they felt about their school experience, what problems they had encountered there, and how they felt school could have been better for them. In the second interview, emphasis was placed on obtaining an account of work experience, particularly for boys out of school.

In the first series of adolescent interviews, difficulty in locating boys after school required that most interviews take place during the school day. Counselors' offices, empty classrooms, corners of auditoriums and school cafeterias, and frequently even the interviewers' parked cars were used. Although the school setting seemed a handicap in some instances, the interviewers were selected for their experience, interest in, and ability to work with inner-city youth, and in most cases they were able to develop rapport and obtain desired information. Because some of the boys were relatively noncommittal and many were nonverbal in communicating with adults, it was found most fruitful to maintain the interview on an informal, conversational level.

By the time the second series of interviews got under way, most boys were high school dropouts. Interviews were made wherever the boys could be located—in the boys' homes, in interviewers' cars, and on street corners. Most of these interviews were made by a research associate, as were the second interviews with parents. This increased the information yield as well as the consistency of quality in the interviews.

By the time the experiment was half-finished, it was clear that our research hypotheses were too simple. Youths who were carefully identified in the seventh grade as similar in mental development and social and educational maladjustment in fact showed differences in their adolescent patterns of response to school and to the Work-Study experiment. They also showed differences in adjustments to community and family life. One subgroup of midadolescent boys appeared to be profiting from their work experience. Another subgroup showed some signs of adapting to school, although with little evident progress in academic achievement. A large number of boys showed various degrees of maladjustment both at school and in the community. Although there were erratic and changing patterns of adjustment among the study group during this midadolescent period, these were the general types of subgroup adaptations.

During the final two years of the study, when most boys were seventeen to nineteen years old, an assessment of each individual's adjustment patterns, independent of any earlier assessment, was made. (See Appendix C for criteria and data employed in assessing late adolescent adjustment.) Only adjustment data collected during this period were used in identifying boys as falling into adjustment subgroups.

Youths in the work adaptive subgroup showed ability to get and hold jobs, and boys in this category were rated by their employment coordinators as showing real progress in moving toward adult work-role identity. Involvement with police was minimal, although a few youths had records of frequent traffic violations and a few had one or two arrests for misdemeanors such as drinking in public, fighting, or disorderly conduct. In the main, however, this subgroup appeared to be relatively free of serious socially maladaptive behaviors during late adolescence.

Youths in the school adaptive subgroup either were in school and showing signs of staying in and adapting sufficiently to meet at least minimal requirements for a high school diploma or certificate of attendance, or had graduated during adolescence. While most in this group achieved at minimal academic levels, they managed to stay in school and achieve success in certain school experiences. A few showed successful adaptation to both the instrumental and the expressive cultures of high school (primarily in athletics). (The instrumental culture is the academic area, where the major business is teaching students subject matter necessary for achieving higher educational levels or for entry into careers. The expressive culture consists of the games, plays, sports, peer group associations, and spontaneous fun and nonsense activities outside the classroom whose purpose is the enjoyment and excitement of the activities without concern for their significance for future achievements.) Among school adaptive youths, traffic violations were the major contacts with police in late adolescence.

Youths who showed both adaptive and maladaptive behaviors in school, work, or community life were identified as the erratic subgroup. Some of these youths were still in school and showed some progress at times but were in frequent difficulty with the police and sometimes with school authority. Some boys showed ability to find jobs and to do satisfactory work for a while, but were involved in various delinquent pursuits outside work which created problems on the job through absences for frequent court hearings. Although these youth showed ability to adapt successfully in certain situations and under

certain conditions for periods of time, such periods were interspersed
with periods of seriously maladaptive behavior indicating conflicting
values and needs or situational or emotional stress. For a few boys the
problem seemed to be that subcultural life styles conflicted with the
expectations of the larger society.

Boys who had dropped out of high school, were out of work,
or had held only very few menial part-time jobs and who showed little
initiative in seeking employment were identified as the marginal subgroup. Some of these boys were in frequent trouble with the police,
but mainly for misdemeanors such as drinking in public, disorderly
conduct, or fighting. Some spent time at the county farm or in the
city jail. The predominant characteristic of this group was a kind of
aimless drifting without apparently much thought of the future or even
of their current life situation.

Youths in the seriously maladaptive subgroup were clearly
identified by their arrest records for serious offenses and their commitments to correctional institutions. They were recidivists; only a few
had held jobs, and these were for brief periods of time. All in this
group had dropped out of high school. These boys appeared to be
hard-core delinquents whose values and way of life differed most from
those of the larger society. Of the total group of four hundred youths,
15 per cent were not assigned to late adolescent adjustment categories
because information about them was considered inadequate. The distribution of the five types of late adolescent adjustment among the
study group is summarized in Table 1.

Table 1. LATE ADOLESCENT ADJUSTMENT

Race	Total Number Identified	Serious Maladap.	Marginal	Erratic	Work Adaptive	School Adaptive
			Per Cent			
Negro	202	28	16	17	15	24
White	139	13	15	21	31	20

2

The Community

Most of the 422 boys identified for the study grew up in Kansas City, Missouri, a midwestern metropolis with a population of approximately 500,000 in 1960. The city is primarily a distribution and agricultural center and is almost in the center of the United States. During 1959, 1960, and 1961, the years when study group boys were identified as likely to become marginal unskilled adults, Kansas City's unemployment rate was relatively high compared with national rates. The percentage of unemployed, mostly unskilled workers, varied from 6.6 to 7.8, in contrast to the national average of 5.5 per cent. Part of Kansas City's high rate was due to occupational dislocation caused by reduction of livestock operations, part was due to automation. The result was a general decrease in demand for unskilled labor. These factors particularly affected young, inexperienced workers, but older Kansas Citians were also dislocated from semiskilled jobs which were becoming obsolete.

As in other large cities, there was an increase in the number of people coming into the urban center to live and work. The pace accelerated following World War II, and from 1940 to 1960 the population of Kansas City increased 50 per cent. The most significant features of this increased population were its racial composition and the marked change in racial characteristics of neighborhoods as increasing numbers of white residents moved to areas further south or into the suburbs.

17

In 1940, Negroes were only 11 per cent of the city's population, and most of them lived in congested, segregated residential-business areas in the old North Central city district. By 1960, Negroes composed 18 per cent of the population. The old core city still remained a congested segregated Negro community, and city areas further south and southeast, predominantly white in the 1940s and 1950s, had become predominantly Negro. The trend is most clearly seen when the 1950 and 1960 racial compositions of schools in the area are contrasted; schools formerly completely white had become completely Negro. This process was not steady or continuous. In certain parts of the old central city to the northeast and northwest there were minimal movements of white people and for the most part these communities remained segregated and white in 1960. Thus, in 1960, Kansas City was beginning to feel the impact of changing technology, increasing population, and changing racial and socioeconomic situations. Although problems were not as vast as those confronting larger metropolitan centers with massive ghetto and slum populations, there were clearly recognized problems and portents of problems to come.

For a considerable proportion of Kansas Citians, however, 1960 was a relatively prosperous year. The economic status of citizens and the level of business and industrial activity appeared healthy, and plans for future development seemed promising. In spite of relatively high unemployment, half the city's families in 1960 had incomes of $6,500 or more in contrast to the national average of $6,200. Seventeen per cent of Kansas City families had incomes of $10,000 or more. For these citizens, most of whom lived in new residential communities far from the old central city, Kansas City was a community of spacious, well-tended homes with two-car garages, green lawns, wide, tree-lined avenues and parkways, schools with ample space, beautiful parks, fountains and plazas, and large modern shopping centers.

The slum and low-income areas were located, as in most large cities, in the old, central sections of town. After World War II, a great influx of people from rural and impoverished backgrounds entered these inner-city areas. During the 1940s and 1950s, the congested core neighborhoods, impelled by the mass of new people, began to extend their boundaries into adjacent lower-middle-class and middle-class neighborhoods. After the exodus of whites, these areas were filled by a variety of people, mostly from minority groups and generally less affluent than the previous residents. By 1960 the increased percentage of socially disadvantaged families was clearly visible. About 75 per cent of all such families among metropolitan Kansas City's one million people were among the half million population of the city itself. The largest proportion of these families were further concentrated in five of the city's ten school districts, located in or adjacent to the old parts of the city. These five school districts together defined the geographical areas of the inner city where the study group boys lived in 1960.

The 65,000 families living in these five districts composed approximately 60 per cent of the city's population. One-fourth of these families existed on three thousand dollars or less, and one-fifth of the 30,000 children age eighteen or younger growing up here lived with only one parent, in 90 per cent of the cases the mother. Half the adults had completed the ninth grade, but one in three had less than an eighth grade education, and one in four was employed in unskilled or semiskilled work. Police records were twice as frequent among the adult population as among adults in the city as a whole, and delinquency and high school dropout rates were almost twice as high as that found among youths in other areas of the city. The five districts did not contribute equally to the proportion of socially disadvanaged people. Some communities were relatively homogeneous in unfavorable socioeconomic conditions and characteristics of families. Others were much more heterogeneous, with a wider range of socioeconomic levels and life styles evident among residents.

The West Side and North Central areas of the city came closer to being ghettoes in 1961 than did any other parts of the inner city. The West Side was once an area of fine homes for the city's elite, but since about the turn of the century it has been a residential section inhabited by low-income families and some transient and itinerant workers. Racially, it is the most mixed of the five inner-city areas in the study, with Negro, Mexican, and white families in close proximity although for the most part in segregated neighborhoods.

On the West Side more people live on less land than anywhere else in the city, in dwellings which rank among the most inadequate in the inner city. Many families live in small frame houses built on the steep hill which leads to the West Bluffs, once called "tin can hill" because of the shacks housing impoverished immigrants. Housing here was still substandard in 1961. At the top of the hill some families live in old, brick apartment buildings and some in what were once stately homes, now converted to low-rent rooming houses and apartments.

The highways which run through and along the southwest boundary of the West Side tend to fragment communities in this area, as does the topography with its steep hills and dead-end streets running perpendicular to the bluffs and terminating at the edge. Racial and cultural differences also isolate neighborhoods; Mexican, Negro, and white residents tend to stay in their own neighborhoods. Thus, a minimum of organized community action or planning for civic improvement characterized the West Side during the 1950s. Of all areas in the city, this district had the highest recorded incidence of repeated delinquenecy among young people.

During the 1950s the population of the West Side remained relatively stable. In 1960 about 70 per cent of the people were white, about 5 per cent were Negro, and about 25 per cent were Mexican-Americans in one of the oldest ethnic settlements in Kansas City. The Negro population here had increased slightly in the middle of the 1950s when Negro mothers with families moved into a housing project, but little in-migration of other Negro families had occurred.

Although there were parks and play areas on the West Side, their use was limited by lack of recreation personnel. In the summer, when supervised recreation was provided by the city, many West Side children participated. However, when unsupervised the play areas were often dominated by a few older, aggressive youths whom other children were reluctant to challenge. Some youths also had to cross hostile territory to reach play areas and, rather than risk being beaten up, they stayed away. A community center, a Salvation Army center, and a center primarily for Mexican children were operating in 1961. Although they were favorably accepted by the community, lack of facilities and qualified personnel for these organizations seriously limited the numbers of West Side children and families they could serve.

In 1961, fifty-five of the boys in the target group lived in West Side communities. Forty-two of them lived in three of the West Side's twelve census tract areas. These three areas were among Kansas City's most blighted communities. Shortly after the boys were identified as seventh grade school misfits, interviewers visited the families in their homes and recorded the physical conditions of the home and surrounding neighborhood. The examples given are representative of the different kinds of living conditions found among the West Side target group.

In 1961, B, his parents, and seven brothers and sisters lived in what had once been one of many elegant mansions gracing the West Side's quality residential section in the 1890s and early 1900s. Most of the mansions had been demolished, but a few had been remodeled into rental property. The building where B lived little resembled the stately mansion it had been, although a grand staircase swept majestically up to the second floor. The staircase was now badly cracked and splintered and the banister and steps bore many carved messages and doodlings. The steps and the second floor hallway were littered with cans, trash, garbage, and an odd assortment of broken toys and games. On the second floor lived three other large families, all sharing with B's family the only bathroom, which opened off the hall. The apartment B and his family occupied consisted of four rooms which were of necessity filled with beds for the ten occupants; there was little other furniture. The apartment was entered through the kitchen, a small room filled with dirty dishes, sacks of garbage, tin cans, and bottles lying on greasy linoleum.

The apartment had a small glassed-in back porch which would have been a nice play area for B's smaller brothers and sisters, except that it opened onto an unprotected, old, and unsafe wooden fire stair. In any case, there was little room to play because of broken appliances lying about, including a washing machine with its parts strewn on the floor. Outside in the yard there was only packed earth, barren of vegetation because of the many children and dogs who constantly played there.

C, a West Side Negro boy, lived several blocks from B. His family of six had a seven-room apartment in one of several two-story brick apartment buildings of a housing project. His mother, widowed and unemployed, received Aid to Dependent Children (ADC) of less than three thousand dollars a year and paid about six hundred dollars a year for rent. The family had lived in the project almost four years. Although the interior was of plain painted cement blocks, it was evident that efforts had been made to create an attractive, livable home. Furniture, although somewhat sparse, consisted of a chair, a sofa, and a TV set in the living room, all in good repair and neatly arranged. Lace curtains, freshly laundered and ironed, were at the windows. The linoleum floor was spotlessly clean, as were the walls. There was no debris on the floor, although five young people under eighteen lived in the apartment. The kitchen, also spotlessly clean, was most adequately furnished with modern appliances and a small breakfast table.

C's mother acknowledged the improvement in her family's living conditions from four years before but voiced concern about the West Side and its isolation, particularly for Negro boys. She saw the problem mainly as one of "nothing for young boys and girls to do," and "not enough chance for boys to have the guidance of or association with adult men."

D's home was on a street where small frame houses on narrow lots predominated. Most people rented their homes, but there were a few homeowners who had bought property many years before or who were second-generation Americans whose immigrant parents had settled in the area. Although there were notable exceptions, most of the small houses were old and needed extensive repair. Some appeared structurally unsound and unhealthy. The house D and his family lived in was one of these. The interviewer graphically described the home and its effect on him.

> The first thing I noticed as I walked toward the house was a distinct sewer odor. I saw a small stream of water running across the walk. The mother told me this was due to water seepage from a clogged or broken sewer, commenting, "we have a back-up in the basement quite often, but if we're careful it drains out." The home was scantily and drably furnished. A divan covered by an army blanket, a table, and an ironing board were the sole contents of the living room. In the dining room there were a few chairs and a small table. The floor was partially covered by a beige shag rug, badly soiled by food and drink. Scattered about the living room floor were papers, drinking cups, and playing cards. As I sat talking to the mother, I could see small bugs crawling in and out of the loops in the rugs. Cockroaches crawled across the floor and climbed the walls. Plaster had fallen out of several places in the walls, and signs of further deterioration were evidenced by the very noticeable cracks in the other areas. The windows were dirty and covered by broken and torn venetian blinds. Two strips of colored plastic hung over them. The sole wall decoration in the living room was a large felt hanging of the "last supper."

Such dwellings were not uncommon on the West Side. R also lived in this community, but his home was atypical. It sat on a narrow lot as did other houses here, but it was larger than most, consisting of two stories and eight rooms. R, a second generation Mexican-American, lived with his five brothers and sisters and his parents who had begun buying the home several years before. The green asbestos exterior siding was in excellent condition and the front porch had a new concrete floor and wrought-iron railing. The small yard was uncluttered, although there was no grass because the area was the principal playground for young children. Inside, the home was furnished comfortably with furniture which was somewhat old but very clean and in good repair. Everywhere there were signs of efforts to maintain a comfortable, orderly, and clean home. This was one of the few West Side families interviewed who seemed to have ample room for living and for privacy when desired. R had his own room, as did an older brother. The very adequate state of repair of this one-family dwelling contrasted sharply with the deterioration of surrounding houses.

Living conditions among the fifty-five boys living on the West Side in 1961 varied between the extreme congestion, dirt, and disorganization of the homes of B and D and the ample space, comfort, and cleanliness of R's home and, to some extent, C's home. Despite such differences in family dwellings, most of the fifty-five boys had similar exposure, outside the home, to social and cultural forces and experiences associated with blighted communities. For example, in the communities where most of the West Side target group lived, the population density was more than twice the average for the city as a whole. These extremely congested conditions exposed children to many adults, adolescents, and other children outside the primary family group. In these communities the proportion of relatively marginal adults and adolescents was higher than anywhere else except for certain North Central communities.

Almost half the adult males had less than an eighth grade education, and one in three worked at menial, unskilled jobs with little opportunity for advancement. However, this West Side working class was a fairly stable group, and when work was available their unemployment rate was relatively low. West Side youths of high school age, following adult patterns, typically dropped out of school as soon as possible. This was usually when they became sixteen or upon completion of the ninth or tenth grade in the West Side's junior high school. Adult expectations reinforced this dropout pattern as did the absence of a four-year senior high school in the area. Out of school, many of these teen-age youths were without jobs, and in a typical year one in four would have some kind of contact with police. While there were no well-structured gangs, there was one group formed by Mexican boys chiefly for protection of members and the defense of certain turfs. This group was not particularly known for its aggressiveness, although it sometimes became involved in fights with other loosely organized groups. However, individual members were frequently involved in assaults and street fighting, and police suspected that the gang was fairly well organized for shoplifting. Young children growing up in crowded West Side homes and communities were exposed to the influences of these older, street-wise youths.

Many of the young people in these neighborhoods were without fathers in the home. In some neighborhoods one out of twelve families received public assistance, usually ADC, and one-fourth of the children under eighteen lived with only one parent, usually the mother. Many youths on the West Side had never lived in a family situation where an adult male had a job and provided for his wife and children. As we shall see, however, West Side boys were not unique in this respect.

The North Central district, like the West Side, is one of the most extensively built up and congested areas of the city and contains a high percentage of the city's most impoverished and dependent families. Unlike the racially mixed West Side, the North Central district, one of the city's oldest Negro communities, continued to be relatively homogeneous in 1961. The area has many ghetto characteristics, particularly in communities close to the central, downtown districts. Here, mixed with residential dwellings, are pawnshops, secondhand clothing and furniture stores, cheap ($1.50 a night) transient hotels, bars, pool halls, dance halls, liquor stores, shoeshine parlors, and so forth. Used car lots with "easy credit" proclaimed on large signs abound, as do small manufacturing concerns and junkyards piled high with scrap metal and heaps of rusting, wrecked cars. Incongruously, the city's modern sports stadium stands in this deteriorating section.

In these mixed business and residential areas, families live in rooms and small apartments above the bars, pool halls, and business establishments. In 1961 half the buildings stood empty and condemned, abandoned for better facilities and customers further south. Interspersed among these condemned buildings were dwellings, also in serious disrepair, where families continued to live. In certain primarily residential areas, alleys behind rows of old apartment buildings were cluttered with garbage and trash, providing a natural breeding place for rats. Broken beer and whiskey bottles, paper, and trash littered the parkways, sidewalks, and streets in these areas. In sharp contrast were the occasional nearby communities of brick and frame houses in neat rows, which, although old, were in relatively good repair. The small yards were well tended and some painting and repair work was going on. Here the parkways and streets were relatively clean.

Some inroads on the housing problem in this North Central area were being made in 1961. Several public housing projects had been completed and were largely populated by mother-only families, many of whom were dependent on ADC grants. These housing projects with their clean lines, yard space, and play areas contrasted sharply with the deterioration of the neighborhood and dwellings around them where most North Central families continued to live. The inadequacy of housing and space for play and study for many families here was not offset by availability of community facilities. The recreational programs and parks available were insufficient for the large numbers of youths competing for them. In some communities, conflict frequently flared between rival groups of adolescents. It was in these neighborhoods that two of Kansas City's four or five loosely organized gangs operated. These youths, most of whom were unemployed and out of school, tended to congregate around recreational areas, thus limiting their availability to younger children and non–gang members except during the summer when the city sponsored supervised recreational programs. Most of the time the street or sidewalks provided the most accessible play areas. In the mixed business-residential sections, play areas consisted of alleys and sidewalks in front of bars and pool halls. Although there were several child-service agencies in the North Central district, many families who needed help did not avail themselves of these services. As on the West Side, shortages of qualified personnel limited coverage of children and families needing assistance.

In 1961, 23 per cent of the total study group (all Negro boys) lived in almost completely segregated Negro neighborhoods in the North Central district. Nine out of ten of these youths lived in communities ranked among the bottom quarter on indices of poverty for the city as a whole. Researchers found much the same general conditions in the homes and neighborhoods here as in West Side neighborhoods, but they also observed differences. The main difference seemed to be the somewhat greater frequency of extremely congested and deteriorating environments in certain North Central neighborhoods, as well as extremes in adequacy of physical home environments for boys

living in the same neighborhoods. The following examples are typical
of the different physical conditions described by interviewers.

J lived in an apartment building in a mixed residential and
business community. The other apartment dwellings around it were
in much the same condition.

> This is a very old run-down brick tenement building
> located in a slum area. There are a couple of bars down the
> street, a pool hall, and a loan and pawnbroker shop nearby.
> There are many kids around, and most of them seem to be
> playing in the street since there isn't any other place for them
> to play. Several windows are broken and the window frames,
> porches, and doors are badly in need of repair and paint. The
> porch sags, and the three steps up to it are broken. In the
> hallway, the paint is almost completely peeled off, and large
> scribbled writings continue from this hallway up into the long
> hall leading to the apartment units. There is a stench of
> cooked cabbage which is almost overwhelming. The apart-
> ment J lives in has five small rooms in which ten people live.
> The apartment floor is encrusted with dirt, and the few sparse
> furnishings are very old and in various stages of deterioration.
> There are no pictures or draperies nor any signs of books or
> magazines around. I smelled the strong odor of urine, which
> I believed came from a bathroom located off the room where
> I talked with J's mother. J shares a room with four brothers.
> The only light source observed was one naked fifty-watt bulb
> in the center of the room, and this seemed to be the case in
> the other rooms. The family had lived here almost two years.
> The mother said she would like to move into a better place
> but that she just can't afford it.

L lived in a neighborhood which was mainly residential.

> L lives in this house with his mother and seven siblings.
> It is a small frame house with six rooms. Both the exterior and
> interior are in very poor condition, with repair and paint badly
> needed although this probably wouldn't help much since the
> building itself seems to be structurally unsound. The whole
> house seems to sag and inside there are wide cracks in the
> plaster. The furnishings and floors are as clean as one could
> expect with this large family living in such crowded and inade-
> quate circumstances, but the furnishings are very old and dilap-
> idated. While the mother seems to be making some attempt to
> keep the living quarters clean, the material conditions here are
> depressing. This feeling is enhanced by the deterioration which
> is evident in the neighborhood. Most of the houses nearby

have been condemned as unsafe and are standing empty in various stages of collapse.

M also lived in a North Central area which was mainly residential. Here the houses and yards appeared to be generally well tended and cared for. M's home is an exception.

> Generally this is a pretty good neighborhood with fairly well kept yards and houses in good repair. M's house, however, is one of the most inadequate I've ever seen, and I've seen and been in many in the inner city. The house is a frame structure that looks like a shack. Paint, nails, shorings are badly needed, but even this probably wouldn't help much. Inside, the stench and filth are so strong that I had great difficulty staying for the interview. There was obviously no attempt to clean, scrub, or air out the house. The ten family members along with a dog shared the five small rooms. Cots and blankets were everywhere, and there was little evidence that bedclothes were changed or washed frequently. Everywhere there were diapers and the smell of urine mixed with other smells which were almost nauseating.

P lived in the same neighborhood as M yet in much different circumstances.

> P's home is a brick and frame bungalow with a small but cared-for lawn. The exterior of the house has been painted, and cracks in the foundation have been repaired, as have the porch steps. Inside the house is clean and has a fresh smell. The furnishings are typically middle-class in some respects. A comfortable sofa, several lamps and tables, bric-a-brac on a shelf, were part of the living room furnishings. I did not see books or magazines, although the local newspaper was lying on the coffee table in front of the sofa. There are six people living in this six-room house. While the mother states that they feel they need more room, she likes this house and neighborhood.

Like boys on the West Side, North Central youths were exposed to similar kinds of experiences and associations outside their family life. The facts perhaps most significant to the question of identity achievement were the relatively large number of marginal adult males in these communities and the number of boys living in homes without fathers. In many neighborhoods more than half the children lived in incomplete homes. Many families depended on public assistance. In one-third of the fifteen residential areas in this district, almost one in every five families required public help. In one community which included a high-rise housing development, 40 per cent of the families were dependent in this way.

The proportion of marginal adults in some of the North Central communities was considerably greater than in the core neighborhoods of the West Side. In some communities where Work-Study boys lived, half the adult males were unskilled workers. Their educational level was the lowest in the city and family income averaged less than three thousand dollars a year. Unemployment was common among adult males. In some neighborhoods the rate of unemployment was almost three times as high as that of the city as a whole.

The East Central inner city extends farther south than any of the other areas in the inner city. In the early 1950s its still predominantly white population represented a fairly average socioeconomic group. At that time there were several lower-class and lower-middle-class neighborhoods in the northern part of the district, as well as a few upper-middle-class communities in the southern section, but such extremes were few. With the exodus of white families to the suburbs following World War II, socially mobile Negro families, including professional and business people, began moving into these desirable and spacious residential areas. Also, working-class people and others began to settle here as redevelopment and highway projects in the inner city dislocated them from their homes. By 1961 the transition from a segregated, relatively homogeneous, white middle-class population to a segregated, somewhat more socioeconomically heterogeneous, Negro population was well under way. In that year 60 per cent of the residents were Negro. Families living here then showed a somewhat higher living standard than core inner city residents. Adults were generally better educated and better skilled. The median family income, lower than that for the city as a whole, was still considerably higher than the median for West Side and North Central residents. A higher proportion of families were buying homes, fewer were dependent on welfare, and the 7 per cent unemployment rate in 1960, while higher than the city rate, was still lower than that of the core inner city.

By 1961, however, there were signs that the number of lower-middle-class and lower-class families was increasing. Median income decreased, and the upkeep of property declined. Some new residents could earn only a limited income and could not maintain their homes and property adequately. Others were forced out of their central core dwellings by redevelopment projects and highway construction and brought with them life-styles and values which hindered their adaptation to middle-class standards of property upkeep and community responsibility. Several neighborhoods adjacent to the core North Central communities contained small houses, very tiny yards, and seriously deteriorated buildings. In these neighborhoods 10 per cent of the workers were unemployed, and median family income was much lower than in other East Central communities.

Twenty-nine per cent of the 422 youths screened for the Work-Study Program lived in East Central areas in 1961. All but one of these boys were Negro. Transition from white to Negro residents was almost complete; 95 to 98 per cent of the population was Negro in neighborhoods where study group boys lived. Eighty-five per cent of the boys screened lived in five of the district's fifteen census tracts. These five were among the poorest in the district; two of them ranked as low as North Central communities on poverty indices.

Interviewers reported living conditions to be much the same as in West Side and North Central communities. Neighborhoods were congested with limited play areas. Adults appeared to be both educationally and occupationally marginal. Half the adult males had less than a ninth grade education, and one-fourth were unskilled workers. One out of three families lived on three thousand dollars or less a year, and one out of three children lived with only one parent. These East Central neighborhoods differed markedly from other East Central communities farther south where median income, education, and other socioeconomic characteristics of Negro families were at or above the levels for the city as a whole. There were some differences between the relatively poor East Central neighborhoods and the poor West Side and North Central neighborhoods. Youths growing up in East Central areas had contact and opportunity for experience with a much wider variety of people. Even in poor neighborhoods where overall socioeconomic indices indicated similarity to core poverty areas in the West Side and the North Central district, there was a wide range of age groups, family composition, income, and education of people. The old and the young, the married and the unmarried, the poor and the middle class lived in close proximity. Youths growing up here were exposed to a wide range of experience and life styles. Most of them attended the elementary and high school together, where they were exposed to varied socioeconomic and cultural backgrounds.

The Northeast inner city district, like the West Side and the North Central district, is an older part of Kansas City, yet it has a quite different character. In 1961, the people here were mostly white and working-class, as they had been for several decades. The population was relatively stable, with in-migration limited to a few Negro and Mexican-American families who in the early 1950s settled in the western area adjacent to the North Central district. All economic classes were represented in the population, although working-class families predominated. In 1960 income ranged from low average to average, with extremes from very low to above average. Although median education for adults was the eighth grade, two grades below the city's median, there were relatively fewer families on welfare, less unemployment, and a much larger proportion of homeowners than in West Side and North Central communities.

The very poor lived in the industrial bottomlands in small frame houses surrounded by railroad tracks, warehouses, and factories. The houses, unpainted and badly in need of repair, had small yards lacking grass, shrubbery, or trees. Streets were without sidewalks. In one such community, known locally as Dog Patch, the families were known not only for being poor but also for being very independent and stable. Long-term residents for the most part, they raised large, close-knit families and took care of them. In spite of their general poverty, records showed that only one Dog Patch family had sought welfare assistance. Children from these poor communities had to be bused to school, which limited their participation in school activities and their use of school recreation facilities. Their own neighborhoods usually contained small parks, but these were limited to wading and baseball facilities. The children in Dog Patch had much more outdoor play space than did children in core inner-city areas. In summer the city supervised recreation programs which were well attended. Although the high school dropout rate was high, little delinquency was reported and adults had no police records.

Other neighborhoods in the south part of the Northeast district consisted of small frame houses built close together with little yard space and of old three- and four-story brick apartment buildings. These neighborhoods generally were clean, and the houses and yards showed some care. Many children lived here, and the two nearby parks were not adequate for their needs, although the school was close enough so that there was some access to recreational facilities. The Northeast also contained middle-class neighborhoods with ranch style houses, large, well-tended lawns, and numerous parks nearby. In the Northeast, as in the East Central district, children from very low-income families went to school with children from relatively high-income families.

The East inner city district in 1960 was more solidly working-class, with less contrast in socioeconomic characteristics, than any other part of the city. Although almost one in four adults had an eighth grade or less formal education, only 15 per cent were unskilled workers. The median yearly income of six thousand dollars ranked with the median income in the city as a whole. In 1960 the population was predominantly white. There was some in-migration of Negroes, primarily in sections adjacent to the North Central district, and a few neighborhoods were becoming integrated. A few others were becoming resegregated as Negro families replaced white families. Essentially, however, the East inner city in 1960 remained a segregated white working-class community. A relatively stable family life characterized youths growing up here. There were fewer broken homes than anywhere in the inner city, fewer families with incomes under three thousand dollars, and fewer families dependent on welfare. While there were some congested neighborhoods, most appeared relatively well cared for; buildings were structurally sound, and children had considerably greater amounts of outdoor space and parks in which to play than in other inner city districts. Of the forty study group boys in this district, 80 per cent lived in family dwellings which interviewers rated as average or above average living conditions.

It is clear that a large percentage of study group youth lived in communities where adult males were frequently uneducated and unskilled, where unemployment was relatively high among males, and where male employment was typically menial, uncertain, and poorly paid. Thus, many study group boys had few adult male models around whom work-role identity could develop. In Table 2 the five late adolescent types of adjustment are contrasted on socioeconomic variables characteristic of the communities where the boys were living when screened in the seventh grade. Relatively more seriously maladaptive boys lived in communities where families appeared most disadvantaged; relatively fewer school adaptive boys lived in such communities. When contrasted with the marginal, erratic, and work adaptive subgroups, as well as school adaptive boys, the seriously maladaptive group appeared significantly different (.01 level) in having lived more fre-

Table 2. LATE ADOLESCENT ADJUSTMENT AND SOCIOECONOMIC STATUS (SES) OF COMMUNITIES

Socioeconomic Categories (based on ranking census tracts by poverty index)[a]	Total Group (N = 325)	Serious Maladap. (N = 75)	Marginal (N = 51)	Erratic (N = 63)	Work Adaptive (N = 63)	School Adaptive (N = 73)
			Per Cent			
Lowest SES (Census tracts ranked below first quartile on poverty index)	48	61	43	43	49	38
Low Average SES (Census tracts ranked between first quartile and median)	43	31	49	44	43	52
Average SES (Census tracts ranked at or above median)	9	8	8	13	8	10
						χ^2 not significant

[a] This index was developed in 1966 by the Census Bureau as part of its work for the Office of Economic Opportunity. The index for each census tract in the city is a numerical value based on composite census tract data including percentages of (1) families with less than three thousand dollar annual income, (2) children under eighteen not living with both parents, (3) persons over twenty-five with less than eight years of school, (4) unskilled males in the labor force, (5) dilapidated housing.

quently in lower SES neighborhoods. Relatively few seventh grade study group boys, whether they became adaptive or maladaptive in late adolescence, lived in communities of average or above average socioeconomic levels. In the next chapter we examine some of the socioeconomic variables among study group families at the time of screening and we report the study of the association of these variables with late adolescent adjustment.

3

The Family in Childhood

For most youths the direction and shape of emerging identities are highly influenced by early family experiences and relationships. It is in the family that the young child learns about the world and what he can expect from it. Usually his value orientations, his concepts about himself and other people, and his modes of relating to and coping with the world are fairly well established before he actually becomes involved in the world outside the family. It is in the family that the young child learns whether he is adequate or inadequate, loved or unloved, with or without some control and mastery over his fate.

Although early childhood experiences are acknowledged as vital, social scientists still do not know why some individuals approach the ultimate in development while others fall far short. It is relatively clear why a considerably larger proportion of children from middle-class backgrounds complete their education and move into relatively stable and productive careers than do children from disadvantaged families. However, some disadvantaged children do grow up and move into middle-class society, and some move into skilled blue collar jobs. Others, although able to hold only unskilled jobs, support their families, stay out of serious trouble, and generally live stable lives. What makes the difference between these individuals and those who are unable to adapt to even the minimal requirements of modern society? Is the absence of a responsible, productive adult male in the early life of

34

some disadvantaged boys significant? Or is the accessibility of unsuitable male models a problem? What is the effect on boys of a socially deteriorating neighborhood? Does the effect of these conditions depend on whether a boy lives in a relatively stable family or in one where family relations are noncohesive or where family structure is disorganized or deteriorating? (Family deterioration refers to a complex of factors including broken home, no consistent authority, conflict among family members, shifting of parental roles, amoral, asocial, or antisocial adult models in the family, inadequate child-rearing practices, improper parental care, brutality, and lack of nurturant adults.) Does being Negro or white make a difference in the shape of work and social roles emerging in late adolescence from the various conditions and circumstances of early family life in the inner city?

In this chapter we look at some of the conditions, circumstances, and characteristics of the four hundred families as they appeared when the boys were identified in the seventh grade. (The first parental interviews and school, police, juvenile court, and welfare agencies provided the data for this study.) We examine the proposition that inner-city boys showing signs of social and educational maladjustment in the elementary grades live in families in various stages of disorganization or deterioration, as well as under economically, socially, and culturally depriving conditions. The association of these varied early childhood family characteristics with late adolescent adjustment is explored.

In our society education is stressed as the major avenue for achieving a satisfactory adult work career and the major process through which the adolescent is readied for the role of responsible adult worker and citizen. In middle-class families this educational model is relatively well established for most children. What about inner-city children who already show unmistakable signs of estrangement from school by the time they are in the seventh grade? What educational models exist for them in their early childhood years?

Seventy-six per cent of all study group fathers were school dropouts. About half had less than nine years of school (median was 8.7 years), and 35 per cent of those who quit school did so during the elementary grades. About one-fourth completed twelve grades and 5 per cent had done some college work. Mothers showed similar patterns, although they generally had more years of formal schooling. Half had attained the tenth or higher grade (median grade was 9.8), and although 70 per cent were also school dropouts they tended to leave school later than fathers. Of parents who did not complete high school, 44 per cent of mothers in contrast to 26 per cent of fathers remained in school past the tenth grade.

White and Negro fathers showed similar median numbers of years of formal schooling (8.6 and 8.7 years) and similar percentages of school dropouts (77 per cent and 75 per cent). However, white fathers tended to leave school earlier. Of those dropping out, 41 per cent of white and only 28 per cent of Negro fathers dropped out before completing the eighth grade. White mothers reported a slightly higher median number of years of schooling (10 years) than Negro mothers (9.6 years), and slightly more white than Negro mothers (33 per cent and 26 per cent) completed high school.

In both Negro and white families, mothers reported more years of formal education than fathers. In Negro families the difference appeared to be mainly that mothers stayed in school longer before dropping out. In white families the difference seemed to be that more mothers (33 per cent) than fathers (23 per cent) completed high school and that of parents who were school dropouts only 18 per cent of mothers in contrast to 40 per cent of fathers left before completing the eighth grade. Of all parents, white fathers had fewest years of formal schooling.

Only about one-fourth of study group boys lived with parents who had completed twelve grades of school; 5 per cent lived in homes where at least one parent had some hours in college. However, parents of the majority of boys identified as school misfits in the seventh grade had educational levels considerably lower than those of the general population. (National data indicate medians of 12.1 years of schooling for white male and female adults and medians of 9.2 and 10.0 years for nonwhites.)[1] Is there any significant association between parents' education and the late adolescent adjustment of study group boys? Table 3 summarizes our findings. Only in the white families of our sample did the father's education seem in some way associated with the work and social adjustment of the son in late adolescence, although generally as parents' educational levels increased the relative numbers of late adolescent maladjusted boys decreased. However, a number of

[1] Office of Policy Planning and Research, United States Department of Labor, *The Negro Family: The Case for National Action* (Washington, D.C.: Government Printing Office, 1965).

Table 3. PARENTS' EDUCATION AND BOYS' LATE ADOLESCENT ADJUSTMENT[a]

	Negro Boys		White Boys	
Parents' Educational Status	Maladaptive	Adaptive	Maladaptive	Adaptive
	Per Cent			
Fathers	(N = 84)	(N = 67)	(N = 60)	(N = 65)
Early school dropout	26	18	40	20
Dropout after eighth grade	61	64	40	54
Completed twelfth grade	13	18	20	26
		(Not significant)		(.05 level)
Mothers	(N = 114)	(N = 77)	(N = 60)	(N = 65)
Early school dropout	25	14	17	9
Dropout after eighth grade	52	55	55	54
Completed twelfth grade	23	31	28	27
		(Not significant)		(Not significant)

[a] Five late adolescent adjustment types reduced to general categories (maladaptive and adaptive) to increase N's for chi-square analyses.

boys with poorly educated parents showed adaptive adjustments in late adolescence, and a sizeable number with relatively well educated parents showed maladaptive adjustment.

A basic assumption of work experience programs and particularly of the Kansas City study is that families of socially maladjusted inner-city youths are generally limited in providing adequate adult worker models for their children and particularly for boys. How valid is this assumption for our sample? In the initial home interview we asked about current employment of parents as well as about their work history. (See Appendix B.) From this information an occupational rating scale was developed using income, security of employment, and estimated level of skill required as criteria. On this four-point scale a rating of one indicated lowest work status (manual labor, poor pay, unsteady employment, no advancement) and a rating of four indicated highest work status (skilled work, employment security, good pay, marketable skills).

The distribution of these ratings tended to substantiate the anticipated low work status among adult males in the families of boys screened. This was particularly the case with Negro families. Of the 227 Negro parents interviewed (mostly mothers), one in five had no knowledge of the father's current or past work or would not reveal the information. In almost all these families the father lived outside the home. In the 178 Negro families offering occupational information about fathers, 61 per cent of fathers were employed in unskilled, low-paying jobs, 21 per cent in semiskilled work, and 9 per cent in skilled but not highly technical trades. Work status ratings among white fathers indicated a relatively higher level of occupational employment. There were relatively fewer fathers for whom occupational information was not available (one in ten). Of the 160 white fathers with work status ratings, 26 per cent worked in unskilled jobs, 46 per cent in semiskilled jobs, and 18 per cent in skilled occupations. Forty-one per cent of Negro and white mothers were employed full or part time. Like the fathers, they generally held jobs at low occupational levels; again this was particularly true of Negro families.

At all educational levels white fathers held somewhat higher status jobs than Negroes. While there was some association of education to work status for both Negro and white fathers, race appeared to be more significant than education. Negro fathers at all educational levels were significantly more frequently employed in unskilled jobs than white fathers. Negro unskilled fathers averaged 8.40 years of school; unskilled whites averaged 6.95 years. However, the relatively low work status of both Negro and white fathers is clearly defined when compared with general and local populations of adult male workers. For example, among Negro workers in our sample six out of ten held unskilled jobs in contrast to less than two in ten adult Negro workers in the general population and almost three in ten among Negro workers in the inner-city study area. About one in four white fathers in our group held unskilled jobs compared with about one in twenty-five white adults in the general population and about one in five white workers in the inner city.[2]

Some Negro and white boys appeared more disadvantaged than others. More than one-fourth of all boys (29 per cent) lived in families where the male parent was absent. Most of these fathers were out of the home permanently through divorce, separation, or desertion. A few (one in five) provided some support for their children, but in most instances this was irregular and insufficient. In a considerable number of such families the absent father's occupation and whereabouts were unknown to the mother. In a few instances where mothers reported boys born out of wedlock there was no information at all about the father. In the 126 families with absent fathers, 59 mothers (47 per cent) worked full-time out of the home. Two-thirds of these mothers provided the family's full income with no outside assistance. Another 8 per cent of mothers were employed in part-time jobs, and the remaining 45 per cent depended on outside sources, usually ADC and general welfare.

Study group boys were considered relatively advantaged with respect to the male adult worker model if fathers were present in the homes and employed in relatively skilled jobs for which they received fairly adequate wages. Fathers of other youths appeared to be steady workers, as evidenced by several years' employment with one employer, yet their jobs were unskilled or semiskilled, paid poorly, and were essentially dead-end. In many of these families income had to be supplemented by the mother's full- or part-time work.

From our overview of the work role of study group parents,

[2] National data from U.S. Department of Labor, *Manpower—Challenge of the 1960s* (Washington, D.C.: Government Printing Office, 1960), p. 20. Data for inner-city of Kansas City, Missouri from Bureau of Labor Statistics, Department of Commerce, *Statistical Abstracts* (Washington, D.C.: Government Printing Office, 1960).

particularly of fathers, it appears that many boys in our study were seriously limited or handicapped in beginning identification with an adult worker by the absence of adequate adult worker models in their early family experience. As was noted in Chapter Two, within their neighborhoods these boys were also limited in the availability of suitable male adult models. Yet about four out of ten boys screened as social and educational misfits in the seventh grade showed signs of remission of problem behavior and appeared to be making progress in social adjustment and work role development in late adolescence. Were these the boys whose childhoods were spent in families where there were relatively adequate male worker models?

In assessing these associations we found 277 father-son pairs with appropriate ratings. This represented 84 per cent of the 341 study group boys for whom we had late adolescent adjustment ratings. We found that although boys who showed maladaptive adjustment in late adolescence tended to have lived in families where the father's work status was lowest, the association was not statistically significant. The most pronounced association was between skilled and semiskilled work status of fathers and work and school adaptive adjustment of boys. Of boys whose fathers were skilled or semiskilled at the time of the seventh grade screening, over half (55 per cent) showed progress in social and work role adjustment in late adolescence. In contrast, only 36 per cent of boys whose fathers were unskilled showed such progress in late adolescence. Seventy-one per cent of the work adaptive and 60 per cent of the school adaptive group had fathers working at skilled or semiskilled jobs, in contrast to 46 per cent of the seriously maladaptive boys and 53 per cent and 45 per cent of marginal and erratic subgroups.

When the association of race and father's work status to late adolescent adjustment was examined, no statistically significant association for either Negro or white youths was found. Again, there was a tendency for boys with fathers in unskilled jobs to have adjustment problems in late adolescence. This was particularly true of Negro boys, with 67 per cent of those whose fathers worked at unskilled jobs showing maladaptive adjustment, in contrast to 53 per cent with fathers working in skilled or semiskilled jobs. In spite of such trends we concluded that there was no direct association between boys' social adjustment and work role development in late adolescence and their fathers' work status at the time of screening.

The association of chronic economic stress with family deterioration and consequent social maladjustment has been documented in many studies. In study group families, economic deprivation was expected to be a major characteristic because the study area was specifically selected to include low income families. Although our screening did not include indices of families' economic status, it became evident when such information was collected after screening that our sample did include a large percentage of low-income families. Yet there were marked variations from low to high income levels; one-fourth of the boys lived in families with incomes close to the median for the entire city. Although these higher incomes were associated to some extent with high work status of fathers, they were primarily associated with two-parent families in which both parents were employed. At the low end of the scale 37 per cent of study group families (in contrast to 22 per cent of all Kansas City families) had yearly incomes of less than three thousand dollars.[3] Negro families were relatively more disadvantaged than white families in our sample just as they were in the general population.

The economic problem for many families in our study was clearly evident in the fact that not only was family income lower than average, but families were larger than average. At the time of the initial survey the average number of persons in Negro and white families in our sample was 7.50 and 6.70 persons respectively, in contrast to the national averages of 4.30 and 3.58. Did study group boys who differed in extent of material deprivation in childhood also differ in late adolescent adjustment? At time of screening, families of boys who later showed maladaptive adjustment had on the average more family members but less income than families of boys who in their late teens showed adaptive adjustment. However, these differences were not statistically significant. While many of the most seriously maladjusted youth did come from the poorest and largest families, 47 per cent of the 115 boys from the poorest families (income less than three thousand dollars) showed adaptive adjustment in late adolescence in contrast to 43 per cent of the 99 boys from the relatively most advantaged families (income five thousand dollars or more).

In Chapter Two we described certain characteristics of differ-

[3] Income level for general population of Kansas City from Kansas City Bureau of Labor Statistics, Department of Commerce, *Statistical Abstracts* (Washington, D.C.: Government Printing Office, 1960).

ent neighborhoods and dwellings where study group boys lived while in the seventh grade. From our initial interview data we gave examples of the physical conditions of dwellings typical of those rated as poor or inadequate, fair, and good family living conditions. Did the different living conditions have any association with race or with late adolescent adjustment? Also, did the extent of the physical mobility of families (number of dwellings lived in) during the boys' elementary years show association to late adolescent adjustment?

At the time of screening 37 per cent of the boys lived in family dwellings rated as substandard. Another 32 per cent lived in dwellings where there appeared to be some effort to maintain the home and keep it relatively clean. In many families this was a difficult task, since there was limited space for the many children and family income was insufficient for necessary repairs and replacement of worn furniture and household equipment. In about a third of the families the physical conditions for family living appeared good. In these homes there was evident and successful effort not only to maintain the home in good repair but also to provide attractive surroundings and comfortable living conditions. These families were fairly well distributed among the four income level groups of our sample, so a clean, attractive home in good repair was not necessarily associated with higher income. However, as might be expected, larger families (eight or more members) with income under three thousand dollars a year most frequently lived in substandard dwellings.

Crowded living conditions characterized many families. For the total group the average dwelling had six rooms or an average of .86 rooms per person in the average household of seven members. However, 43 per cent of all families lived in dwellings averaging 4.4 rooms. One-fourth of these families had eight or more members. Wide differences in living conditions and style characterized our supposedly homogeneous group of boys and families. There were families of four or five members living in relatively large dwellings with six to ten rooms (13 per cent of total). Only 23 per cent of these families were in dwellings rated substandard. Moreover, one-third of all large families (eight or more members) were in homes of eight to twelve rooms where space did not seem to be a significant problem. However, 51 per cent of these dwellings were rated as physically inadequate. This was only slightly lower than the 54 per cent of large families living in smaller houses where conditions were rated as poor.

For slightly over one-fourth of all families (27 per cent) the dwelling rated in the initial survey had been home during at least the previous five or six years. Another 42 per cent of families had lived in two to four different dwellings (frequently in the same neighborhood) during this period. The remaining one-fourth of the families had moved relatively often, averaging one or more moves a year during the previous five or six years. Within each of these three subgroups of families there were differences in the general physical conditions of the surrounding neighborhood and the socioeconomic status of people in the community. Of families who had lived in the same dwelling for several years, 51 per cent had lived continuously in the most blighted areas of the inner city during the childhood years of study group boys. Of the 42 per cent of families who had lived in two to four different dwellings, about one-third had moved from one blighted area to another, and more than one-third had moved in and out of such neighborhoods. In highly mobile families frequent moves did not change the blighted physical conditions of the neighborhoods. Among families who had moved occasionally or frequently there was little indication that change in family dwelling was associated with social mobility, although there were a few families who had moved into communities at or above the median on socioeconomic indices for the city as a whole.

The assumption that living in disorganized and physically deteriorating dwellings and neighborhoods is associated with the development of social maladjustment is supported to some extent by our findings. As we have seen, however, not all families in our sample lived in blighted areas or in impoverished physical circumstances. What relevance do differences in childhood environments have for the late adolescent adjustment of study group boys? Our study indicates that those study group boys who lived in the poorest physical circumstances in childhood and whose families frequently moved about in the inner city tended more often than other boys to show maladaptive adjustment in late adolescence. However, differences between maladaptive and adaptive boys in these variables appeared mainly to be differences between the seriously maladaptive and adaptaive school subgroups. Work adaptive boys appeared slightly favored over the seriously maladaptive and erratic types but considerably less favored than the school adaptive and somewhat less favored than the marginal youth. In all comparisons on environmental variables the most striking differences were between the seriously maladaptive and the school adaptive subgroups.

Many studies have shown a statistical relationship between broken homes and adolescent maladjustment. Our findings tend to confirm this; by age thirteen or fourteen over half of study group boys (53 per cent) had experienced the loss of one or both natural parents from the home. Of these boys, 42 per cent had experienced additional changes in family structure and parental authority when new adults were introduced in the family setting, usually through the mother's remarriage. While many of these new adult males appeared as father surrogates, others appeared to be just part of a sequence of men who moved in and out of the lives of the mother and her children. In some broken homes, relatives, including even older siblings, came into a new or different relationship with the boy when they became parental surrogates in the absence of the natural parents. Table 4

Table 4.   FAMILY STRUCTURE AT TIME OF SCREENING

Adults in the Home	Total Families (N = 418)	Negro Families (N = 240)	White Families (N = 178)
		Per Cent	
Both natural parents	47	43	52
Mother and stepfather	11	9	13
Father and stepmother	4	4	6
Mother only	29	33	22
Father only	2	3	1
Other (Includes grand-parents, aunts and uncles, older siblings, foster parents, friends of family, shifting from one parent to another.)	7	8	6

summarizes data on family structure when the boys were screened in the seventh grade. The broken home as a distinctive characteristic of our study group families is indicated by the absence of 22 per cent of white and 33 per cent of Negro fathers in contrast to 7.9 and 22.9

per cent of white and Negro fathers absent from the general population of families in the United States.[4]

We were interested in whether coming from a broken home had any relevance to the late adolescent adjustment of inner-city boys who had been clearly visible as socially and educationally maladjusted by the seventh grade. Table 5 summarizes our findings. These findings

Table 5. FAMILY STRUCTURE AND LATE ADOLESCENT ADJUSTMENT

	Negro Boys		White Boys	
In the Home at Time of Screening	Maladaptive (N = 119)	Adaptive (N = 79)	Maladaptive (N = 62)	Adaptive (N = 73)
	Per Cent			
Both natural parents	37	50	62	52
Natural parent and step-parent (78% mothers)	13	8	13	20
One natural parent only (94% mothers)	41	30	18	21
Other family structures	9	12	7	7
	χ^2 not significant		χ^2 not significant	

indicate a slight association of broken homes with maladjustment in social and work role development in late adolescence among Negro youth. However, this was not demonstrated for white boys. In fact, more white boys showing maladaptive adjustment in their late teens had come from complete families.

Although findings reported so far do not indicate strong statistical associations, they do tend to show that in our sample relatively more maladaptive than adaptive late adolescent boys came from the most disadvantaged childhood backgrounds. We have seen that youths having trouble in social and work role development in late adolescence tended to come from families where parents were least prepared to successfully compete for jobs paying adequate wages. Large families, poor physical settings, and crowded conditions for family living were

[4] Taken from Office of Policy Planning and Research, United States Department of Labor, *The Negro Family: The Case for National Action* (Washington, D.C.: Government Printing Office, 1965).

more often found in combination in the family backgrounds of boys who in late adolescence were having difficulty in social adjustment and work role development. Yet, we have also seen in our sample boys from similarly poor childhood environments who somehow were managing in late adolescence to move toward adaptable modes of behavior and a work-role identity. In what ways were these boys different from those continuing to show maladaptive adjustment in their late teens? Did differences in the quality of family life in childhood experience partly account for differences in late adolescent adjustment?

The quality of family life as defined for our study essentially has to do with family relationships and the way family members feel toward one another. The sense of joint identity which exists among family members is a key factor. To investigate this area, interviewers in the initial home interview with parents inquired about child-rearing practices, discipline problems, nature of supervision, and the feeling of closeness in family relationships. Parents were asked about the kinds of things the family did together, the expectations they had for their children in the way of responsibilities, and any problems they had encountered in bringing up their children. These data provided ratings of family cohesiveness on a four-point scale based essentially on the Glueck and Glueck[5] social background scale. (See Appendix B.) Table 6 shows the distribution of cohesiveness ratings.

Although Negro families showed a slightly higher percentage of noncohesive ratings than did white families, the differences were not statistically significant. In both groups of families more than one-third of the boys lived in families in which primary relationships appeared marked by tension, conflict, or indifference. The remaining families appeared relatively free of these characteristics. About one-third of all boys screened as socially maladjusted in the seventh grade lived in relatively cohesive families.

What is the relation of family cohesiveness in childhood to late adolescent adjustment of study group boys? Were the boys who experienced "good" family relationships during childhood the ones who showed promise in late adolescence? Table 7 summarizes our findings. Of all characteristics and areas of family life studied, it was family cohesiveness that was most significantly associated with late adolescent adjustment.

[5] S. Glueck and E. Glueck, *Unraveling Juvenile Delinquency* (Cambridge, Mass.: Harvard University Press, 1950).

Table 6. FAMILY COHESIVENESS AT TIME OF SCREENING

Categories of Cohesiveness	Total Families (N = 341)	Negro Families (N = 199)	White Families (N = 142)
	Per Cent		
Noncohesive families[a]	42 (N = 143)	44 (N = 88)	39 (N = 55)
Partly cohesive	27 (N = 92)	27 (N = 53)	27 (N = 39)
Cohesive	31 (N = 106)	29 (N = 58)	34 (N = 47)
	$\chi^2 = .85$; df = 3; not significant.		

[a] For chi-square analysis rating values of 1 and 2 designating noncohesive families have been combined into one category.

Table 7. FAMILY COHESIVENESS AND LATE ADOLESCENT ADJUSTMENT

	Negro Boys		White Boys	
	Maladaptive (N = 122)	Adaptive (N = 77)	Maladaptive (N = 68)	Adaptive (N = 74)
	Per Cent			
Noncohesive families	59	19	51	28
Partly cohesive families	19	38	25	30
Cohesive families	22	43	24	42
	$\chi^2 = 31.21$; df = 2 Sig. Level = .001		$\chi^2 = 9.42$; df = 2 Sig. Level = .01	

The significance of family relationships to late adolescent adjustment regardless of family structure is indicated in Table 8. These findings indicate that, regardless of family structure, boys growing up in cohesive families have a considerably better chance of developing socially adaptive styles in late adolescence than do boys from noncohesive families. For Negro boys in our sample living in two-parent

Table 8. FAMILY STRUCTURE, COHESIVENESS, AND LATE
                 ADOLESCENT ADJUSTMENT

| | Negro Boys | | White Boys | |
	Maladaptive (N = 115)	Adaptive (N = 80)	Maladaptive (N = 67)	Adaptive (N = 75)
	Per Cent			
Both parents in home				
Cohesive family	47	53	40	60
Noncohesive family	83	17	59	41
Broken family (Primarily mother only)				
Cohesive family	34	66	21	79
Noncohesive family	77	23	70	30

families where there was tension, conflict, or indifference, the chances of late adolescent maladjustment were slightly higher than for Negro boys living in broken noncohesive families.

Regardless of whether a study group boy had lived in a complete or broken family during childhood, his developing patterns of adaptive or maladaptive behavior in adolescence appeared to be significantly linked to the quality of childhood family life. Although there is a significant association of family cohesiveness with late adolescent adjustment, we must note that about one-third of boys with such favorable childhood backgrounds showed maladaptive adjustments in late adolescence. In the remaining pages of this book we examine conditions, circumstances, and experiences of adolescent boys growing up in the inner city which may influence the emergence of such socially maladaptive behaviors.

4

The Elementary School

When the four hundred boys in the study were identified in the spring semester of the seventh grade, they were scattered among six Kansas City elementary schools. These six were feeder schools for the five junior and senior inner-city high schools selected to participate in the Work-Study Project. These six schools were located in the lowest socioeconomic areas of the inner city. Sixty-seven per cent of the study group had lived and attended school in these communities during all of grade school. A smaller group (20 per cent) had attended all but the first two grades in Kansas City elementary schools, while the remaining boys (13 per cent) had been in such schools only one or two years. These more recent students were mostly from families which had moved to Kansas City from rural communities in Kansas and Missouri. There were also a few Negro boys whose families had recently moved to Kansas City from rural areas in the Deep South.

When screened as socially and academically maladjusted in the seventh grade, the four hundred boys represented approximately 6 per cent of all seventh grade Kansas City boys and about 10 per cent of thirteen-year-old inner-city youths. The multiple screening criteria for school maladjustment ensured that the boys selected were the ones in this age group who would most likely be early high school dropouts or in conflict with police and juvenile court authorities in adolescence. In this respect they were homogeneous. Yet there were differences among them in terms of how marked the signs of school and social

maladjustment were. Some boys were borderline on sociometric measures of aggressive maladjustment, that is, scores were at or slightly
above the seventh grade median score which was established as the
lower cutoff point for screening. Other boys, however, scored higher
than 75 per cent of their classmates on such measures. Likewise, the
boys screened were relatively homogeneous in measured intelligence
in that none scored above average on the Otis Beta IQ test used in
screening and yet none were considered retarded. However, there were
differences of thirty-nine IQ points between scores at extremes of the
IQ distribution. (The Otis Beta test was the standard paper and pencil
group test administered to all students in the fifth and sixth grades.
It is a measure highly influenced by language facility, attitudes, and
social and cultural factors, and therefore disadvantaged youth are particularly handicapped. However, as a measure of functioning intelligence applied to learning tasks, it has been found to be a relatively
valid predictor of school success. Approximately 11 per cent of boys
screened had IQ scores below the cutoff level of 80 on the Otis. These
youths were included in the group because they met other criteria and
their earlier Stanford Binet IQ scores indicated average ability. The
inclusion of these youth was necessary in certain schools to increase
the numbers of youths participating in the research project.)

In spite of the range of scores, half the boys did score at low
average or below average IQ levels and therefore were relatively homogeneous in terms of measured functioning intelligence. When IQ
scores from the Stanford Binet test administered in the first or second
grade were assessed, a somewhat more heterogeneous distribution of
IQ scores emerged. Moreover, the general level of the earlier Binet
IQ scores was higher. One-fourth of the study group earned scores
in the first grade in the average to superior IQ range. Six boys had
IQ scores from 120 to 132. Some of the changes from first testing to
second testing could be accounted for by the phenomenon of regression toward the mean. However, the trend of IQ scores shifting downward toward the mean is considerably greater than those shifting
upward.

When individual patterns of changes in IQ scores were studied, it was found that 70 per cent of the total group showed higher IQ
scores on the Stanford Binet test when they first started school than
they did on the Otis Beta test in the sixth grade. Of these 70 per cent,
almost half had Binet scores higher than their Otis scores by ten or

more IQ points. Several of the boys who had IQ scores of superior and above levels on the Binet earned low average to below average IQ scores on the Otis. This pattern of decreased IQ scores over the six elementary grades did not hold for all boys. Thirty per cent showed a reverse pattern with Otis scores indicating better potential for school work than did Binet scores. This included about 9 per cent of the study group with Otis scores ten or more IQ points above Binet scores.

Not only did boys screened for the Work-Study Program compose a somewhat heterogeneous ability group as they entered school, they also showed differences in kinds of adjustments, extent of problems, age when school problems began to emerge or first became noticed. These different patterns were indicated in individual cumulative school records which contained various kinds of information about each child's progress from year to year as perceived by his teachers. Included in these records were teachers' numerical ratings on personal and social adjustment as well as comments concerning various aspects of progress or lack of progress. Teachers recorded their observations at the end of each school year and rated students on several trait dimensions. Teachers' assessments emerged out of their work situations and were meant for their colleagues. That these teacher-based reports and ratings are of value is given some credence by a number of studies which have shown that teachers can identify with considerably better than chance probability those pupils who in adolescence become delinquent or who need psychiatric help.

Table 9 shows the percentile distribution of teachers' trait ratings of study group boys at the end of the first, third, and sixth grades. As boys in the study group moved toward the seventh grade, their teachers increasingly identified them as showing regression in or little progress toward development of attitudes and behaviors essential to both satisfying school experience and educational growth. The single most significant problem appeared to be organizing for study and completion of assigned tasks, that is, work and study habits. For almost two-thirds of the study group this problem was clearly identified by the sixth grade; it was to plague many of them in high school as well as in their later adjustment to work.

In most of the other areas rated, there was some increase each elementary year in the percentage of boys rated by their teachers as showing signs of school difficulties. By the sixth grade almost half were identified as showing difficulties in self-control. Slightly over half were

Table 9. TEACHERS' RATINGS ON PERSONAL TRAITS
AND ADJUSTMENTS

Rating Categories and Levels	Grades		
	First	Third	Sixth
Work habits		Per Cent	
Below average	39	51	62
Average	42	36	33
Above average	19	13	5
Responsibility			
Below average	24	46	54
Average	54	35	35
Above average	22	19	11
Self-control			
Below average	30	38	49
Average	52	49	40
Above average	18	18	11
Attitude toward school regulations			
Below average	22	31	43
Average	48	43	37
Above average	30	26	20
Getting along with others			
Below average	19	30	34
Average	55	46	45
Above average	26	24	21
Personal habits			
Below average	24	29	31
Average	41	40	37
Above average	35	31	32

seen as indicating little sense of responsibility in the school situation. Two out of every five boys in the study group were identified as showing little respect for school rules and regulations. There were, however, variations in the patterns of these ratings with respect to indicating extensiveness and chronicity of school problems among the four hundred boys.

When the patterns of ratings were assessed for each trait across each elementary grade, it was found that 47 per cent of the study group had been rated consistently over the four elementary years prior to screening (third through sixth grades) as showing unsatisfactory personal adjustment in one or more of the areas rated. Slightly more than one-third of this chronic problem group were consistently rated below average on one of the traits over the four-year period. Another 20 per cent were consistently rated below average on two traits, and the remaining 47 per cent were below average on three to eight traits. Low ratings on work habits and initiative characterized 75 per cent of boys with these chronic patterns. Very few of them rated above average on any other traits, with the patterns of ratings typically fluctuating from average to below average over the four grades. Thus, for almost half the total group of boys, different teachers saw the same kinds of adjustment and personal problems in individual boys over a four-year period beginning when the boys were eight or nine years old. (The phenomenon of labeling, the perpetuation of labels, and the effect on those labeled, must be considered. Teachers' ratings and impressions are recorded on the permanent record and they follow a child through his school career. We are not concerned here with the validity of these ratings but only with their relevance for describing boys as their teachers perceived and described them for their colleagues. We will later be concerned with the association of these ratings to various outcomes and adjustments during adolescence.)

There were two subgroups whose adjustment problems did not appear to be chronic at the time of screening. One of these, comprising about one-third of the total group, had ratings indicating relatively average adjustment up until the fifth or sixth grade. At that time there was a marked change in pattern, with most of these boys rated below average on two or more traits including work and study habits, initiative, and responsibility. The extent of indicated maladjustment varied markedly among these boys. For about one-fourth of them, difficulties were indicated in only one or two major areas (again mainly in work and study habits, initiative, and responsibility), while for about one-third, adjustment problems were identified in five or more of the areas rated. The other group of boys, comprising about one-fourth of the total, were not identified by teacher ratings as seriously maladjusted until the seventh grade.

In order to assess these elementary school careers in more individual terms, teacher comments recorded on cumulative cards over the elementary years were studied. It was found that teachers' statements could be divided into five categories which included both negative and positive description.

Teacher comments on adjustment to group and peers indicated behavior which affected other pupils in the classroom either negatively or positively. "Bothers others," "trouble maker," and "destructive" are examples of negative descriptions. Positive statements indicated cooperative group behavior, responsibility, and respect for the property of others, such as "a good citizen."

Statements on personality traits and emotional responses indicated students' emotional responses to instruction, to learning tasks, and to correction. Negative statements indicated pupils' disagreeable reactions, resistance, and erratic emotional responses, for example, "hard for him to accept correction," "nervous," "confused," "resents criticism," "flighty," "stubborn." Positive statements indicated generally acceptable responses in the classroom situation, such as, "accepts criticism well," "easy to reason with," "very stable," "mature attitude toward school work."

Statements on social orientation and self-esteem included comments on social aggressiveness as well as on self-concept. Negative statements indicated seclusiveness and lack of confidence or self-assertion, such as "timid," "lacks confidence in his ability," "appears lonely," "retiring," "is not as aggressive as he needs to be." Positive statements described boys in such terms as "good mixer," "likes to be with others," "self-confident," "very outgoing," "likes people and makes friends easily."

Statements on work habits dealt with methods employed in completing classroom work. Negative statements referred to lack of perseverance, planning, or concentration in finishing an assignment or to laziness, sloppiness, or carelessness, for example, "cannot stay with lesson till completion," "works by spells," "procrastinator," "very messy with his work," "poor effort," "bad planning of work," "wastes time." Positive statements were those indicating diligence, perseverance, initiative, carefulness, and so forth in doing assignments.

Statements on attitudes toward school indicated boys' responses to school experience in general. Negative statements indicated apathy, hostility, or opposition to school as an institution, lack of interest in and enjoyment of school work, and need to be coerced or pushed, such as "a don't-care attitude," "needs constant push to accomplish anything," "able to work—won't," "indifferent to school," "does not try to learn." Positive statements indicated involvement in school work and a general interest and liking for school, such as, "interested in school," "wants to learn," "makes every effort to learn."

For each boy these cumulative card statements were abstracted and coded and frequency tallies were made of both negative and positive statements in each adjustment category for each elementary grade. The results showed that teachers tended to see more unfavorable than favorable signs of adjustment among the study group even in the early grades. Moreover, teachers' impressions of unfavorable development increased with each grade, particularly with respect to personality traits and school attitudes. Over two-thirds of the boys in each of the grades were considered by their teachers to have serious enough adjustment problems to be noted in the students' permanent school records. Surveying individual patterns of negative statements across the span of six elementary grades revealed that 78 per cent of the boys were consistently seen by different teachers as showing signs of serious difficulty throughout most of their elementary school careers. These chronic patterns, defined by negative statements from four or more teachers during the six elementary grades, included various combinations of the five problem categories, although poor work habits and poor school attitudes were most frequently included.

While the general trend of teachers' ratings and comments emphasized attitudes and behaviors handicapping boys in their adjustment and progress in school, teachers also frequently described what appeared to them to be more basic problems underlying unfavorable classroom responses. For example, failure to achieve prerequisite skills essential to further learning, particularly reading, was seen as a major factor contributing to school maladjustment. By the sixth grade general academic problems were indicated for almost 60 per cent of the study group. Teachers also frequently attributed classroom problems and unsatisfactory behavior to conditions and circumstances external to the school setting, that is, they perceived them as manifestations of problems or conditions originating outside the classroom. A survey of cumulative records revealed that slightly more than one-third of the boys had been identified in teachers' statements as handicapped by such external problems.

Among the problems identified were poor cultural background, family and related problems such as frequent absences, tardiness, changes of school due to family's frequent moving, emotional or personal difficulties created by problems outside the classroom, and physical problems of various kinds. Family conditions and circumstances, along with physical problems, were most frequently identified as major sources of problems. Twenty per cent of the boys were seen as handicapped by conditions at home. The following are typical examples of problems described:

> A divided family—many problems affect boy's school adjustment.

> Mother is employed—family conditions have much to do with boy's school attitudes which are very poor.

> Very poor home conditions—father can't keep a job—the boy has an improper diet.

> The boy gets no help from home. Parents are indifferent.

> Complex unstable home life is having definite effect on boy's school adjustment.

> Mother abandoned child—ran off—left him with grandparents—boy very upset.

> Frequent family moving has kept boy out of school. He cannot keep up.

> Chronic absences hinder progress—boy is kept out of school frequently to care for younger children.

As Chapter Three indicated, it appears likely that family problems affecting school adjustment were more prevalent than indicated in teachers' statements. The referral of 41 per cent of the boys and their parents to visiting teachers during the elementary years tends to confirm this belief.

Learning and adjustment problems of some boys were attributed by teachers mainly to physical handicaps which required help which teachers felt could not be provided in regular classrooms. The records show that 37 per cent of the study group had been identified by their teachers as handicapped in some way at some point during grade school. Twenty-five per cent of the boys were referred for speech difficulties, 9 per cent for visual problems, 4 per cent for hearing problems. Only 2 per cent were referred because of emotional problems. These percentages probably underestimate the actual incidence of physical and emotional problems among the study group. In interviews with parents, physical and emotional problems were occasionally described that were not indicated in the boys' school records. Teachers did not refer many boys for psychiatric help. Whether this was because they saw them as primarily socially rather than emotionally maladjusted or because of the unavailability of psychiatric help can only be conjectured. In teachers' cumulative card statements, however, serious emotional problems were suggested for several children whose records did not indicate referral for professional help. Even according to these possible underestimates, the incidence of handicaps among this group of boys is considerably greater than that for Kansas City grade school children in general. This is particularly true with respect to speech difficulties identified among 5 to 10 per cent of all children in contrast to 25 per cent of the study group.

Another problem area associated by teachers with school maladjustment is the pattern of frequent change of schools and excessive absences among disadvantaged children. The data on school attendance for the primary years reveal that for about half of the study group absences were a relatively minor problem. One-fourth of the boys, however, lost one or more school months a year through absences, with the accrued loss over the six grades amounting to almost half a year, or, for many, considerably more than half a year. Likewise, frequency of changing schools, to which some teachers attributed adjustment problems, appeared to characterize the school careers of less than half the study group. However, more than one-fourth did experience changes in the school setting on the average of once every grade and a half, and some did so much more frequently.

How, if at all, were these indicated problems and characteristics related to racial characteristics of boys or to late adolescent adjustments? Table 10 summarizes the relevant elementary school data. Negro and white youth generally did not differ significantly in measured abilities or in school attendance during the elementary grades. Relatively more Negro than white youths (22 per cent and 13 per

Table 10. ELEMENTARY GRADE SCHOOL VARIABLES

Variables	Negro	White
IQ scores		
Binet median IQ	91.0	94.0
First quartile	85.5	88.0
Third quartile	99.0	102.0
Range	70–118	69–119
Otis median IQ	88.0	90.0
First quartile	83.0	86.0
Third quartile	95.0	95.0
Range	69–103	74–101
Teachers' ratings of adjustment		
	Per Cent	
Chronic adjustment problems[a]	49	52
Extent of chronic problems[b]		
One or two	60	55
Three or four	19	32
Five or more	21	13
Absences during elementary grades		
Median absences Grade 1	15 days	15 days
Median absences Grade 3	10 days	10 days
Median absences Grade 6	8 days	9 days
	Per Cent	
Three or more school changes	55	43
Physical handicaps	36	48

[a] Refers to percentage of boys who were rated below average on one or more of the same adjustment traits over the four years of third through sixth grades.

[b] Refers to the number of problem areas consistently rated below average by teachers over the four-year period.

cent respectively) were identified by teachers as showing chronic patterns of maladjustment over the four grades preceding the boys' selection for the Work-Study Program. However, slightly fewer Negro boys showed multiple problems of adjustment than did whites. Negro boys tended to change schools somewhat more frequently than white boys. Fewer Negro youths had records indicating physical handicaps or referrals for help with such problems.

When the IQ scores of the five late adolescent adjustment sub-groups were compared, there were no significant differences in IQ scores among subgroups. The school adaptive group showed somewhat better potential for school work on the Stanford Binet test administered in kindergarten or first grade, but this advantage was not apparent in the Otis Beta scores obtained in the sixth grade. For all subgroups there was a general downward shift in IQ scores from early measures to those administered in the fifth or sixth grade.

When the association of teacher ratings to late adolescent adjustment is assessed, some associations are found. Table 11 summarizes relevant findings. It is evident that boys who showed maladaptive adjustment in late adolescence also experienced greater difficulty with school rules and regulations, self-control, and study habits in the sixth grade than did boys who showed adaptive adjustment. Moreover, these difficulties increased each year of grade school. Both maladaptive and adaptive late adolescent subgroups showed an increasing percentage of boys rated unsatisfactory in growth from one elementary grade to the next, but the increase was much more pronounced for the maladaptive groups.

When patterns of teachers' ratings over the elementary years were assessed for each boy and compared across late adolescent adjustment subgroups, certain significant differences were found. Table 12 summarizes these data, and indicates that problems with rules and regulations, characteristic of the maladaptive group in late adolescence, appear to have had their beginning in the early elementary grades.

When chronicity of adjustment problems during elementary grades was assessed in association with later adjustment, it was found that relatively more boys showing late adolescent maladjustment showed problems throughout grade school. Seventy-two per cent of seriously maladaptive boys, 68 per cent of marginal boys, 64 per cent of erratic boys, 59 per cent of work adaptive boys, and only 50 per cent of school adaptive boys showed chronic adjustment problems during grades three through six. However, this association is not statistically significant, and all late adolescent subgroups had a considerable percentage of boys with chronic patterns of grade school maladjustment.

Other school variables and late adolescent adjustments did not show statistically significant associations. Data on elementary grade handicaps indicated that maladaptive subgroups were not referred for

Table 11.   LATE ADOLESCENT ADAPTATION AND TEACHERS'
RATINGS OF ADJUSTMENT

Trait Rated by Teachers in 6th Grade	Maladaptive (N = 179)	Adaptive (N = 141)	χ^2	Signif.
	Per Cent			
Work habits				
Below average	66	49	10.26	.05
Average	26	44		
Above average	8	7		
Responsibility				
Below average	60	44	6.82	.05
Average	28	39		
Above average	12	17		
Self-control				
Below average	55	36	10.42	.01
Average	32	43		
Above average	13	21		
Attitude toward school regulations				
Below average	52	28	16.54	.01–.001
Average	31	41		
Above average	17	31		
Initiative				
Below average	60	49	6.47	.05
Average	26	40		
Above average	14	11		
Getting along with others				
Below average	43	30	5.68	.05–.10
Average	33	41		
Above average	24	29		
Participation in group activities				
Below average	35	28	4.70	.05–.10
Average	41	38		
Above average	24	34		

Adjustment Area	Level of Adjustment	Maladaptive N	Adaptive N	χ^2	Signif.
Work habits	Chronic problem[a]	76	46	6.04	.05
	Erratic[b]	51	44		
	Satisfactory[c]	35	43		
Responsibility	Chronic problem	49	38	15.27	.01
	Erratic	75	41		
	Satisfactory	39	60		
Self-control	Chronic problem	46	26	4.17	.05
	Erratic	69	58		.10
	Satisfactory	50	52		
Initiative	Chronic problem	59	36	6.79	.05
	Erratic	63	53		
	Satisfactory	38	50		
Attitude toward school regulations	Chronic problem	36	19	17.80	.01
	Erratic	78	42		
	Satisfactory	52	75		

[a] A chronic problem is defined as a specific trait which is rated below average by three or four teachers (third grade through sixth grade), indicating an adjustment problem which does not seem to improve.
[b] Erratic adjustment is defined as ratings by teachers over the elementary grades which indicate both adequate and inadequate adjustment.
[c] Satisfactory adjustment is defined as teacher ratings indicating average or above adjustment in the trait area over the four-year period.

help more frequently than adaptive boys. In fact, seriously maladaptive youth tended to be less frequently referred than school adaptive boys. Seriously maladaptive boys also tended to have changed schools more frequently than the other adjustment subgroups, with the marginal and erratic groups also showing a somewhat higher frequency of school changes than work and school adaptive boys.

In substance, boys screened for the Work-Study Program composed a rather heterogeneous ability group at the time they entered the elementary grades. By the seventh grade, however, this rather wide range of differences in measured potential for school had narrowed, and the group of boys appeared to be a relatively homogeneous group of socially maladjusted nonachievers with very limited potential for success in junior or senior high school. This chapter documents the fact that whatever learning experience these children had during their elementary years in school, family, and community was not conducive to progress in school. This chapter also suggests that the nature and extent of problems and the period of time during the elementary years when they first emerged differed among the boys screened. Children who showed maladaptive late adolescent adjustments tended to be identified earliest in the elementary grades as having adjustment difficulties. They were more frequently rated by teachers as having greater difficulty with school rules and regulations, self-control, and study habits.

5

The High School

The 422 boys in the experimental and control groups started the study in the eighth grade of five junior high schools—all the schools which served predominantly working-class populations in Kansas City. They spent two years in junior high school and a third year in the tenth grade of senior high schools, reaching the end of the Work-Study curriculum at the close of the tenth grade. Some of them stayed in senior high school for a time, and about 18 per cent of them actually completed high school with a diploma or a certificate of attendance.

These boys were marginal to the school. They had been getting failing or inferior grades. Their measured intelligence was below average or average. They were seen by their teachers and their age-mates as maladjusted to school and generally hostile and aggressive. Even in schools of the lowest socioeconomic status, these boys stood out as "bad actors."

Every school has two cultures, the instrumental and the expressive. The instrumental culture of the school is its obvious business —teaching boys and girls the subjects of the curriculum and so preparing them for higher levels of school or for a vocation. The expressive culture is the set of things that go on outside the regular business —games, extracurricular activities, nonsense activities that pupils carry on, all without any goal outside the activities themselves. The expressive culture is partly conducted by the school as a means of making life more enjoyable to pupils and teachers and partly conducted by the pupils underground as part of their peer culture.

How did study group boys relate to these two cultures? The dominant instrumental culture was the locus of much of their failure. Most of them had not learned the mental skills of the school culture at passable levels. Within the target group of 422 boys, half were reading at the fifth grade level when they entered junior high school. One-fourth were reading at or below fourth grade level; only 10 per cent were reading at the appropriate grade level. This pattern occurred in other skills. Four out of five boys were below grade level in arithmetic fundamentals; half of these were at or below fifth grade level. Already hopelessly behind, many of these youths had given up trying to learn the instrumental culture even before they entered junior high school where the academic pressures increased. Some of these youths were capable of passable achievement. However, their hostility, ambivalence, or indifference toward school and the conflict between their subcultural values and habits and those of the dominant school culture made it difficult for them to become involved in or apply themselves to school work. It took patience, acceptance, tolerance of hostility, and much resourcefulness to work effectively with such boys.

The problem of teaching the boy whose skills were far below par is illustrated by the experience of a thirty-year-old woman who was working for her teacher's certificate. In her last year of training, she took part in a practicum which involved classroom observation and some tutoring of pupils who were doing poorly. She was assigned to one of the Work-Study classes. In a daily log she recorded her impressions of learning problems she encountered. Her log describes her experience with Ned, a sixteen-year-old experimental group boy in the ninth grade.

> Today the class was pretty agitated. They had a substitute and things were disorganized. I was to work with Ned today, so I took him into the hall and we tried to find a quiet place to study. The hall was full of kids, so we went into the cafeteria and sat in one corner. There was a good deal of noise coming from the clean-up work and from the kitchen, as preparation for lunch was going on. These weren't the best conditions and Ned couldn't concentrate at all at first. He was restless and distracted.
>
> I had brought a simplified illustrated copy of *The Count of Monte Cristo* which I gave to Ned. We're going to

write a book report on it if we ever get finished with it. I read him the first chapter. What I hoped to do was give him a form or method for getting the meaning of the story. I had him write down the setting, the characters, and a brief summary of the plot in Chapter One. At first it was like before. I had to tell him the sentences word by word before he could write them down. He had an unbelievably difficult time identifying in his mind the names and the particular characters they represented. It took about a half hour to get this so he remembered it. He has an awfully short attention span, but I could see why. He isn't making any mental connections of individual facts. The names and the people who were doing things were totally unrelated to him.

He did get it at last and seemed delighted, although it was a struggle and he didn't seem to enjoy it very much while he was trying to grasp it. When we got into the plot, he became frustrated again. He didn't seem to be able to comprehend any stream of continuous characters and their meaningful interaction. Then suddenly, he said, "Oh, I see," and he just beamed with delight after many minutes of intense frowning. A few minutes later he said, "You know this is really interesting." I had the feeling that maybe this was actually the first time he'd ever seen that stories were really stories of things happening instead of just word after word of single unrelated meanings.

However, he had such a difficult time. He needs constant encouragement and would never proceed on his own. It just takes too much time and too much energy. Another interesting aspect of his learning is that when he tries to write about what he has read he concentrates so hard on this that he forgets his trend of thought and carelessly leaves out words. He has such a difficult time retaining or holding relationships in his head. I did some of the reading, and I know he was listening; but when I finished it, it really seems that he hasn't heard a word. It doesn't seem to register at all. Here and there he will pick up certain bits of information which struck him as interesting, but usually they are irrelevant facts. When he reads he has to concentrate so hard on the words that he can't get the meaning. I can't help wondering how much he is getting out of these sessions. I get a little discouraged because it seems that it takes the whole period just to get him to the same place he was at the end of the last meeting.

Difficulties study group boys had in the instrumental culture were clearly pointed out in observing and assessing their learning and achievement in specific academic tasks. In one eighth grade Work-

Study class, an arithmetic test showed the majority of the group below sixth grade level. The teacher was using a workbook with the boys, and we noted one day that she was far behind in checking on the boys' work. Many of them were making mistakes in their workbook problems, but these mistakes were not corrected by the teacher. Thus the boys were "learning" to make mistakes. We secured a set of programed workbooks for fourth grade arithmetic. Each lesson had an answer sheet which could be used by a boy to correct himself. We gave each boy a workbook and gave the class a pep talk suggesting that they could have fun checking their own progress. The boys appeared to take to this game, and within a month almost all of them had finished the workbook. Then we gave a standardized arithmetic test and compared the scores with scores on another form of this test taken by the boys before the experiment. The average of the class had hardly changed. A few boys had performed almost at grade level on the first test and maintained this position. They had not needed the workbook practice. Boys who scored at about the fourth grade level or lower gave evidence of being unable to read the simple directions for some test items or to read simple word problems involving arithmetic concepts. Thus, the difficulty the boys had with reading caused them difficulty with other subjects and made the instrumental culture of the school a source of frustration to them.

The Work-Study Program added what might prove to be an important element to the instrumental culture of the school—a systematic work-experience which was viewed as a means to the end of becoming a competent adult worker. Thus, the experimental group boys were given a supplementary instrumental curriculum. Only a fraction of the boys—the work adaptive subgroup—made successful use of this alternative instrumental culture of the school when they were placed in it. The other boys apparently did not have motives or habits that fitted with the Work-Study curriculum.

What the school organized officially as its expressive culture had little or no attraction for most study group boys. They did not like to take part in organized sports. They did not enjoy school assemblies. Few took part in group singing in school. Thanksgiving, Christmas, Washington's Birthday, and Easter celebrations did not involve them except occasionally as distant onlookers. They had their own peer group culture which was essentially expressive and which played an important part in their lives in school and out. The peer group culture

of such boys is somewhat different from the peer group culture of the
majority group in the school, even though the majority group may
have the same socioeconomic status and skin color.

Characteristic habits of the marginal peer group culture included use of an extreme amount of profanity and obscenity, with
little attempt to hide it in the classroom; restless, fidgety behavior in
the classroom, instigated by one or another boy and contagiously imi-
tated by the group; stealing, generally from figures in the Establishment, such as proprietors and school personnel, but also from weaker
youths who are not members of the particular gang or in-group; and
limited, though sometimes picturesque, language patterns which did
not express complex relations.

Motives and values of the marginal group included desire for
excitement, which might come from any of a variety of law-defying
and authority-defying behaviors—stealing an automobile and going
for a joyride, staging a gang fight, or raiding a party in a private
home or in a church or a community center; display of masculine aggressive behavior, lording it over others, swaggering in "cool" clothes,
name-calling, and defying teachers; desire for immediate gratification
of wants, which included preference for being paid by the day over
by the week or month, need for praise or other kind of assurance of
success while working, and inability to work well toward a distant or
abstract goal.

The life of a boy in the tough areas of the city was made tol-
erable or even pleasurable if he made friends and joined a peer group
organization, however loose and unstructured it may have been. This
made it useful for a boy to move from junior high school to senior
high school as one of a group. To move into a senior high school alone
and as a stranger was very difficult. Thus, a few boys, after finishing
tenth grade in a school that went only that far, had to make their way
into a strange senior high school. One such boy said, "Most of the
boys at M have been there two years and have friends, so they don't
want to make up with new boys. You know, man, a guy needs friends
at M." Another boy dropped out of junior high school upon reaching
the age of sixteen. He had moved into the neighborhood with his
mother, and he found that he had to fight other boys every afternoon
after school. He decided that his mother needed his earnings, and he
got a job and quit school.

When a group of boys are together in this kind of area, the

peer culture shows itself clearly and may even be imposed on boys
who have not yet learned it fully because they are younger or share
more of the standard peer culture. We were aware that some of our
experimental group boys might be seduced by the deviant majority in
the group. Work supervisors and teachers of the experimental group
came up against this deviant peer culture quickly and disturbingly.
They had to learn to cope with it or quit their jobs. Work supervisors
had to face it in what was a relatively new and unstructured group
work experience for the boys. Initially, freedom from the classroom
and great physical space to move in during the half day of group work
seemed to stimulate deviant behavior among the boys. Since we had
chosen as work supervisors men of a masculine type who had some
acquaintance with lower-class mores, we expected them to get along
with this alienated peer culture and even to modify it in the direction
of harmony with the standard peer culture of the school. There was
a period during which men and boys took each others' measure.

Two work supervisors were unable to cope with these aggressive, acting-out youth. One man quit on his first day when the fifteen
boys assigned to him broke into a wild free-swinging fight on the
school grounds. Another man, who had no previous experience with
tough boys and was extremely sensitive to their language, was unable
to be tough with them and quit after three months. Each of the other
work supervisors stayed on the job at least two years and worked out
his own approach to the boys. Each testified that he gained satisfaction
from the work, although it was not easy. The initial approaches of
some teachers and work supervisors appeared to enhance or at least
prolong the period of disruption and acting out behavior which characterized experimental youth in the first year of the program.

Mr. M was a physical education substitute teacher and was
attempting to become certified for public school teaching in Kansas
City. He supervised a work group for three years. His first year was
frustrating and very unrewarding. He later revealed in an interview
that his whole approach to these boys was based on his belief that they
needed understanding and guidance and that this could be achieved
through reason and discussion. However, Mr. M could not help showing his feelings of being let down when the boys did not behave. He
took it very personally. He would do nice things for the boys, then expect them to do nice things for him, that is, behave. When they did
not, he felt he was being manipulated and he would blow up. He

wanted to be liked by the boys and to gain their respect and confidence
and was much concerned about his failure to do this. His behavior
in trying to develop a workable approach, however, was inconsistent.
One time he would try firmness, another time he would waver and
be indecisive, and still another time he would explode with profanity,
revealing his frustrations and vulnerability to the group. Although
Mr. M was physically strong he never resorted to physical strength to
maintain order or discipline unruly boys. He had been told that this
would only make his job harder and would destroy his chances of developing a working relationship with the boys. He also refrained, with
considerable effort, from verbal, caustic interchange with individuals
in the group and from ridiculing his major antagonists. He was afraid
this would crystallize the group against him.

An incident in Mr. M's group the first year illustrates the problems confronting him and the turning point in his career as work supervisor. This incident was reported by a Work-Study teacher who
also worked as a work supervisor and who was developing relatively
successful approaches to working with some of the toughest boys in
the program.

> I was in my classroom on the third floor when I hap-
> pened to look out the window and saw three or four Work-
> Study boys in Mr. M's group on the ledge of the second floor.
> I knew he and his group were meeting in a room down there
> to plan the group work for the afternoon, but I was amazed
> and had started for the door when I heard this terrible racket
> down on the second floor. I dashed down, and when I got
> there I found Mr. M standing spread-eagle in the door hold-
> ing on to the door jambs for dear life, trying to keep the boys
> from getting out of the room. Two of them were trying to
> crawl through his legs, and two more were back of him push-
> ing. There was whooping and hollering in the room. Well, I
> grabbed the two trying to get out and yelled for M to grab the
> other two, and we tossed them up against the back wall. Then
> I saw some boys over by the windows. They had chased three
> or four boys out on the ledge and wouldn't let them back in.
> I grabbed several of these boys and threw them over in the
> corner, and M followed suit. He's a big burly guy and could
> have handled them by himself, but he didn't want to use force.
> After that incident he began to change for the better. The
> boys realized then that he could take care of them any time
> he wanted to or felt like it.

At the end of three years with the Work-Study program, Mr. M discussed his experience and what he had learned.

> Usual techniques don't always work with these kids. They are a heck of a lot sharper than we give them credit for and they are always looking for the Achilles' heel. I was floundering until I began to get sore and crack back at these kids. I cracked back hard and found myself feeling a lot better because I began getting respect. Now, these boys are past masters at putting you down, but I found I could give them tit for tat and often a little more for their money. I crack back hard, and when a kid continues to get out of line I just take him aside and say, "Now look, I'm going to begin cracking you in front of the boys, and I mean hard. I know a lot about you, boy, and if you don't think I won't use it, you just try me."
>
> Course, I'm primed because I know they are going to try and best me—but when they do I'm ready, and I crack back and the victim squirms, but the rest of the boys roar. Actually, they seem to want me to come out on top. They respect someone who can really do this. Before I wised up to what was required here, I was miserable. Their classroom teacher told me one day that in class they were discussing me, and several boys chorused "We like old M but he sure can't take it." Well, it's true. Until I learned to take it as well as dish it out, my life was miserable and I had nothing but trouble from those kids.

Mr. M was asked how he thought his "cracking back" affected his relations with the boys.

> Oh, I see this cracking back as just part of working with these boys. You've got to first find some way of communicating, which I find comes from first gaining their respect. I never hesitate to talk to these boys about problems that come up. I just get them together, explain the situation, and then we discuss it. I keep them involved in it because I feel they have got good sense, and I tell them that I know they are smart enough to figure things out, and by golly they are, too. Now we talk and discuss. I couldn't have ever done this if I hadn't changed my tactics and met their challenge. I wouldn't say that the language I use or this method is acceptable to most educators, but we are working with kids who don't accept what usually works for most kids.

Another work supervisor with a Negro group used controlled physical aggression to gain and hold their allegiance. The project director did not discuss this method with him critically and took no formal notice of it. The decision was that each man should be allowed to work out his own relationships within broad limits set by the director. This man, himself a Negro, found himself challenged by some of his boys, who were nearly as big as he and who would refuse to take orders on the work-task. He knew that this group of boys had an unwritten rule that a show of fighting was acceptable but not to be taken seriously if it consisted of punching the opponent on his chest, not on his head or abdomen. The fighting could be apparently quite fierce but harmless as long as this rule was obeyed. Fighting with a knife or other lethal weapon was something else and serious business. This supervisor simply stood up to two or three of his boys when they refused to follow orders and punched them on the chest, hard enough to knock them down. Once he had done this, he had no more trouble from these boys or others in the group. They might grumble about things and curse, but they accepted him as boss of the work crew.

Another work supervisor refused to use force on his boys, except rarely to hold a boy's arms to restrain him from fighting another boy or damaging property. This man had a difficult time at first. His group was quite hostile to him. One of them slit the seat cover of his car with a knife after he had been bawled out for some misbehavior. This man maintained his patience, often scolded boys as well as praised them, and built up a great deal of personal knowledge and understanding of each boy in his group. Gradually the boys settled down with him, and paid him a kind of grudging respect. At the close of the project, after the work groups had been disbanded, members of this group continued to visit his classroom, call him on the telephone about their doings, and invite him to their weddings and similar occasions.

Classroom teachers also had difficulty with the deviant peer culture of these boys, although they did not come into as much raw contact with it. Male classroom teachers, particularly the inexperienced, were constantly challenged until they were able to establish authority and control. Female classroom teachers were treated somewhat less aggressively although they were usually subjected to a period of testing and shock treatment (obscene words and profanity). Mrs. B, a Negro teacher with considerable experience with slow-learning pupils, taught one of the Negro groups. She was notably patient with the group and got better results from them than a male Negro teacher

who set high standards and then seemed bewildered when the class
failed. Mrs. B was most concerned by the open profanity and obscenity
used by the boys. She commented about one boy.

> S is very vulgar. He is always using sexual terms. In
> fact they are terms that you just don't use. Like he will use
> the word *fuck* right in the classroom—right in front of me.
> And, of course, he uses the word that we don't like [*nigger*].
> It's abhorrent, yet he uses it constantly. Of course the other
> boys use it, and when they do, I tell them, "Now of course
> when the other group calls you that you get quite mad, but
> you call each other that name." I have really tried to break
> that down but I still have it used a lot in the classroom and
> other bad words like that. They'll say, "Oh, Nigger, hey, Nig-
> ger, say what's the matter with you, Nigger?"

Mrs. B was able to gain the respect and cooperation of her
group, mainly by being tolerant and trusting of them. A mark of what
she accomplished is the story of her handbag, which contained some
money and personal things and also her keys for school supply cabinets.

> I leave my bag on the desk. I let them get the keys,
> and you know they would take the keys out of my bag and
> put them back and close my bag, and sometimes you see them
> sitting and holding it—my bag. Never have I missed anything
> from my bag. But we cleaned out the cabinet on Monday.
> They took everything they could. That was school property,
> not mine. But sometimes they would take my lunch. I used to
> sometimes bring my lunch and leave it on the top of my desk
> if I didn't get a chance to take it to my locker on the second
> floor. Then I might come into the room and find my lunch
> gone. So I would say, "Someone took my lunch." Then they
> would say, "I did, Mrs. B" or "We did." They had fun with
> me that way. Then they would tell me, "Now, Mrs. B, any-
> thing you want? We steal anything you want." Most of them
> had police records, but they would say to me, "Mrs. B, we
> wouldn't hit you for nothing." That's just the way they would
> put it. Now guess where my bag was stolen? Right there in the
> main office, but not by Work-Study boys. I had a ten-dollar
> bill and I changed it during lunch period and I had $9.75 and
> charge plates and what not. So evidently some pupil saw me
> set the bag on a chair while I was talking about my grade
> reports with the clerk. They just saw a good chance and took it.

Miss G was a competent classroom teacher, about thirty-five
years old, who became relatively successful with a mixed racial class.

The surprising thing to me is the contrast between their group behavior and their individual responses in a person-to-person relationship. In a group they are often so difficult. Each one seems to have to outdo the other. I was startled the first few weeks at the hyperactive level of behavior. They were like separate, individual entities of pure, raw movement exploding in all directions at once. It was unbelievable.

However, individually, these children, when they come to know and trust you, can talk to you and really communicate. They will listen quietly, and you really wonder what makes the difference. But then you realize that the problem is that they just can't hold steady for very long. They are just too easily triggered by any kind of change or distraction in the situation. They just seem to have to hold the center of the stage by being louder, more daring, and more profane than any of the others.

As individuals, however, you just can't help finding them very likeable and attractive youngsters in many respects. At other times you just want to brain them. Let me give you an example. The other day I had the boys out on a field trip. I stopped along the way to pick up some raffle tickets for a friend of mine. As we got back on the bus Bobby came up to me and said softly with real warmth, "Gee, I hope your friend wins." The next day he came up to me the first thing in the morning and asked if my friend had won. Now, I know this sounds like a small thing, but here is a boy who at times is a holy terror, yet he does have it inside himself to be a warm, responsive person. The sad thing is that he doesn't have the chance to express this side of himself. There are just too many pressures on him and he just doesn't have enough opportunity to express this warmth and responsiveness. So many of the boys are like that. It takes so long for some of them to feel secure or safe enough to show this side. Some of them have been badly burnt in their relationships with adults. Bobby, for example, tells me his mother got rid of him so that she could remarry. I know this bugs the boy because he mentions his mother frequently, wondering where she is and asking why she didn't take him with her. He wants to talk to me about it and I let him, but I keep telling him it's bugging him and that's probably part of his trouble. He says talking about it helps. I don't know. When you understand both the inner and external pressures on these kids you can't help but respect their struggle.

Miss G was asked how she managed to get the boys involved in classroom work.

Well, in the first place I have a wholesome respect for
these boys. I try to communicate to them, not only in words
but by presenting problems to them which we discuss in class.
These are practical ones like how does the group help each of
us learn. This leads far afield, but I usually find that the boys
develop the point fairly effectively. One thing I learned quickly
was that when the classroom session was not planned, the boys
made the most of it and shaped it into that with which they
were most familiar; aggressive horseplay, cracking each other,
teasing, et cetera. So I try always to be well prepared and involve them just as soon as they come through the door. I tried
a number of things. For example, I found they were fascinated
by the tape recorder and hearing themselves on tape, so I
came to use this frequently. I also learned that music had a
quieting effect upon them.

I could well understand the boredom they felt and
their restlessness when attempting to solve academic problems
for which they were not equipped. So I tried many kinds of
things to help them discover that using the mind wasn't a
painful experience. We went on field trips to museums, picnics, and we played popular as well as classical music in the
classroom. I'm afraid we didn't follow the usual textbook procedures, but in my class of boys I had a range of ability from
good average to way below average, and the range in achievement was just as extreme. I really felt that the country school-
teacher approach was essential in getting any movement at
all educationally. One thing I feel very definite about is the
class size for boys like these. It must be small, not more than
fifteen or twenty in the group, and preferably smaller, although that would probably be impossible because of the increasing number of students.

Quite a different point of view was held by a classroom teacher
who had the group for about two months before he left to go back to
the university where he was working toward a master's degree. This
man had a class of Work-Study boys who were nearly all white—the
same group Miss G had taught earlier.

Well, I have often felt that I would have to quit—
that I just couldn't take it. I just can't teach these boys. I try,
but these kids won't or don't want to get with it. I've never
had such abuse as I've had from them. Some of them are
mental cases. Nobody has ever talked to me the way these
boys have. The vile language, the profanity, and the name-
calling are unprintable. I feel education and discipline in
school have diminished greatly during the last ten years,

Everybody in the school seems to pass it off to the next person, and then the principal's office coddles the boys, talks to them a little, pats them on the shoulder, and sends them back to the classes. I've tried to teach, but lectures won't work with these kids—they aren't receptive. They call me all sorts of names. When I go home at night I'm upset—my stomach is churning and I can't enjoy my family or friends. This has sure been a bad experience for me.

Another man, Mr. D, spent two years with a class of white Work-Study boys and came out with positive attitudes. He was able to capitalize on some of the advantages of the work program. For instance, he got the boys to open a group savings account in a bank and showed them how to keep records of their savings. On Fridays, when they were paid their weekly allowance, he encouraged them to put some of this money into the savings account. Like the other male teachers, he had to take a good deal of verbal hostility from the boys.

Teaching this type of boy is very difficult compared to teaching regular classes. You have much more name-calling, such as "Fuck you," and "You big fat pig, shut up!" Beating on kids for such remarks would only lead to more name-calling and more hatred. These boys talk to each other the same way. But this would not be as apparent in the regular classes, where the presence of girls would tend to keep them from getting so rough.

The boys get to be more socially conscious and show that they care about the attitudes of other people in the school —especially the girls. I notice when girls come into the room to deliver bulletins from the office, several boys will cover their faces or slouch down in their seats because they don't want to be recognized as being in this problem class. Four of the boys, especially, talk about being ashamed of being in the program. Yet the fact that they have money in their pocket and some of them have jobs gives them confidence. Being out in the world of work and associating with older people at work has given some of them more positive attitudes.

A questionnaire was answered by eight Work-Study teachers and work supervisors in the spring of 1963, at the close of the second year of the project. They were asked to describe their attitudes toward the program, their perceptions of its reception by school principals, and their perceptions of problems and good features of the program. All eight respondents had positive attitudes toward the Work-Study Program, as is indicated in Table 13. Three were with the program

Table 13. Attitudes of Teachers and Work Supervisors Toward the Work-Study Program

Teachers	Initial Attitude	Attitude During Program	Final Attitude
B (male)	Uncertain. Did not know what would be outcome of program.	Developed awareness of the special needs of this type of boy.	Program is needed. Boys look forward to something. They experience success for the first time.
B (female)	Very doubtful about success.	Observed change in boys. Became aware of their potential but need for individual help.	Feels personal experience indicates that boys are being helped and is no longer doubtful that these boys can be helped.
G (female)	Interested in boys of this type. Felt a need to try and help them.	Developed broader view of these boys and their problems. Developed awareness of their alienation from school and community.	Feels program makes it possible to focus teacher effort on understanding boys and developing relationships which are sorely needed by this type of boy.
D (male)	Favored basic approach.	Uncertainties stimulated by discipline problems and non-acceptance by school administration.	Continues to favor program and the basic approach. Feels problems encountered are due to newness of curriculum and personnel and not to the basic approach. Feels depressed at times because gains seem slow.

E (male)	Felt a definite need for this type of program.	Developed awareness that some boys can be helped, but some are so emotionally mal-adjusted that the Work-Study Program cannot help them substantially.	Feels essentially the same way as initially. Feels boys have been let down by not obtaining jobs for them more quickly.
M (male)	Felt boys could be helped through under-standing and discussion and showing that you liked and trusted them.	Learned that boys first had to have firm limits set or you would lose control.	Boys can accept limits, and then counseling and learning about themselves are possible. Feels boys can be helped to find themselves once they are aware of limits and the consistency of authority.
G (male)	Felt a need for this type of program.	This need has been further emphasized.	Feels that with some modifications and changes the program will be beneficial to the community as well as to the boys.
H (male)	Uncertain. Had doubts as to being able to really help this type of boy.	Saw some boys change for the better; bringing about such a change became a challenge.	Feels that all boys who actively participate will profit from the program.

from its beginning. One teacher, while favoring the program, expressed a need for a change in jobs. While the attitudes reflect differences in program operation from school to school and from the vantage points of various individuals, some general assessments can be drawn from this survey. The consensus was that a program of this type was needed in the schools, but there was some doubt about how well it would succeed. Most of the respondents viewed their interaction with the program as a learning experience.

Evaluation of school principals' influences ranged from "[He] has been an inspiration to me," to "The principal did not want the program, and we have been neglected from the day we entered." Four respondents reported positive influences from principals, three reported neutral influences, and one was negative. In one school with positive influence, however, the teacher reported that the vice-principal didn't like the program, and felt that "you can't help these kids."

Suggested modifications of the program included shortening study time to prevent monotony, paying work groups by the job and not by the hour, enrolling boys in the sixth grade rather than the eighth, providing working areas better than the cramped and poorly lit ones in at least one school, and focusing on work which the boys would like and which would be useful when employment was eventually sought. One work supervisor felt a need for transferring the groups away from the school setting. His group worked and studied at the Rotary Club camp while weather permitted and during this period was one of the most successful groups in the entire program. Another suggestion was that boys should not do menial work around their schools where they could be observed by their peers unless they received some special recognition for their efforts.

Among the best liked features of Work-Study were the small size of classes, the flexibility which accommodated individual needs, the grouping of boys of similar ability and socioeconomic background, and the close association of boys and adults. One teacher felt that the boys could learn self-control in this setting but would likely be "kicked out of school" in a regular program. It was said that the program "gives the boys hope and a sense of belonging . . . a kind of reprieve in order to find themselves."

Among the most difficult problems was insufficient time for record-keeping and counseling with the boys. Selling the program idea to parents, teachers, administrators, and the boys was also listed. One teacher reported that her colleagues did not accept either program or boys and were quick to accuse them of any misbehavior. The lack of adequate kinds and amounts of group work during Stage One was mentioned three times, as was an inadequate number of part-time job openings in Stage Two. One teacher reported that his group was meeting in a small converted storage room. They used folding chairs and old benches and did not have a blackboard. A later interview with this teacher disclosed the irony that a bright, roomy study room was just across the hall from the storeroom; Work-Study boys were barred from this room. In other follow-up interviews with teacher and work supervisors, conditions and circumstances specific to each school were revealed as significant factors influencing teachers' attitudes and behavior. Teachers' morale, for example, was directly affected by their acceptance in the school, by the physical facilities and supplies at their disposal, by the support received from administrators in crisis situations, and by their being recognized as special teachers of boys with learning and social adjustment problems. Some administrators did not recognize the special morale problems of teachers who worked daily with and were responsible for the school progress and behavior of socially maladjusted boys. One teacher who had been particularly effective during the first two years of the project showed real concern about his professional status and his acceptance by his colleagues. In the middle of the third year he talked with a research associate about his feelings.

> I feel in a way that the Work-Study boys and myself are actually degraded somewhat. I personally feel alone and isolated here. Now I think I'm accepted by other teachers in the school, but I don't think they understand what I'm trying to do or the aims and objectives of the program. I think these are misinterpreted. I was promised a chance to discuss this program with the faculty but it never materialized. You know, after a while, you get to feeling like you're a foreigner on the faculty. I feel the other teachers think I have some kind of Mickey Mouse program. I'm always getting comments from other people here about wasting time and money on these "punks." Why, I overheard [the vice-principal] say to someone the other day that he thought it was a crime to spend all this time and money on "troublemakers" and not do anything for the kids keeping out of trouble.

The control group received only the normal treatment given to boys in high school. They were not identified to teachers. Their parents were not alerted unless a problem arose in the usual course of school events. Researchers interviewed them at the age of about sixteen and again at eighteen, but in a nondirective fashion. To see how control group members were perceived by their teachers, the eighth and ninth grade teachers in all the junior high schools in the study in the spring of 1963 were asked to nominate the three worst- and the three best-adjusted boys in their classes. Poor adjustment was defined as poor study habits and attitudes and little interest in school, accompanied by aggressive behavior and possibly by excessive absence and tardiness and by not working up to ability. The teachers questioned had in their classes at the time the majority of boys in the two control groups, together with fourteen boys from the experimental groups who had transferred back to the regular program. About 70 per cent of the boys were named by at least one teacher as among the three worst-adjusted boys. But 17 per cent were identified as among the three best-adjusted boys. Since the control group made up about 7 per cent of the total enrollment of each grade, this meant that, on the average, a class of fifteen boys contained one control group boy. Each boy was in the classes of four or five teachers; thus he had several chances to be named, and often he was named by more than one teacher. On the basis of chance alone, a boy had about a 20 per cent probability of being chosen as worst-adjusted or best-adjusted. The high number rated worst-adjusted indicates that control group boys were highly visible as poorly adjusted, as were the experimental group boys who had returned to the regular program (79 per cent rated worst-adjusted). The fact that 17 per cent of the boys were named among the best-adjusted is probably mainly due to chance factors, although some of the boys had average academic ability and special interest in such subjects as industrial art.

The principals of the five senior high schools which received Work-Study groups and had to provide space for them in the tenth grade were asked to fill out brief questionnaires and to respond to follow-up interviews concerning their perceptions of the Work-Study Program. These principals were somewhat more distant from the program than were the junior high school principals, who had helped set up the program in their schools and had had Work-Study groups in both eighth and ninth grades. Only one principal, of a school with grades eight through ten, had experience with all three years of the Work-Study Program.

One of the four items on the questionnaire asked what principals felt were the major problems confronting the Work-Study Program. The varied responses among the five principals reflected to some extent problems unique to specific school settings. For example, principal D was concerned with providing nonsolid credits to Work-Study boys when they both worked and studied away from school. This concern stemmed from a special arrangement, carried over from junior high school, by which Work-Study boys both studied and worked at the Rotary Club camp away from the home school during the fall and spring. In the follow-up interview, principal D was the only principal who did not emphasize behavior and discipline problems. It is relevant that his was the only school with Work-Study boys out of the school setting for weeks at a time. This, of course, alleviated the day-to-day discipline problems experienced by other principals. Additionally, since the teacher and work supervisor had the responsibility of dealing with discipline problems at Rotary camp, when they returned to the school setting they were expected to continue this practice. Thus, administrative involvement with behavior and discipline problems of Work-Study boys was very slight in principal D's school.

In contrast, principals A and C, with Work-Study boys in and about their school each day, emphasized behavior and discipline problems. It was in these two schools that the principals were most directly involved with the discipline problems of experimental boys. This was made necessary by the inability of Work-Study teachers in these schools to deal with such problems and by their constant referral to the office of boys causing problems. At these two schools several changes in teachers were made in attempts to improve the classroom situation, but, because of difficulty in obtaining experienced teachers, the classroom situation at these two schools remained relatively poor. Principals A and C also felt strongly that the seriously maladjusted boy had no place in the Work-Study program or any other present school program. Principal C did indicate that he felt the poor quality of teaching in the Work-Study classrooms contributed to many of the discipline problems coming to his office. However, principal A focused on the personal maladjustment of about one-third of the Work-Study group as the major problem. This principal acknowledged the importance of a good teacher in any classroom situation, but with the Work-Study group he did not see poor teaching as the main problem. In his words, "The teacher didn't have anything to do with Joe extorting money from smaller boys in the boys' restroom or in Donald's bringing dynamite caps to class."

Principal A did feel that the physical space and facilities of the Work-Study classroom in his school were inadequate and had probably contributed to many classroom problems. This classroom was the converted small storage room mentioned above. The space was so cramped that a boy shifting in his seat came into physical contact with other boys, which frequently triggered disruptive behavior. The surrounding classrooms were large, airy, and well ventilated, and they contained new furniture and such classroom fixtures as maps, globes, pictures, and charts. Although Work-Study boys were told that they were assigned this room because they were a small group, they still considered it a stigma and expressed this feeling frequently.

Principal A had seventeen boys in his tenth grade Work-Study class and said he thought the program had helped about ten of the seventeen. The other seven, he thought, were a detriment to the program and to the school. He argued that these seven boys should be eliminated from school, together with others not in the Work-Study Program. These boys were involved in severe fights, in theft from students' lockers, and in extortion of money from smaller boys. For instance, three of the Work-Study boys told another boy that if he did not bring them each a nickel the next day they would whip him. The next day the boy came without the money and they actually beat him in the hallway of the school. Parents had come to him, the principal stated, demanding that he exclude boys causing this kind of trouble. As the principal, what course should he take? His conclusion was that next year he would lay down the law at the beginning of the year and eliminate students who flagrantly disobeyed.

Principal B, only recently appointed acting principal in his school, was the only other principal who saw physical space as a major problem. His concern was somewhat different than that of Principal A, however. In his school, Work-Study boys attended class in a regular size classroom for two and a half hours a day. In the follow-up interview, Principal B focused on the administrative problems this created for him in assigning rooms for regular classes. He noted that the small Work-Study class tied up badly needed space, making it necessary to overcrowd math and science classes. Although in the questionnaire he indicated behavior of Work-Study boys as a major problem, this was much less emphasized in the follow-up interview. This principal, formerly vice-principal, had not been as directly involved with the operation of the program during the previous year and a half as had the former principal who dealt directly with Work-Study boys and their teacher when the need arose. This former principal was not available for the questionnaire or interview.

Principal E was the only principal who focused on the work part of the curriculum as a major problem. While all principals touched on this problem in the follow-up interviews, it appeared to have particular significance to principal E. His school was the only one of the five that did not have provision for boys to continue their education into the eleventh and twelfth grades or to attain high school diplomas. In this school, a job at sixteen was the desired goal, since few boys anticipated further education. In the follow-up interview, principal E noted the increase in discipline problems and the lower morale of Work-Study boys when jobs which they perceived as promised were not immediately forthcoming in the second year of the program.

Although only principal C indicated credits and transfer of credits in the Work-Study Program as a problem in the questionnaire, all principals expressed concern about this in the follow-up interview. All emphasized the need for some kind of guide to handling boys who transferred back to the regular school program or to another school. The principals also emphasized the need for some projected structure of the program so that they could plan teaching and classroom schedules for the eleventh grade. All of them wanted to know what was going to happen the next year.

The second questionnaire item asked principals to state what they saw as advantages or disadvantages of placing Work-Study boys in their own special classrooms. Three of the principals agreed that grouping the boys in this way was preferable to having them scattered through regular classrooms. The other two saw no advantage, with one principal stating that grouping the boys resulted in their "cooking up too many conflicts among themselves." The three principals who felt that special classrooms were preferable emphasized different reasons. One emphasized the therapeutic aspects, commenting that in regular classroom work experimental boys would be frustrated, which would result in much higher incidence of discipline problems. This principal also saw the possibilities of group counseling in special classrooms. Another principal felt that grouping boys made possible "better control in a group where they are responsible to one teacher for a half day." The third principal saw the advantage primarily in the reduction of pressure on teachers and students in regular classrooms. In his words, "grouping experimental boys has been of considerable value to teachers and students in other classrooms in time saved from dealing with discipline problems as well as in the improved morale of individual teachers."

The third questionnaire item asked principals what they felt to be the advantages of full-day regular school over the half-day work and half-day study curriculum for experimental boys. Two principals expressed the opinion that these boys would not stay in regular school programs. The other principals saw advantages in the regular curriculum, mainly in terms of the presence in classrooms of socially adjusted, education-oriented youths who might contribute to the improved school and social adjustment of study group boys. In the follow-up interview, principals were not as optimistic as their responses to the questionnaire suggested. It seemed evident that the questionnaire responses of three principals reflected hoped for adjustments rather than predictions based on concrete evidence. For example, the large numbers of dropouts among controls and the fact that 70 per cent of control group boys were nominated by their teachers as poorly adjusted suggest that the advantages of the regular program for this type of youth were not being demonstrated.

It must also be noted that many of the problems principals experienced with Work-Study boys resulted from the fact that heretofore few such boys remained very long in senior high school. Boys in the Work-Study Program tended to remain in their home schools; that is, being a member of an experimental group acted as a kind of school stabilizer. Control group boys, on the other hand, distributed themselves among other schools as they sought or were helped to find more suitable school settings. Thus, not only were experimental boys grouped and therefore identified as a special group, but they also tended to remain in the same school setting. It seems probable that Work-Study boys appeared more seriously maladjusted when the seriously maladjusted control boys initially in the same school were no longer available for comparison.

The last questionnaire item asked principals what changes in the program should be made to better serve everyone. In the area of Work-Study staff, principal A suggested stabilizing the staff, reducing the shifting in and out of teachers and work supervisors. He also suggested hiring specially trained teachers, social workers, and psychologists to work with the boys. Principal C suggested in-service training of teachers through workshops. He saw a need to recruit "dedicated teachers who are master teachers with background in understanding problem behavior." Principal B commented that the teacher, work supervisor, and counselor were all doing a very good job, but said, "Our experiences indicate it [the Work-Study Program] is not doing what we had hoped to achieve."

In the area of selection of boys, principals B, C, and E saw a need for change. Principal B felt the seriously maladjusted or disruptive boy should be eliminated early in the program. Similarly, principal C suggested eliminating serious delinquents and all boys returning from institutional commitments for delinquency. Principal E urged "a better home interview procedure with consistent facts about the program presented to parents, student, and school" and "use of teachers, counselors, and administrators in student placement into the program."

In the area of curriculum, principal A suggested more emphasis on remedial help, particularly in reading, and better scheduling of work. Principal C urged "more meaningful job experience for Work-Study boys" and obtaining permanent jobs for boys entering eleventh grade. Principal D felt a need for a further program after tenth grade, similar to the Cooperative Occupational Educational Program (C.O.E.), but with modification to meet the achievement levels of the boys. Principal E wanted "a better organized work program for the first year" and "practical trade courses which will meet the ability and educational levels of these boys."

"We always get blamed for everything around this school. If anything's missing, why we took it. We do a little bit of it, but we don't do nearly all the things they say we do. I don't care. If they are going to blame us all the time why not do it? That's the way I feel." Joe was almost sixteen when he said this, and he was constantly in trouble for fighting on school grounds and occasionally in the halls. He was a member of an all Negro Work-Study group in one of the two almost completely Negro high schools. The theme of unfair treatment and persecution, and the response of defiance and desire to get even was characteristic of the boys' perceptions of and response to teachers and administrators in the school setting. Boys varied in the degree to which their suspicions of others and sense of injustice were important determinants of their school adjustment; most of them, however, voiced some sense of being objects of discrimination. This was particularly true of the early school dropout.

Bart, a control youth, was interviewed after he dropped out of the ninth grade.

> I quit 'cause I couldn't get along with those people up there at school. Every time I did anything they wanted to send me to the office. If I asked them why, then they would say, "I'll give you an eighth hour and if you don't like that, I'll give you two eighth hours." Then when you go up to the office they give you another one because they'd say you were smarting off at the teacher. I just didn't like that.

Bart felt that when he made a real effort to do his best he was not encouraged and that in fact his effort was rejected.

> I was suspended the last part of last year and just didn't go back, but then at the beginning of this year I went back and tried to do my best. But every time I did, I wasn't given no credit for it. Like they'd give me homework, I'd bring it home and work on it for a while, and then I would go to work [part-time evening job], and then I would work some more on my homework. But then when I'd give it to the teacher he'd just throw it in the wastepaper basket and say it was too late. Then when I would get my grade I'd still get a F. So I just quit.

Bart was asked if he would like to go back to school.

> No. If I did it would just be the same. Up there they're always smarting off at you or kicking you out for a few days. Me and a buddy took off from school one day, and a cop picked us up on the street and took us to school. Well, they just left us sitting out there from the second hour to the fifth, just left us sitting there all that time. They could have talked to us before then. Finally they took us into the principal's office and this big wheel asked us what we were doing. So we told him, playing hooky. Well, now he's always saying something smart, and so he said to a teacher who had just come in, "Do you know these boys? Well, they're fishermen, and if they don't straighten up, they're going to have to be good ones, 'cause I'm going to kick them out of here for good and they're going to have to fish for a living." Then he says to us, "How would you like that?" So he just suspended us.

While many boys did believe specific adults at school treated them unfairly, only a few, like Bart, expressed marked hostility toward school and school personnel in general. In the series of interviews with the boys when they were about sixteen years old, 50 per cent expressed generally favorable attitudes toward school, 26 per cent seemed indifferent and saw school as something one had to go to, while the remaining 24 per cent were either highly critical of specific adults in the school (15 per cent) or hostile toward school in general (9 per cent). In spite of these relatively positive school attitudes in interviews, the boys' responses to various attitude measures, as well as their behavior, indicate that many of them experienced considerable ambivalence about school. In an attitude measure administered in the tenth grade, experimental boys in general agreed that school was a worthwhile place to be. In their responses to specific items, however, significant facets of their school experience appeared to be particularly frustrating. Several descriptive statements from this questionnaire and the percentage of boys ($N = 64$) agreeing are presented in Table 14.

On a sentence completion test administered at about the same time, approximately half the boys responded with innocuous completions while the remainder expressed feelings about their current status and school experience quite directly. The following kinds of responses were elicited on the stem "I wish teachers . . . would understand me. . . . would understand my ways. . . . would know the whole story before judging. . . . were not so bossy. . . . would get lost. . . . would stay home. . . . would learn to keep their noses out of people's business. . . . would drop dead. . . . would be sick for a year." Fifty per cent of the boys responded with these and similar completions.

On sentence completion stems designed to elicit expressions of attitudes toward specific learning tasks in school, responses indicated that many of these youths rejected the instrumental culture. Responses to the stem "When I have to read. . . ." point this up clearly: "I feel like I don't want to. . . . I get all nervous and can't read. . . . I get sick. . . . I need all the help I can get. . . . I hide. . . . Don't like it much."

Although some experimental boys could express their feelings of concern and anxiety about school on measures such as these, many of them in their contacts with school personnel and peers feigned a cool indifference to their obvious failures in both the expressive and instrumental cultures. They put up a front to those outside their own special group and tried to impress the "squares" with their "cool cat"

Table 14. ATTITUDES TOWARD SCHOOL

Statement	Per Cent Agreement
Too much nonsense goes on in school	65
School can be very boring at times	86
There's too much importance placed on grades	62
Most pupils learn what they have to learn, not because they want to learn	60
Too much of what we have to study does not make sense	47
Pupils have to keep reading and studying the same old things over and over	53
Teachers expect too much of pupils	61
Most pupils are not interested in learning	61
Some pupils are always making fun of other pupils in the classroom	91
Teachers are too bossy	62
Teachers always seem to like some pupils better than others...	74
Pupils do not have much freedom in school	62
Teachers really do not understand children	54
Pupils are treated fairly in school	49

qualities. It became important to them to seek status by developing reputations as tough, virile, worldly-wise males who defied school rules and adult authority. However, observation of these boys over time and in various school settings and situations revealed that in many of them these qualities were superficial and easily stripped away. In one school, a completely segregated white school where the boys and Work-Study personnel felt little acceptance, the boys expressed marked ambivalence about their membership in the experimental group. In individual interviews when they were about sixteen years old, 65 per cent stated that the Work-Study Program was helping them. Yet observations of these boys indicated that many of them felt their status threatened by being in the program. In some situations they expressed rather directly their fear of being held up to ridicule or singled out as inferior. For some of them, loss of face was to be avoided at all costs. The work supervisor for this group reported his observations of one type of situation when the boys were between fifteen and sixteen years old.

> Some of these boys seem to feel threatened when they are in the bus around the school. [Buses were used to transport the boys to various work sites.] These are old buses, but they are painted yellow and don't look too bad. One day though, we passed a county bus, and the boys started complaining that even "jailbirds" have better buses than Work-Study.
>
> Some of the boys seem to really have a thing about being seen in the bus by other students. They ask me to park it in an area so the others won't see them when they get on it. Then in the evening when I take them to where they get off to go home, several boys insist that I let them out two blocks away from the avenue where they are supposed to get off. They make me do that even if no one is around. They don't want to take chances of anyone seeing them. One time I stopped by a bookstore, and they all laid down in their seats so no one would see them. When I go around a school where they think somebody might know them, they all slump down in their seats so as not to be seen. If we are coming back to school after working, and school is just dismissing at that time, boys insist that I stop and let them walk to school because they don't want to be seen getting off the bus.
>
> It's a funny thing. They don't care who sees them as long as they aren't acquainted with them. We can go over to other school grounds and do some work and the boys don't complain unless some of the students make derogatory remarks, but they practically have a tizzy if they feel kids they know see them. One boy dives into the corner of the bus to avoid being seen by girls on the street. Several boys, regardless of how dirty the bus floor is, will get right down on the floor to avoid being seen by kids around their own school.

In spite of these experiences, a surprising number of boys remained in school for the eleventh and twelfth grades. While the criteria for selecting these boys in the seventh grade were highly predictive of nongraduation, conditions changed during the following few years so as to put pressure on pupils to stay in school and to graduate if possible. There was a national public relations program, and federal funds were given to local school districts to pay for the time of high school counselors to telephone or visit pupils who were likely to drop out. The high school nongraduation rate dropped, in a five-year period, from about 35 per cent to about 25 per cent nationally, and Kansas City reflected this drop. Consequently, a considerable number of boys selected by the screening criteria remained in school who probably would not have done so under 1960 conditions.

Probably the Negro boys were considerably affected by this change in general attitude toward high school graduation. A further factor was the lift in Negro morale given by the Civil Rights March on Washington in 1963 and by the subsequent civil rights legislation. In September following the March on Washington, thirteen parents in one of the Negro schools requested that their sons be removed from the Work-Study program, commenting that they saw the program as preparing their boys only for menial work. One parent said, "I wants my son to gets an education." Another commented, "This is not slavery days." The boys were shifted back to the regular program if the parents insisted on it after discussion with the school counselor. Nearly all these boys dropped out of school shortly afterward. But the more positive attitude of parents toward education for their sons had some effect.

Furthermore, there was evidence that some experimental group boys remained in school longer because they had found responsive adults in the persons of work supervisors, job placement supervisors, and classroom teachers who made them feel accepted in the school and gave them an emotional reward for making the effort to stay in school. Since the Work-Study curriculum ran only through the tenth grade, boys who stayed in school for the eleventh and twelfth grades had to enroll in regular school programs, although the programs were often reduced in scope to permit some of the boys to work at paid jobs during school hours. Control group boys, of course, were in regular school programs if they remained in school during this period.

The fifth year of the project began for Group One with the fall semester of 1965–66 and for Group Two in the fall of 1966. By the beginning of the fifth year, all youths in Group One and 98 per cent of Group Two were beyond the legal dropout age of sixteen. The median age for Group One at this time was seventeen years, seven months; one-fourth were between eighteen and nineteen and one-half years of age. For Group Two, the median age in the fall of 1966 was seventeen years, eight months; one-fourth were seventeen years, eleven months old or older.

For students who had been enrolled continuously since the eighth grade without repeating any grades, the fifth year of the program was the last or fourth year in senior high school. In Table 15 enrollment data by research groups and race are summarized for this fifth year. These school data indicate that over one-third of the 422 youths continued some kind of association with high school considerably beyond the time they were legally old enough to drop out. However, the attrition rate was relatively high, and about one-third of those enrolled the fifth year dropped out before completing the school year. The most striking difference in school status was between control nonconsents and the larger control and experimental groups. When the racial composition of these subgroups was considered it was clear that Negro youths tended to continue their association with school longer than did the white group. This tendency was fairly consistent over Groups One and Two.

While it had been anticipated at the beginning of the program that a few youths, both experimental and control, would probably "find themselves" after a few months in high school, continue in school, and graduate, school records indicate that at the end of the fifth year a total of sixty-one youths had completed high school and had received either a high school diploma or a certificate. Several additional boys in Group One continued in school during the 1966–67 school year, and four of them completed requirements for graduation. At the end of the 1966–67 school year, 15 per cent of the original 422 youths had graduated from high school. A number of Group Two youths were enrolled in the 1967–68 school year and some graduated, increasing the percentage of the total group completing high school to 18 per cent. Graduation data at the end of the 1966–67 school year are summarized in Table 16. Relatively fewer experimental than control youths from Group One had graduated from high school by the end of the 1966–67 school year. In Group Two the pattern was somewhat reversed; experimental youth showed a slightly higher percentage of graduates than controls. In both groups, the control nonconsents contributed a relatively greater number of graduates.

As noted previously, it was assumed that parents of youths in the larger control groups would have accepted or rejected the Work-Study Program, had they been asked, in about the same proportion as did parents who were invited to enter their sons in the program. Since youths whose parents refused consent tended to stay in school longer than either experimental or control group boys, it was inferred that such parental nonconsents are in some way associated with boys' re-

Table 15. Enrollment in High School After Conclusion of Work-Study Program

Group and Race	Enrolled at Beginning of 5th Year				Enrolled at End of 5th Year			
	Total Group	X's	C's	CNC's	Total Group	X's	C's	CNC's
				Per Cent				
Total group	35	27	38	60	25	18	29	45
Negro	42	33	47	73	31	21	40	60
White	26	19	23	53	19	14	15	38
Group One	41	31	47	57	28	14	39	43
Negro	47	37	53	88	30	23	27	71
White	30	23	27	48	20	9	27	33
Group Two	30	24	31	63	24	21	23	47
Negro	37	31	41	63	30	24	33	50
White	24	18	64	18	18	18	12	46

Table 16. HIGH SCHOOL GRADUATION IN THE RESEARCH GROUPS
AS OF JUNE, 1967

Group and Race	Total group	High School Graduates		
		Experimental Boys	Controls	Control Nonconsents
		Per Cent		
Total Group	15	11	16	32
Negro	16	11	19	33
White	15	11	11	31
Group One	19	8	27	36
Negro	20	10	27	42
White	18	6	27	33
Group Two	12	13	9	26
Negro	12	12	11	25
White	12	14	6	27

maining in school. The inclusion of a hidden subgroup of control nonconsents within the larger control groups would tend to increase differences between experimental and control boys and to decrease differences between controls and those control nonconsents identified by parental refusals. Therefore, an attempt was made to correct the control group numbers by estimating the size of the hidden subgroups of control nonconsents. The numbers of Negro and white youths thus estimated were in proportion to the number of nonconsents among Negro and white parents who were asked for consent when experimental groups were formed. The numbers of boys who stayed in school past dropout age and of high school graduates in the control groups were reduced in proportion to the number among Negro and white nonconsents encountered in the initial selection of research groups.

Taking into account in this way the effects of the hypothesized control nonconsent subgroup within the larger control group did result in changes in the expected directions. However, in only two instances were the differences reversed. These reverses were between experimental and control white youth in Groups One and Two. Prior to removing control nonconsents from the figures, 27 per cent of white control boys in Group One were in school the fifth year, in contrast to 23 per cent of white experimental youths. With control nonconsents removed, only 14 per cent of white control youth remained in school. A similar change occurred in the data for Group Two. Additionally, in Group One differences in relative numbers of high school graduates favoring experimental youth were increased with removal of control nonconsents from the larger control groups.

In summary, about one-fourth of the total group of 422 continued some association with high school five years after being identified as school misfits in the seventh grade. About one in six of the total group graduated or received a high school certificate by the end of the sixth year. It should be noted, however, that almost all (93 per cent) of the boys who did finish high school were in the bottom half of their class in school marks. Fifty-six per cent were in the bottom one-fourth, and 73 per cent were in the bottom one-third. Many of these boys received a certificate instead of a diploma, the certificate being awarded to students who took the required number of courses but did not make grades high enough to qualify for the diploma.

The characteristic thing about the boys who completed school was their willingness to adapt to the school, to stay with it under difficult circumstances. This characteristic promised well for stable careers as workers and citizens, although careers probably not to be marked by economic success. These boys who stayed in school composed the school adaptive subgroup of our sample. Did these youths show early signs of being able to cope with the high school situation? Did their school adjustment and classroom achievement in the eighth and ninth grade differ from those of the other four late adolescent adjustment subgroups? Our findings showed that boys who differed in adjustment patterns in late adolescence also tended to differ in school adjustment from the very beginning of junior high school. The most pronounced differences were between the maladaptive and school adaptive subgroups; the seriously maladaptive and marginal subgroups, in particular, showed considerably higher percentages of youth having apparent difficulty, as measured by poor or failing classroom work, high rate of absence, or dropping out of school completely, in their early high school experience. The erratic and work adaptive subgroups showed relatively similar eighth and ninth grade status characteristics, although a considerably higher percentage of the erratic subgroup dropped out of school before the tenth grade. Work adaptive boys generally showed less favorable response to the school setting than the school adaptive subgroup.

Half the seriously maladjusted and marginal boys missed a month or more of school during the eighth and ninth grades. Over one-fourth of these two subgroups were out of school two or more months during the ninth grade, which probably accounts for the high rate of below average classroom achievement among boys in these groups. The erratic and the work adaptive subgroups showed a similar pattern; their absences were considerably fewer than those of the seriously maladjusted and marginal groups, but considerably higher than that of the school adaptive group. In all five subgroups, a higher percentage of boys were identified as showing unsatisfactory adjustment and achievement in the ninth grade than in the eighth. The rate of this increase was most pronounced for the seriously maladaptive and marginal subgroups.

Teachers' ratings of boys' personal adjustment in the first two or three years of high school were distributed among late adolescent adjustment subgroups in a pattern similar to that in the elementary grades. The seriously maladaptive and marginal subgroups were more often rated as having problems in the eighth grade than other subgroups, and this trend accelerated the longer these boys remained in school. The erratic and work adaptive subgroups showed similar distributions of ratings; boys in these groups were less frequently seen by their teachers as school problems early in high school, although in their last year of high school about three-fourths of them were considered to be seriously handicapped in work habits and sense of responsibility. Boys in the school adaptive subgroup differed markedly from the other adjustment subgroups. From the very beginning of their high school career through their last school year, most of them were rated about average in personal adjustment.

Among our disadvantaged study group were some boys whose family lives appeared to show aspects of middle-class orientation. In the eighth and ninth grades, teachers of experimental youths were asked to rate their Work-Study boys in terms of twelve different values, attitudes, and behaviors. Half these twelve descriptions were considered to represent lower-class orientations while half expressed middle-class values. The rating scale was a forced-choice measure requiring that

Table 17. TEACHERS' RATINGS OF VALUES IN THE EIGHTH GRADE AND LATE ADOLESCENT ADJUSTMENT

Rating[a] Categories	Total Group		Negro Boys		White Boys	
	Maladaptive (N = 101)	Adaptive (N = 60)	Maladaptive (N = 64)	Adaptive (N = 23)	Maladaptive (N = 37)	Adaptive (N = 37)
	Per Cent					
Middle-class	34	57	36	65	32	54
Neutral	13	7	12	9	14	5
Lower-class	53	36	52	26	54	41
	$\chi^2 = 8.05$ df = 2 sig., .02 .01		$\chi^2 = 8.01$ df = 2 sig., .02 .01		$\chi^2 = 3.97$ df = 2 sig., .20 .10	

[a] Middle class included items such as: "This boy wants more education even though he may not be a good student." "This boy likes to work; he gets right down to business and stays with the job." Lower class included items such as: "This boy likes to fight; he is physically aggressive and gets real enjoyment out of fighting whether he is on the winning or losing side." "This boy is very hostile to school; he says school has never done him any good and he will be glad when he can get out of school forever."

teachers rate a certain proportion of the class as most like each attitude or behavior. Thus only those individuals who stood out from the group in the particular behavior would be identified. Three sets of scores—middle-class values, neutral values, and lower-class values—were obtained. Table 17 gives the results of a chi-square analysis of the association of teachers' ratings in the eighth grade to late adolescent adjustment of experimental boys.

These data indicate that as early as the eighth grade boys screened as socially maladjusted seventh graders could be differentiated by their teachers in terms of "lower-class" or "middle-class" orientations and that these identifications had a significant association with late adolescent adjustment. It is apparent, however, that not all experimental boys rated lower-class or middle-class by their eighth grade teachers showed such orientations in late adolescence. For Negro boys the association was relatively significant, but among both Negro and white youths there were many whose middle- or lower-class orientation in the classroom setting had little relevance to the modes of social behavior and work role development observed in late adolescence.

6

Work Experience

The Kansas City Work-Study Program was developed to serve the 15 per cent of high school age boys who are seriously maladjusted.[1] It was an attempt to create for these boys a situation similar to that of similar boys in the first two decades of this century. The intent was to create this situation for an experimental group of boys, record and evaluate their experience, and then decide whether this kind of program should be extended and applied to larger numbers of boys. The objectives were to help the boys acquire the basic habits and attitudes of industrial persons, learn to use and care for tools, learn to work for employers, and choose and prepare for occupations. It seemed too late to start such a program at or just before the age of sixteen, when boys could legally quit school. At least the first phase of this program should start while the boys were all in school.

In the first year of the program there were four groups of eighth grade boys, one at each of four schools. Each group had a school bus to take them to work sites some distance from the school when necessary. Each group had a work supervisor with an assistant. The work supervisor was a licensed teacher, usually a physical education or industrial arts teacher. A Negro man supervised one of the Negro groups. After the first semester a second Negro supervisor was

[1] This chapter was drafted by Ralph Berry, Director of the Work-Study Project of the Kansas City Public Schools. It has been edited by Robert J. Havighurst.

98

appointed to work with the other Negro group. Their assistants were young men, mostly students in the local junior college. In the second year of the program a group of eighth grade boys was recruited at a high school which was predominantly white but contained several black boys.

Each group was limited to twenty-five boys. The West Side group was somewhat smaller due to the smaller size of the junior high school. Since no new boys were added to the experimental groups after they were established, they all decreased in size as boys dropped out for one reason or another. The groups were held intact as boys moved from junior high school into senior high school. Work in groups was discontinued after the tenth grade since all boys were in Stage Two, individual part-time employment, by that time.

The first group work assignment was landscaping at various schools and in city parks. It varied from raking leaves to cleaning out flower beds, transplanting, trimming hedges, and making pathways. This work was not generally liked by the boys, mainly because much of it was done in full view of their schoolmates, who teased them a good deal. Some of the boys objected to the work on the ground that it was mainly busy work, of little value to them or to the community. The work supervisors at this time were trying to create work attitudes and to teach the care and use of hand tools. For the first time in the lives of many of the boys, they were confronted with the need to use tools properly. The tools were simple ones—rakes, shovels, small hand sickles, and garden hoes. The boys immediately became aware that if they destroyed or misused the tools they would not have to work until replacement tools could be obtained. Some of the boys would deliberately strike their rakes or hoes on cement curbs or blunt their sharp tools.

There was some fighting among the boys. The first task of the work supervisor was to control aggression among these aggressive boys; each supervisor worked out his own methods of control. Out of a group of twenty to twenty-five boys, at least half were outspokenly aggressive, both in words and action. In the early phases of group work it was very difficult to get the boys to work together. They threw rocks, dirt, and tools at each other. In many cases the boys would not work with each other and would purposely do the opposite of what the supervisor told them to do. In each group there seemed to be at least one boy, and in some cases more than one, whom the group liked to pick on. They would usually make life miserable for him. In spite of all the aggressive behavior among the youngsters in the work groups, there were very few injuries and no serious ones.

With the coming of cold and wet weather at the end of autumn, inside work became necessary. On the whole this went better than the yard work. Some jobs, such as moving and storing materials, were found in the warehouse of the school system. The principal job, and one that grew in importance, was the refinishing of school furniture, mainly old wooden tables and desks whose surfaces were deeply scarred. These had to be sandpapered and surfaced with shellac or varnish. Principal tools were hand sanders, power sanders, and paintbrushes. During this phase of work, many boys began to develop some skill and to take pride in their work. They particularly liked to use power sanders, and some of them enjoyed the varnishing and shellacking.

Still there were difficulties in controlling a group of boys, often working in a small room with an inadequate supply of tools. And some of the boys continued to sabotage the work by damaging their tools. A favorite trick was to set a power sander free on a table and let it run across the table at full speed, catching the cord just in time, and sometimes too late, to stop it before it fell to the floor. Constant supervision was needed. Some of the assistants had no skill in controlling or disciplining boys, and the supervisors found discipline their major concern. One supervisor gave up at the end of the first semester.

The eighth grade boys needed a good deal of attention to the details of their work. They could not follow complex directions. They had no mental grasp of a two- or three-step operation. They would do one phase of an operation and then stop and wait for directions. For example, if they were sanding desks with coarse sandpaper, someone had to tell them when to change to finer sandpaper, and once the sanding was completed they had to be told to wipe off the dust before putting sealer or varnish on the wood. There was constant bickering among the boys as to who was and who was not doing his share of the work. If one boy sat down and stopped work for a minute, the others would be after him. Some boys complained that they were not paid adequately. One group, led by a smart and aggressive youngster, tried to strike for more pay. Yet the dollar a week was appreciated, and absences were very few on Fridays—paydays. It was difficult to get the boys to wear work clothes. If they had good-looking clothes they wanted to wear them no matter what kind of work they were doing. It was found that the boys tended to work better in pairs than alone or in large groups.

Despite all these initial difficulties, as time went on the boys followed directions well, showed respect to the work supervisors, and gained in self-confidence. This matter of self-confidence was important for boys with rather severe academic disabilities which placed them at the bottom of their school classes. By spring of the first year, and for the next two years, the group work was being chosen and organized with much greater success. A most successful work project was carried on at the Rotary Club camp. This camp for disadvantaged children was used mainly in the summer. Its cabins were badly in need of repair, and road-building, fence-repairing, and general landscaping were needed. The boys of one work group were bused to the camp five mornings a week. Their academic instructor came with them, and they did classwork with him a half of each day. This situation had two distinct advantages. The group was undisturbed by their schoolmates, and they could see themselves completing a job. They could celebrate when they finished work on a particular cabin, and they could see the entire camp take on a new appearance as they worked.

Another away-from-school project was carried out at a county park. Ten ninth grade boys were assigned to do landscaping, grass-cutting, and so forth. They were paid fifty cents an hour at first. Their work was continued during the summer when they were paid $1.25 an hour. The park supervisor commented that these boys did as good work as had the high school graduates and college boys who had formerly worked on this job at $1.65 an hour. This group of boys showed almost no delinquency or police contacts during the summer work periods.

The main work project of Stage One remained the refinishing of furniture. A work group would move from one elementary school to another, refinishing all the desks and tables that needed attention, using a basement room as their workshop. During the summer a number of boys were employed to work on cafeteria tables and desks in the high schools. They worked in groups of ten or twelve, under supervisors, and were paid fifty cents an hour at first and more later. These boys worked steadily and well.

Supervisors rated the boys on their work orientation. These ratings served as a partial basis for identifying the boys by type of adjustment in midadolescence. A good rating meant that the boy liked to work and did whatever was asked of him. An average rating meant he did not like to work but did what he was asked or instructed to do. A poor rating meant he disliked work, disrupted group work, and refused to work when he could get away with it. Boys were rated unstable if they were erratic in work habits, working well one day but not the next. Only about a quarter of the ratings were good and another quarter were average. Fully a quarter of the boys were rated as poor.

As soon as boys reached the age of fifteen they pressed for paid part-time jobs. They were anxious to earn money. The work supervisors, however, felt that many of the boys were not mature enough to be placed in competitive employment and to hold jobs. Furthermore, the number and variety of available jobs were small at first because the boys were under sixteen years of age. This barred them from certain kinds of work; some labor unions had age limits for certain jobs. An employment coordinator was employed to seek out jobs and connect boys with jobs. He filled a key role since he had to introduce the project to employers and to convince them it was socially useful even though the boys might not add much profit to their businesses. Several men filled this role effectively.

One major problem was finding employment for Negro boys, especially in 1963 and 1964. It became somewhat easier later, although the type and quality of work experience for Negro boys remained more limited than for white boys. The jobs generally available to Negro boys were as busboys and kitchen workers in restaurants and cafeterias. A few additional jobs appeared later in automobile service stations, in stockrooms of wholesale houses, for trainees in automobile body and fender work, and for delivery boys.

Not all the boys in the Work-Study Program got part-time jobs, but the majority of them did. Some boys dropped out of the program in Stage One or early in Stage Two. Sixty-eight out of eighty-one boys in Group One and seventy-eight out of ninety-seven boys in Group Two secured paid work. In Group One, percentages of white and Negro boys placed were similar (79 per cent and 77 per cent), but difficulties in placing Negro boys were clear in Group Two (74 per cent and 61 per cent). The median length of work in Stage Two was forty-two weeks for Group One and thirty weeks for Group Two. White boys tended to stay on each job considerably longer than did

Negro boys, especially in Group One. During the period of part-time employment with private employers up to May, 1966, the average boy held three or four jobs.

Most boys had to learn to work consistently; it did not come naturally to them. For instance, James was placed in a body shop in a garage after some twenty hours of the work supervisor's time were spent arranging for the job; clearances with the union and insurance problems took considerable time before placement. After James had worked a few days the employment supervisor noticed the men were beginning to take a personal interest in him. In fact they were pooling their surplus tools to give James a set of his own. On later visits to the garage the employment supervisor received favorable remarks about the boy from the employer and the men with whom he worked. Their comments were, "He is doing a fine job," "He is a good boy; we like him," and "He tries hard." These comments led the supervisor to believe James was doing very well on the job. After several weeks, when James had received a few pay checks, the employment supervisor noticed that James had bought some new clothes, a bicycle, and other things. He realized that the purchases might have been hastily made, yet he felt they were not out of the ordinary for a boy of his age and temperament. After another week, James quit his job without notice. The employment supervisor was surprised, since the boy had said he enjoyed his job very much. When James was asked why he quit, his only reply was, "I didn't like the work."

Another boy was employed in a shop where glass was replaced in automobile windows. Joe was learning the job of glass-setting while doing other small jobs in the business. After the first week on the job, the employer asked Joe to work on Saturday, explaining that Saturday was usually a busy day. The boy did report for work on the following Saturday, but at ten o'clock instead of the seven o'clock starting time. The employer approached Joe again, pointing out the importance of Saturday's work and of being on time. Joe came to work three more days and then quit, telling his employer he had too many things to do on Saturdays. Talking to the employment supervisor, Joe commented, "I didn't like the job, and besides I don't want to work on Saturday."

This kind of experience was also a learning situation for the other boys in the group, as it provided the teacher with an opportunity to discuss the meaning of the job from various points of view including an employer's. These job discussions were held during a portion of each day to review various phases of work experience. These periods also provided time for role-playing episodes in which one boy would take the role of an employer while another boy took the role of an employee. In these role-playing sessions the boys treated "employees" much more severely than they themselves were treated while working on the job. There was also a development of group feeling among Work-Study boys toward the obligations connected with job placement and retention of jobs. One teacher, for example, told of a boy who was truant from his work: Bill was employed as an attendant in a service station. He called his employer one day at the time he was to report for work saying he had a blister on his heel and wanted to be excused for the afternoon. After permission was granted Bill met a friend and played most of the afternoon on another school's playground. The other boys, finding this out, brought it up in the job discussion the following morning. The group severely criticized Bill for his actions, saying that such actions on his part cooled their chances for job placement. Bill reported the following day with his uniform to show the group and said, "See, I'm going to work today." There was no further trouble from this boy, and it seems likely that group pressure was more effective than a lecture from the employment coordinator would have been.

Several boys set their sights on getting rich with half-time jobs. They did not like to start with what they felt were low wages. For example, Harold and Bernard, two leaders in the group, were offered a job in a letter-addressing establishment. When they were taken for interviews, Harold was not acceptable to the employer, and Bernard was not impressed with the wages he was offered and would not take the job. When they returned to school both boys complained about the employer, the job, and the wages offered. Don, another boy in the group, asked for the job. The other boys made fun of him for accepting the job, but Don did not seem particularly bothered by this, perhaps because he needed the money. After two weeks on the job, Don received an unsolicited twenty cents an hour raise. The employer also promised him a permanent job with a local newspaper, which would become a full-time job later. Don returned to the classroom group telling about the raise and the promise of a permanent job. Harold and Bernard listened to the story as told by the boy they had previously labeled a "jerk." The teacher reported, "This is one time the two leaders in the group had the wind taken out of their sails, because they now realize they turned down a good thing by their hasty decisions."

The importance of finding the right job for a boy is shown by the experience of Tony, who was hired as a helper in a greenhouse. He seemed so interested in his work that the employer decided to teach him the complete operation of a greenhouse and florist shop. The teacher reported, "Tony is very enthusiastic about his job. He banks a portion of his money, saying, 'Some day I want to own my own greenhouse and florist shop.' " Tony's parents expressed to the employment supervisor their happiness with the boy's job, saying, "Tony has found something he is interested in for the first time in his life. We feel it is good for him because it keeps him busy."

Marvin was placed in a wholesale grocery firm taking orders. He had a private desk and a telephone at work, which gave him a feeling of importance. This feeling may have been partially responsible for the complete transformation of the boy. Marvin had always dressed in a careless, slovenly way at school; after he was employed he became conscious of his clothes and personal cleanliness at school and work. His clothes were neatly pressed, and his hair was cut and combed in a conventional manner. The academic teacher reported, "Marvin can now sit in a classroom without interrupting other people—a habit which used to cause a lot of trouble. I feel this is partially due to the environment in which he finds himself at work. The association with adults and their actions have, in my opinion, been very helpful to this boy."

A part-time job was a source of prestige among many Work-Study boys and proved one of the more constructive experiences. One group contained several boys who tended to boast about their drinking and their sexual experience; less experienced boys listened eagerly. As some of the boys got jobs, the teachers noticed that the jobholders became the center of attention; boys clustered around them asking how much money they earned last week, what kind of boss they had, and whether they knew of other jobs. The most frequent jobs in Stage Two were in the food services and in stockrooms. Negro boys were more likely to work in the food services and white boys in stockrooms.

The Work-Study Program definitely gave most of the boys a great deal more work experience than they would otherwise have obtained. The boys were interviewed when they were just under sixteen years of age and asked to describe their work experience. Of the first seventy-five boys interviewed, 40 per cent of those in the experimental group had had paid work with regular hours and regular pay, while only 15 per cent of the control group reported such experience.

Stage Three was for boys who were ready for full-time jobs. A number of boys did not move into Stage Three because they decided to stay in school and graduate. Forty-four boys from Group One and fifty-three from Group Two were placed in full-time jobs. In each group 60 per cent of boys available for placement held jobs. Again, Negro boys were hard to place—only 45 per cent of those available in each group were placed. Also, white boys again held jobs longer than Negro boys. Full-time jobs were more easily available when boys were over sixteen than part-time jobs had been when they were younger. Furthermore, the barriers against Negroes in certain occupations were being lowered somewhat. Boys were most frequently placed as stock clerks, delivery boys, food service workers, and audiovisual equipment repairmen. One boy was placed in a print shop, one in a motorcycle repair shop, several as janitors, some as hospital aides, one as a whole-sale grocery clerk, one as a baker, and one as a truck driver. Several boys entered the military service at age seventeen or eighteen, where they learned job skills that helped them find high-paying work on discharge from the service. The Negro boys were still overwhelmingly in food service, about 50 per cent of their placements being in that area.

Problems still existed in the placement of boys in Stage Three. There was still considerable job turnover. Horace tried eighteen different jobs in Stage Three and then went into military service. Another boy had seventeen jobs before entering military service. Many boys were unrealistic about the type of work they were qualified to do or the jobs they might hold. Most boys felt that their wages were too low. In contrast, a number of boys did quite well. Jerry tried a number of jobs, but then he got married, had a child, and settled down to a single job as a janitor. Will took over his father's chili parlor when his father became ill and ran it quite successfully.

When late adolescent adaptation and performance in the Work-Study Program were compared, it was found that, as was to be expected, the work adaptive group tended to stay longest in the program. Of those who remained in the program a full three years, 38 per cent were in the work adaptive group. Also predictably, 42 per cent of those who stayed in the program less than nine months were in the seriously maladjusted group. The school adaptive group had the next best work rating to that of the work adaptive group, and they tended to stay longer in the Work-Study Program than all but the work adaptive group. Also, the work adaptive and school adaptive groups received the most favorable ratings from work supervisors in Stage One.

Of course, there was a variety of work experience and adjustment among the boys in each pattern of adolescent adaptation, with something of a modal character emerging. Adaptive work youths varied somewhat in early work adjustment. Some of this group simply continued into their eighteenth and nineteenth years patterns of successful adjustment in full-time employment which had begun to develop during earlier supervised work experience. Ray was one of these. He dropped out of school in the eleventh grade to work full time. By age nineteen, he had been employed by the same firm for about four years. He went to work part-time with this company after completing a year and a half in the supervised group work of Stage One. He first worked as a messenger boy; because of his dependability and responsibility, his employer sent him to a special school to train as a repairman on audio equipment the company sold and maintained. Before he was twenty, Ray was a qualified technician in this field, married with one child, and was buying a home.

Jim's juvenile work pattern was a variation on this adaptive work adjustment pattern. By age nineteen, Jim had shown success on the same job for a year and a half. Unlike Ray, however, Jim did not seem likely to adjust well when he dropped out of school. In fact, during his enrollment in the Work-Study Program he was considered one of the more seriously maladjusted boys. His attitudes toward school and classroom were so negative and his behavior so disruptive that he was suspended from the program for one semester. The next semester he wanted to get back in Work-Study and was permitted to return. Initially there was some improvement in his behavior and attitude. However, he soon became a serious problem again, in both the classroom and group work activity. Unlike Ray, Jim was never considered qualified for placement, nor was he placed in a part-time job during the time he was enrolled in school, although he kept insisting he wanted to work and would do a good job if given the chance. After one final altercation with his teacher, he left school and was unemployed several weeks before seeking help from the Work-Study employment coordinator. Jim was placed in a job with the understanding that this was

on a trial basis only. The employer was well aware of the boy's adjustment difficulties but saw him as a challenge. Jim adjusted well, received pay raises, and, like Ray, can build a future with his company
if he desires.

Another pattern among boys showing relatively successful work
experience in their late teens was a series of unsuccessful job placements prior to successful placement. Mack, for example, by age nineteen had worked in the same job for more than two years. Before this
placement he had worked in four different part-time jobs while he was
enrolled in Stage Two. He was fired from three of these jobs, quit the
fourth one, and held none of them longer than two months. Following
each of these experiences he would return to the work group of the
program and would have to wait until he could again be considered
for placement. He was not yet seventeen when placed in his final job,
and for several weeks his work adjustment was erratic. He was frequently tardy. Some days he showed initiative; other days he appeared
indifferent and lazy, and termination seemed imminent. However, the
employment coordinator worked closely with both the boy and his employer. Soon Mack began showing signs of adapting. After the eleventh
grade he left school to go to work full time with his employer, who
now described him as one of his better employees.

Many school adaptive youths evidenced little interest in working. Among this group were boys who soon returned to the regular
classroom to earn a high school diploma. For them, work experience
and going to work during adolescence was of secondary importance.
Others expressed strong orientations toward work and getting a job
in the initial stages of the program, only to show diminishing interest
in later adolescence. Some indicated real promise in their first work
assignments. However, over time their attitudes toward work became
increasingly indifferent and apathetic, and this was clearly shown by
the poorer quality of their work. For some of these youths school experiences rather than work began to be the major focus of activity and
interest as they moved into middle adolescence. William was an example of this type. He held three Stage Two part-time jobs while he
was enrolled in the Work-Study Program. He succeeded quite well on
the first two, which terminated for seasonal layoffs. On the third job,
which promised a full-time position when he left school, William
initially adjusted quite satisfactorily. However, as time passed he began

showing less and less initiative, was frequently late to work, began to do sloppy work, and finally, following a number of attempts by both the employer and employment coordinator to talk out the problem, was fired.

While William's interest and productivity in this third job slackened, he showed increasing interest and participation in school activities. He was enrolled in ROTC, was in the band, and was active in athletics. All these experiences in the expressive culture of the school developed during the ninth grade and William was beginning to show some proficiency as well as success in these areas. He left the Work-Study Program in the tenth grade, transferred to a regular high school curriculum, graduated, and attended one year of junior college. He transferred to a university on a track scholarship. In the spring of 1968, in his third year at the university, he competed in the tryouts for the Olympics.

Marginal and seriously maladaptive youths also varied in the kinds and amounts of earlier work experience and in their responses to work opportunity. Some had only minimal part-time work experience during early and middle adolescence and in late adolescence seemed unable to find work or to take advantage of opportunities to work. Joe represents this type. Joe is Mexican-American. A dropout at age seventeen, he was without work and had only a few weeks' paid work experience during early and middle adolescence. The employment coordinator made several attempts to get Joe involved in work, but the boy appeared reluctant. For example, a part-time job became available in a Mexican restaurant. The pay was a dollar an hour and free meals. When Joe was told of the job he rejected it, stating that he was too bashful to work around other people. He explained that if he was asked to clean tables and refill coffee cups he just could not do it. He wanted some kind of stock work, although these jobs were not available then. The employment coordinator suggested he think about the restaurant job and then call him at his office the next day. He never called.

The employment coordinator summarized his impression of Joe: "He does appear to be a shy boy. He withdraws from you and seems embarrassed when you talk to him. He appears to be very passive, preferring to stay home rather than to work. His mother frequently puts pressure on him to go out and get a job, and he will go out and fill out a lot of applications, but there is just never any job for him." At age eighteen, Joe was still sprawled in front of the family TV set.

Ralph's work adaptation in late adolescence was much the same as Joe's. He talked frequently about wanting a job, needing money, and so forth, but was unable to hold a job more than a few days. Dropping out of school after the tenth grade and holding only a few menial jobs for short periods of time, Ralph at age eighteen was unemployed and depressed about his chances for work. This pattern was not new for Ralph. His adjustment in the Work-Study group work activity in the eighth grade was, like that of many of the other boys, immature. He showed even less interest than most boys, and the quality of his work was poorer. It was clear that he saw the work period only as a respite from classroom study. However, he did not create problems in the group. He claimed that he wanted to continue in the Work-Study Program. In spite of his poor accomplishments in group work activity, he was one of the more vocal boys in expressing his immediate need for a part-time paid job. Ralph's family was large and also poor. His need for clothes was apparent. However, the employment coordinator was reluctant to place the boy with a private employer until he had demonstrated some capacity to work consistently over time.

After several months of counseling with Ralph, the employment coordinator finally decided to place him in a job, not so much because his work adjustment had improved as because of the boy's obvious need for money. Then began several weeks' search for a suitable job and an employer sufficiently tolerant at first so that the boy would have some time to adapt to the new situation. In the job interview Ralph handled himself well. He was hired immediately and put to work. At the end of the first week he began coming to work late. By the end of the second week he did not show up at all. The employer agreed to accept another experimental boy to replace Ralph. Ralph's reaction to this was somewhat different from the passive or indifferent response frequently elicited from this marginal group. The employment coordinator reported: "I took this replacement to the job, and just about this time in walks Ralph. He wanted to know what was going on. Well, we told him he had lost his job. His employer simply said that he had to have someone he could depend on and that was the reason he was going to hire this other boy. Well, the surprising thing was that Ralph began crying. In front of me, this employer, and this other boy. He seemed very upset. All the way back to class I tried to buck him up a little bit, telling him he could look at this as something he had learned and that this would help him keep the next job. Well he seemed awfully depressed over this and kept saying that he wanted to work and needed to work real bad." The employment coordinator set up several additional job placements. The same pattern occurred. After three years Ralph demonstrated little change in his basic pattern of irresponsible work adjustment, and his job terminations, usually through being fired, were followed by tears and depression.

Other youths who showed marginal adjustment or appeared seriously maladjusted in late adolescence actually rejected opportunities to work and earn money during early and middle adolescence. This was in spite of their early school-leaving, limited family income, pressures from family and probation officers, and proffered help from the employment coordinator. Jay, at age nineteen, appeared to be drifting aimlessly. He frequently called to talk with the director of the Work-Study Program, professing interest and need for work. However, he never followed through or showed up for job interviews. This is the same kind of pattern, reported his employment coordinator, that characterized Jay four years previously in the experimental program. At that time he voiced a desire to work and said he would work at anything as long as it paid something. However, attempts to place Jay in paid work settings were futile. He either did not show up for the job or invented some excuse as to why he could not take a particular job. Following Jay's dropping out of school during the tenth grade, his employment coordinator summarized his efforts and impressions of Jay.

> I stopped by to see Jay. He wasn't home, but his mother was, and she was upset. She told me she had had it with Jay and that he had better get a job quick or she was going to have him committed. She said she'd have him call me. Well about two days later Jay called and said he really needed a job and he'd take anything. So I started looking for a suitable employer. During the three weeks I was looking Jay called the office almost daily saying he wanted to go to work as soon as possible.
>
> I finally found a fairly good job. While it only paid a

dollar an hour it wasn't bad as a start. I called Jay, told him he had a job working from seven A.M. until noon. Jay said he didn't want it, that he didn't want to work until noon and didn't want to go to work as early as seven A.M. Well I laid it on the line because I was getting pretty upset with Jay myself. So Jay said he'd try it. It was about ten A.M. Saturday, and I took Jay over to the job myself, and he worked until noon that day. The boss said he could use Jay the next day, Sunday, but Jay said he couldn't make it and so the boss said he would see him at seven A.M. on Monday. Well Jay arrived at seven-thirty and then informed his boss that he would be late Tuesday because he had to take a physical.

Well the upshot of the whole thing was that Jay was simply stalling. He told his mother he didn't have to go to work till ten A.M., and when I called Tuesday morning early Jay answered and said he was just leaving to take his physical. I called again at ten-thirty when I found he hadn't yet turned up at the job. His mother answered. She said that Jay had just gotten up a short time before and had left for work. Jay, of course, was fired, but he didn't tell his mother this. He gave her some story about the company wanting part-time workers who were going to school so he had been replaced. Now his mother is really upset because she knows Jay lied to her. Besides that he has a girl pregnant, and although he says he will not marry her he has no way to contribute to the support of the child and appears to see it as no obligation on him.

During the intervening years Jay held a few jobs but only for brief periods of time. He did have one job, as a busboy, where he appeared at times to be a hard worker. However, he was fired after several weeks. His employer explained that Jay worked hard when he thought there was a tip involved but where there was not he let the other boys do the work.

Some of the youths in the seriously maladjusted subgroup had only minimal work experience, primarily because much of their early and middle adolescence was spent in confinement. There were several, however, who were actively delinquent during this time but were somehow able to avoid commitment until late adolescence. These youths appeared able to avoid direct confrontation with society's rules and regulations by developing and refining techniques of social manipulation. While giving lip service to the need for school and work, these youths seemed oriented toward avoiding any real investment or involvement in social goals. Some had developed at quite an early age an expressive style which permitted them to control their social environment and reduce pressures for change which would infringe upon their freedom.

7

Family Life in Midadolescence

As we have seen in the last two chapters, study group boys responded and adapted to school and work experience in quite different ways. Some boys appeared to settle down and to begin making progress toward socially desired and acceptable goals in middle adolescence, while others, too many others, seemed to find satisfaction in pursuing socially unacceptable goals. In Chapter Three we saw how certain primary family characteristics in childhood appeared to be associated with late adolescent types of adjustment. In this chapter we take another look at the family and the boy, this time during the period in which decisions to stay in or drop out of school were being made. Because of the crucial significance such decisions may have for career development and work-role identity, we were interested in determining the conditions and circumstances of a boy's family as he approached the legal dropout age of sixteen. We wanted to explore these conditions and circumstances in their association with the kinds of decisions which were made as well as with different patterns of adjustments which were occurring in other areas of experience during this time. We were particularly interested in determining whether there were measurable characteristics of family life and structure in midadolescence which

114

appeared associated with these various kinds of adjustments, including dropping out of school and being in trouble with the police.

In order to get a picture of the family and the boy at this time, interviewers visited the homes and talked with the parents about their children, the schools, and other aspects of family life. Although a non-directive approach was essential for eliciting response, interviewers asked the same questions of all parents, although not in the same sequence since the parents' concerns and interests were given priority as the interview developed. The questions were designed to obtain information about family structure, family relationships, and parents' attitudes toward and aspirations for their children, particularly for the Work-Study boy. Physical descriptions of the neighborhood and family dwellings were also recorded.

By the time study group boys were about sixteen years old, 57 per cent of them had experienced changes in family structures, such as loss of a parent by death or divorce, sometimes with remarriage of the remaining parent. In the study group as a whole, the family unit which had emerged by the seventh grade remained relatively stable into the boys' midadolescent years. However, this was somewhat less true of Negro than of white boys. When patterns of changes for each family were tabulated, it became evident that although most changes first occurred during childhood, one in five boys also experienced some kind of change in family structure during adolescence. Only a few youths (about 5 per cent of the total sample) experienced these changes for the first time during adolescence. For the others, such experiences were second, third, or further changes of adults on whom they were dependent for care and support.

To assess physical conditions and circumstances in which boys lived in midadolescence, interviewers in home visits carefully recorded their observations of the physical environment of family dwellings, including their state of repair, physical facilities, cleanliness, and spaciousness. (See Appendix B.) Ratings of physical conditions were then assigned and these ratings were compared with those made at the time of the screening interview, permitting some assessment of improvement, lack of improvement, or deterioration in the physical environment during adolescence. These data are summarized in Table 18. On the whole, living conditions for both Negro and white boys seemed to have improved somewhat as they moved into midadolescence. Still, slightly more than one-fourth lived in dwellings rated as physically

Table 18. Physical Conditions of Homes

Physical Conditions	Total Group (N = 292)		Negro Boys (N = 170)		White Boys (N = 122)	
	7th Grade	Mid-adol.	7th Grade	Mid-adol.	7th Grade	Mid-adol.
	Per Cent					
Very poor	33	24	35	28	29	20
Minimal standards	27	38	30	40	24	34
Fair to good	40	38	35	32	47	46

inadequate, and for many in this subgroup such conditions appeared chronic, since they had been rated inadequate at the time of the seventh grade screening. At this earlier time Negro boys were generally less favored in their physical surroundings at home than were white boys. In midadolescence this pattern still held, although slightly fewer white boys lived in home environments rated as good than when they were in the seventh grade.

We were concerned with the quality of family relationships in midadolescence because we had found in screening that about one-third of the boys lived in family settings where there appeared to be either considerable tension and conflict or general indifference of family members to one another. It was felt that, if such conditions existed in midadolescence, they might be particularly relevant to the direction and shape adolescent adjustment might take. In the midadolescent home visits, interviewers were chiefly concerned with discovering how family members saw each other and how parents described their children, each other, and their family lives. The kinds of interactions which occurred between family members during the interview and the ease or difficulty of communications between them were given just as close attention as were the parents' responses to questions.

The degree of affection of family members for one another and their interdependence were explored through questions about family activities and relationships among family members. Information about the problems the family faced, their solutions or attempted solutions, and major problems parents perceived in relation to their children and mates was sought for assessing the family life of study group boys at this crucial stage of development. The general inquiry about family relationships followed closely that employed in the Glueck interview schedule constructed for eliciting information concerning family cohesiveness. It included the following questions: What do you and your family have a chance of doing together as a family? What do you like to do together? How about meals—do you all get a chance to be together then? How do the children get along with you, their father, and each other?

Interviewers explored any leads parents provided as they talked about family activities or lack of activities together. Special concern was given to determining whether there were specific problems which affected family relationships, for example, a delinquent child, an alcoholic husband, a retarded child, emotional or physical illness, money problems, and so forth. Interviewers recorded their interviews with parents immediately after the interview, and ratings were assigned identifying various kinds of situations and relationships for each family. The ratings of families on a family cohesiveness scale are summarized in Table 19. Considering the first three categories as representing relatively noncohesive families, these data show that one-third of the total study group lived in relatively noncohesive families in midadolescence. Several examples from the interviews with parents identify the kinds of information which indicated noncohesive or cohesive relationships.

THE NONCOHESIVE FAMILY

"That boy is a thief. He stole my record player and other things and he ought to be committed," said Bert's mother in response to the interviewer's inquiry about how the boy was getting along. Bert's was a noncohesive family. The mother explained her attitudes and feelings, showing marked antipathy toward her son. "That boy is no good. Listen to this—when I'm away from the house, the kids tell me, he gets in bed with his sister [age fifteen]. She's going to have a baby, so I knows he done it to her. And that's not all—he's stole from me lots of times—took money right out of my purse. Oh that boy, he makes trouble for me. I wants him put away for awhile—teach him a lesson."

Four years earlier the mother had told a school interviewer seeking permission for the boy to be enrolled in the special school pro-

Table 19. FAMILY RELATIONSHIPS IN MIDADOLESCENCE

Family Relationships	Total Group	Negro Families	White Families
	Per Cent		
Noncohesive family. Hostility is characteristic of relationships.	10	9	10
Noncohesive family. Indifference and some dissension are characteristic of family members.	11	14	5
General indifference or apathy of family members toward each other.	12	14	10
Both noncohesive and cohesive elements characterize family life.	21	22	20
Generally cohesive family but some noncohesive elements.	6	7	7
Cohesive family.	40	34	48

gram for potential school dropouts, "Well, I wish somebody would take that boy and straighten him out. I beats him, teaches him right from wrong, and he knows he better not sass me. Around home he don't cause too much trouble, but he ain't getting along in school. I gets notes—what am I supposed to do? I got other kids."

"What about his father?"

"Oh, he ain't got no father here. He left before Bert was born, so he ain't never seen him."

"Does he ask about him?"

"Oh, he did when he was little. I just tol' him his dad ain't no good so forget him."

"What do you do together as a family?"

"Huh, what do you mean?"

"I mean like having fun together—like going on picnics, fishing, playing cards, going to church, and this sort of thing."

"Ha. Man, I got enough to do just taking care of the kids. I got three in school and three that ain't, and I ain't got time for nothing but work."

Harry's mother described him to the school interviewer who asked about how he was getting along in school. Harry, sitting nearby, displayed no reaction to his mother's remarks. He gazed out the window with his face blank, appearing to have "tuned out" his mother.

"Harry's my problem child. He never has liked school—always gotten poor grades even in grade school, and now he is having a lot of trouble in senior high. He truants, fights, and mouths off up there at school, and I've had to go up there many times to try and get things straightened out. . . . And now he's got himself involved in something more serious. I've been thinking all day about whether I should turn him over to the police. But the disgrace to the family and all—I don't know." [Harry's head abruptly jerked up. He turned, looking hard at his mother.] "He's been stealing cars."

"Did the police contact you about this?"

"No, my oldest son Jim told me. I know if he told me it's true. He's my model son, and I know he's right. He's been trying to keep Harry out of trouble. Harry told Jim that he almost wrecked a car and took him to the place where he had left three of the stolen cars. Jim told me that he saw the stolen cars but was afraid to go near them for fear he would be picked up by the police as the one who had stolen them."

The mother said Harry had stolen seven cars that she knew of, all within the last few days. When he got through with a car he would turn it over to some of his friends. Harry continued sitting, staring hard at his mother, who began to lecture him about the consequences of what he was doing and emphasizing that it would give him a record and disgrace the family name. Harry did not deny stealing the cars, nor would he say why he had taken them. As his mother continued talking, he returned to his blank, "tuned out" expression. The interviewer, hoping to reduce the tension, asked the mother how her other children were. However, the mother continued focusing on her problems with Harry, pointing these up by contrasting Harry with his older brother Jim, eighteen years old. "Jim has never given me a moment's worry. He did fine in school, and he's working now. He is a whiz at mechanics. He can make a car run better than anyone you've ever seen. Now Harry is just the opposite. He doesn't like anything. He can draw good, but Jim was the one who taught him how."

Harry continued gazing out the window. His fingers were beginning to drum the arm of his chair but his blank expression remained. His mother shook her head, "I don't know what I'm going to do with that boy."

As the interviewer was leaving, Harry's mother commented that she was sorry she had missed him the other evening, but that was one of the two nights a week she just had to get away for a little while from the children. "I'd go nuts if I didn't." She explained that she went to two or three taverns and had several drinks just for relaxation. Although she occasionally dated, she never wanted to get married again. "Twice is enough, 'specially when you picked louses each time." The interviewer had visited at about half-past seven one evening several days before and had found Harry baby-sitting with his four younger half siblings. Two preschool children were upstairs by themselves, screaming, laughing, and splashing in the bathroom. Two other children, seven and eight years old, were watching television. Harry simply announced that his mother was out and that he did not know when she would be home or where he could reach her if anything happened, but he commented, "Nothing's going to happen—it never does." His older brother Jim usually was with his girl friend on Friday and Saturdays so he could not baby-sit. The interviewer asked Harry how he got along with his mother. "When she's here, I'm gone."

Ben's parents were interviewed on their front porch. Ben had recently been released from a county institution for delinquent boys. Ben's stepmother spoke sharply and with finality in response to the interviewer's query concerning Ben's plans about school. "We just don't have enough money to send him to school and buy his books, 'cause all he wants to do is cause trouble, and I ain't going to give him twenty dollars for that without his learning something."

Ben's father stood nearby, leaning against the house with a bottle of beer in his hand. "Well, I don't think he's smart enough to go to school."

Ben's stepmother glowered at her husband. "Keep your goddamn mouth shut. We didn't ask you for any comments."

The father shrugged and took a long drink from his bottle. "Well, if that's the way you feel," and he turned away looking across the street where city tree trimmers were working. "I used to be a tree trimmer," he commented.

Ben, who had been in the house watching TV, joined the discussion. The interviewer asked how Ben and his eighteen-year-old brother got along. Ben responded,

"Okay. When I was in the county institution I ran away four times in the six months I was there and each time my brother helped me get away. I would tell him I was going to run away on a certain day, and he would park my car down at the bottom of the hill, and this made it easy for me to get away. They kept sending me back there and I kept running away, till finally the supervisor out there says, 'Get out of here. I don't want you here.' That's the best way to get away from there. Yeah, my brother helped me a lot."

The interviewer asked how Ben had been getting along since he had left the institution. "Well, I'm happy now I'm out of it. I've been staying out of trouble."

The mother agreed that as far as she knew Ben had not been in any trouble since he got out three weeks before, but she added, "He don't do nothing. He just messes around."

Ben interjected that one reason he was keeping out of trouble was that he got to drive a car now. A heated interchange with his stepmother took place.

"Well, I don't know whether it keeps you out of trouble or not —you know you're not sixteen yet and you are driving without a license."

"It's none of your damn business if I do."

The interviewer commented that in a bordering state parents were held responsible for their children and could be put in jail. Ben responded, "Oh, I don't drive over there anyway."

Ben's stepmother looked hard at Ben. She shook her finger at him vigorously. "If I ever catch you driving a car I'll break your goddamn neck. You better hear me."

Ben sat straddling the porch railing muttering in an undertone, "Oh mind your own business and go to hell." His stepmother appeared not to have heard this comment. She again warned him he better not let her catch him driving a car.

The interviewer attempted to draw Ben's father back into the discussion by asking whether he and Ben had any common interests or things they liked to do together. He responded readily that he liked to hunt and that his wife had bought him a gun the previous Christmas, but that shortly afterwards he had busted a knee cap and had not been able to use it yet. However, he was looking forward to hunting with it this year. The stepmother broke in, commenting that Ben was not interested in hunting and had urged her to sell the gun to get some money. She had not done it because she did not feel it was fair to give her husband a gun and then take it away from him. The father shook his head, emphatically stating that even if Ben was interested he would not take him along because, "He couldn't shoot a gun. In fact he'd probably kill you he's so careless." Ben glowered at his father.

The father continued deriding Ben. Asked if Ben had opportunity to go with him on his trash truck and help out, he responded with feeling. "Hell no. He would probably kill you. He's so careless. See I haul trash in one of these new trucks that has a blade and smashes all the cardboard boxes and trash. I don't want that boy around. He's always trying to get somebody hurt. In fact everything he does he acts like a little kid. I don't want anybody like that around on one of these trucks that can hurt someone and hurt them badly."

When asked about Ben's leisure pursuits, the mother admitted she did not know what Ben did with his evenings. Ben would only say that he messed around with some of his friends. He admitted he stayed out late. His stepmother expressed no real responsibility for seeing that he was home at a reasonable hour or checking his activities. "After all he's old enough to take care of himself. He knows what he wants to do. I've got my work to do so I got to rest. I know he gets in sometimes awful late—sometimes one o'clock, two or three in the morning. One morning he didn't come home all night."

The father commented that he did not like this, but, "If that's what he wants to do, I'll just go ahead and let him do it. He needs an education, but he's just too dumb to get it."

The interview was suddenly terminated when the stepmother snapped, "Finish that goddamn beer and take me to work. I'm going to be late now." Ben's stepmother worked as a waitress in a bar downtown. She commented that she had lost one job because of having to go to court with Ben so often and she did not want to lose another job on his account. As Ben's parents walked off the porch he muttered, "Goddamn old hicks."

THE INDIFFERENT OR APATHETIC FAMILY

"Let's see. I got these younguns here [four preschool children running around the floor with diapers] and the two girls. That makes —Ella, how many kids I got at PS Twelve [elementary school]?"

"You got five at PS Twelve, Maw."

"Yeah, and then I got Frank. He's at PS Fourteen [senior high school] now."

This was Frank's mother's response to the school interviewer's query concerning how many children she had in school. Ella, fifteen years old and pregnant, was one of two daughters in a family of thirteen children. During the interview Ella sat in the darkened dining room listening to the discussion between her mother and the school visitor in the living room. Her mother frequently enlisted her aid in remembering dates and other information about the large family. Ella, expecting her baby any day, got pregnant when she was a sophomore and dropped out of school. Her boyfriend, also a dropout, did not have a job and he and Ella did not plan to get married. Ella's older sister, Jane, eighteen, had also dropped out of high school to have a baby. She likewise did not get married but left home and got a job as a day worker in the south part of town. She now took care of herself; her mother took care of the child in addition to three of her own babies. She said she expected she will take care of Ella's too.

The interviewer asked about her husband and his work. "Oh, he don't live here. We separated. He just walked off."

"How long ago was that?"

"Well, I think it was—Ella, when was it?" The mother and Ella conversed briefly. They were not sure whether he left in 1954 or 1955. Then Ella remembered that she was about six years old at the time, which would make it—after some help from the interviewer— about 1954 when he left.

"It must be difficult taking care of your family by yourself."

"Well, yes, it's been hard. I'm on welfare and my folks help some when they can. Then Jane, she works and takes care of herself now. The fathers of these younguns help out some too. The father of this one here gives me ten dollars a month support, this one here give me five dollars, and this one buys me some groceries every month. This baby here is Jane's, and his father gives me ten dollars a month support. Course if anything comes up I ain't expecting, well I just have to skip some bill for a month, but I try to keep up."

The school interviewer asked the mother how she managed to keep track of all the children. "Well, it's pretty hard. I try to keep the TV fixed so they can watch it, and then I buy comic books for the kids. I try to keep them around here. My younguns don't get in much trouble." She looked over at Ella, commenting, "Now, these girls only have babies when they gets old enough. That's all they is good for is having babies."

She was asked if she thought Frank had a girl friend. "Well, I suppose he does. He's fifteen and I ain't seen many boys that old that don't get themselves satisfied—you know."

"Has Frank been in any trouble?" The mother acknowledged that he had been picked up by the police on several occasions. Recently she had had to go to juvenile court because Frank and several other boys had stolen some watches. She felt much of Frank's trouble was his companions. "He wouldn't be a bad boy if I could just keep him busy and away from those boys that are with him so much. What's their names, Ella?"

"One of them is Lonnie, Maw."

"Yeah, Lonnie and some of that Seventeenth-street gang. If I could keep him away from them he'd be all right. He just don't think for hisself. They think for him. Now last summer the school got him a job and he didn't get in no trouble. He was just too tired when he got home. He just flopped and watched TV. That was a good thing. Course he don't work much now. Jobs is awfully hard to find and like when he's around these boys he don't want to work."

Frank's mother acknowledged that she was unable to keep Frank away from these other boys because she could not follow him around all the time. She said that she expected him in not later than half-past eleven at night but she was not sure just how he did spend his time. "He tells me he is at somebody's house or just playing out on the street. Sometimes he is real late and then I gets on him."

The interviewer asked how she disciplined her children when they disobeyed. "I just beats them when they get into trouble or sass me. My children don't get too big for me. I just start beating them with anything I can get my hands on—my shoe, a stick, just anything. She knows [pointing to Ella]."

"That's right. I ain't got no whippin' for sometime now, but she sure give it to us."

"Just cause you ain't able to get a whippin' right now, that is why you ain't had it."

The mother admitted that Frank was getting too big and she could not make him obey as she could the younger ones. She tried to teach right from wrong and to give her children proper training. Although they did not go to church regularly, she felt, "It don't matter whether you go or where you go, 'cause we have only God to serve." She felt Frank was headed for trouble, but she did not see how she could do very much about it. She did what she could. She provided Frank with cigarettes so he would not take cigarettes from other boys because "they could be hopped up." She said Frank did not drink around the house, but she suspected he did when he was with the boys.

GENERALLY COHESIVE FAMILY WITH NONCOHESIVE ELEMENTS

"We don't do nothin' as a family. How can we? My husband works nights and sleeps all day. He don't want to be bothered. Of course, now if some of his buddies are going fishing, why he takes right off with 'em. But for the rest of us we just stay home."

"Isn't your husband interested in the children?"

"Not that you'd know it. Course he works hard and he does keep us in groceries and a roof over our head, so I guess you can't have everything."

Marty's mother had three preschool children by her present marriage and two boys and a girl in junior and senior high school by a former marriage. Marty, at age sixteen, was the oldest child.

The interviewer asked if it was not difficult at times being tied down to the house without a break. "Well, you learn how to manage sometimes if you have to. I have learned you can kill a cat in other ways. I don't do this often, but sometimes when he get home I just tell him I'm going out someplace and he's got to watch the kids. Then I get out quick before he says anything. So I gets to town when I have to. He's not mean or anything like that, but he just don't want to be bothered with kids or anything around the house. When I get home he fusses a little, but that's all."

"Do you get away from the children that way?"

"Oh heavens no. Well I do, but I don't do it for that reason.

It would be nice though. No, I go to see about the kids in school or I go to the clinic sometimes. Various places like that.

"One time my husband was feeling good about something. I believe he was going on a fishing trip. Well, he gave me two dollars to take to town with me. So I bought some material for baby clothes. That was a thrill. Oh, another time he took us to visit some friends in the country. I had to prod awful hard for that, but we had bad luck. The car broke down before we got there. It cost us thirty-five dollars. Boy, my husband was sore about that. So we don't get no-where anymore."

During this interview Marty's brothers and sisters and three young friends had come into the living room where the school inter-viewer and Marty's mother were talking. They listened as the inter-view proceeded and they occasionally would add a comment.

The interviewer summarized his impressions of this family.

> The family is held together by the mother. The father, while not an aggressive individual, apparently does not take any time or responsibility for the children's rearing. During the interview it was obvious that the children had affection and respect for their mother and each other. If one of them would speak the others listened or would elaborate on what had been said. There was a lot of good-natured kidding. Marty, partic-ularly, was taking the brunt of that, since it seemed that he and a neighbor girl were going on their first date.

The mother was home during the day, so she supervised the children quite carefully. They had an evening curfew of half-past nine and they usually observed it. A neighbor, talking with the school interviewer who was asking directions, stated, "With all the rough kids around here, those kids [Marty and his siblings] are the best behaved kids you'll ever see. They are home usually before nine o'clock and they aren't troublemakers like some of the others in this neighborhood."

THE COHESIVE FAMILY

"Jim's difficulties in school I feel came from his not being taught to read in the first grade. I feel much of his later dislike for school goes right back to that," said Jim's father to the research inter-viewer late one afternoon. The interview took place in the living room of the home, and Jim sat nearby. The father, a railroad dispatcher, explained he was home this time of day because he was working a rotating shift and presently worked nights. His wife, a stenographer in a downtown firm, had not arrived home from work.

The interviewer asked the father why he felt that reading might have been the problem. "Well, my first two children, both girls, didn't have nearly the trouble Jim had, and they both had the same first grade teacher. Jim had a different teacher, and he had trouble from the very beginning. He just couldn't learn the way his teacher taught him. Both my girls started out right and continued without difficulty. My oldest girl graduated from high school this last year, and she's planning to enroll in junior college next fall."

Jim, sixteen at the time of his interview, was still in school. The interviewer turned to him, asking how he had been getting along in high school. "Well, the eighth and ninth grades were rough. Mom and Dad got me some tutoring in reading, but it didn't help me too much. But then last summer they sent me to a reading clinic, and it really helped me a lot, and this year has been a lot better. Now I can pick up the newspaper and read it and other things, where I never could do this before."

Jim's father added that since Jim had been helped with his reading he seemed to have found himself and was generally getting along much better in school. Jim added that he also was doing "pretty good" in sports. "I play in the baseball league over here in this district, and I'm doing fairly good this year. I play a lot of other sports too, like basketball and football. I'm going out for varsity this next fall."

The interviewer asked the father if he and Jim had much opportunity to do things together. "You bet we do! We go hunting about every other weekend during the season. That's about the only thing Jim and I get a chance to do without the ladies. Of course, we all go to church regularly. My wife and I believe in keeping our kids in church. You know we've lived in this neighborhood for a long time. We are buying here, but there are some rough neighborhoods near by, and kids need all the help they can get of this kind."

Jim's mother arrived home from work and greeted the interviewer cordially, expressing appreciation that the school was continuing its interest in Jim's progress. Both she and her husband commented that Jim's teachers in high school had been most helpful. The interviewer summarized his impressions of the family:

> In spite of the fact that it was late afternoon and the mother had not yet gotten home from work when I arrived,

the home was clean and olderly. The interior was attractively furnished; there were pictures on the walls and *Newsweek* and *Life* were in the magazine rack.

During the interview there was an easy give and take between the parents and Jim, particularly between Jim and his father. Both seemed interested in what the other had to say. The parents appeared congenial and seem to share an interest in their family and home. Throughout the interview they showed a healthy interest in their children, an understanding of differences in them as well as knowing pretty well what was going on in their school and social life.

It is clear that Jim's family was one of the more advantaged families in the study sample. The parents' attitudes and values expressed in the interview indicated a "middle class" orientation as did the material conditions of the family dwelling. The family income was sufficient. With both parents working at relatively skilled jobs, family income was slightly above average. While these socioeconomic characteristics were associated with cohesive relationships in Jim's family, the larger percentage of families rated cohesive were not as socially or economically favored.

Mark's family is one of these. Mark and his three brothers and sisters lived with their parents in a small five room frame house in a community locally known as Dog Patch. Many of the people here migrated from rural areas of Missouri and Arkansas and generally were relatively unskilled or semiskilled workers with large families. These families were known as very poor but also as independent and stable people who worked hard and provided for their families. The interviewer summarized his visit to Mark's family.

> They live in five small rooms. The furniture was dilapidated. There was a strong odor. There were no pictures, books or magazines to be seen. In addition to the eight family members there were two or three dogs running in and out, and, on the afternoon of my visit, there were two cousins and an aunt visiting. About seven or eight people were sitting in the small living room watching TV when I arrived. The parents greeted me courteously, and, when I explained my interest in their children, they became very friendly and openly expressed their appreciation for my visit. It was obvious they liked to talk about their children, and several children who were present entered easily into the conversation when their parents would turn to them for their ideas or opinions.
>
> Everywhere there was evidence of family- and child-

centered activities and interests. Bowling balls were lined up against one wall. Bicycles, tricycles, and wagons and other toys were parked in the small dirt yard. The family bowls together every Wednesday and on weekends goes fishing. The parents acknowledged that they had financial problems in making their income stretch (sixty-five dollars a week), but it was evident that much of their income was stretched to include family activities rather than material possessions.

Both parents had less than eighth grade education, and both agreed they would like to see their children get a high school education, but they weren't sure this would be possible for Mark because he had never learned to read well. The father felt that Mark would do just as well by leaving school when he was sixteen and going to work, since he was a good hard worker and could get ahead this way once he was free to work full time. Both parents were enthusiastic about the help Mark was getting in the Work-Study program.

As parents talked about their families and the kinds of relationships we have been describing as cohesive and noncohesive, many of them identified specific circumstances and conditions of family life and family members who were creating problems. Other parents described what appeared to be major difficulties yet did not elaborate on them even when encouraged. These parents seemed unaware that what they were saying about their family life had any bearing on family relationships or the problems of their children. A content analysis of interviews identified several major problem categories which parents identified. Table 20 summarizes this analysis.

Among those problems identified by parents as causing greatest concern were their children's school achievement and adjustment. However, somewhat fewer than half the parents identified these problems in the interview, although the evidence from school indicated that a much larger percentage of the study group were having school difficulties and would most likely drop out as soon as they could. Parental attitudes toward the school were felt to be important determinants of whether boys would continue in school or terminate as soon as they reached the legal dropout age of sixteen. In the interview the parents' attitudes toward school were explored through the following questions: How do you feel about the schools your children attend? What do you think could be improved or changed? What would you like to see especially changed? Interviewers noted whether parents were critical of the schools and explored their criticisms as well as any positive statements

Table 20.   MAJOR PROBLEMS AND CONCERNS OF PARENTS WHEN
STUDY GROUP BOYS WERE IN MIDADOLESCENCE

Problems and Concerns Indicated by Parents in Interviews	Total Group (N = 400)	Negro Boys (N = 231)	White Boys (N = 169)
	Per Cent		
No major problems or concerns indicated or recognized	37	32	40
One or more problems indicated:	63	68	60
Poor living conditions of family	21	25	15
Boy's poor behavior in community and bad companions	32	35	28
Boy's poor school adjustment	45	43	48
Family problems in relationships and social maladjustment of family members	20	22	17
Boy's personal and physical problem	17	14	22

about the schools. Examples of specific areas of criticism and approval were sought. Each interview protocol was rated independently by two raters on an attitude toward school rating scale. Table 21 summarizes the distribution of ratings on a five-point school attitude continuum.

At the time most boys were almost of legal dropout age, one-third of them lived in family settings where parents indicated generally positive attitudes toward the school. Parents who expressed hostility toward the school were only a small percentage of all those responding. However, combining these parents with those expressing indifference to the schools their children attended shows that 40 per cent of Negro and 27 per cent of white study group boys lived in families where support for staying in school was probably not very strong. It must be noted that some parents were unable or reluctant to express their per-

Table 21. PARENTS' ATTITUDES TOWARD SCHOOL WHEN
BOYS WERE SIXTEEN YEARS OLD

Attitudes Toward School	Total Group (N = 308)	Negro (N = 163)	White (N = 145)
	Per Cent		
Negative—very critical of school and school personnel	12	16	8
Relatively indifferent— school just a place to send the kids	21	24	18
Generally approve the school but without much knowledge[a]	12	11	12
Ambivalence—some positive feelings yet also criticism of some features	23	18	28
Generally positive feelings about school, express some knowledge about school	32	31	34

[a] Although this attitude suggests a positive orientation toward the
school, its relative rank in the value hierarchy was considered to be
lower than ambivalence, which indicated knowledge of the school
and a more realistic appraisal by the parents.

sonal feelings and thoughts in the interview, and these parents' responses may have appeared indifferent. These ratings of parents' attitudes were not distributed among the five late adolescent adjustments
in a way that might have been anticipated if parental attitudes had no
relevance to the school adjustment of children.

Additional information concerning parents' attitudes toward
the Work-Study Program was sought. Parents were asked about any
special school program in which their boy was participating. If they
did not mention the Work-Study Program, they were asked if their
boy was participating in such a program. Whether or not the program
was voluntarily mentioned, parents were asked the following ques-

tions: How do you feel about the Work-Study Program for your boy? Have you seen changes in your boy since he was in the program? What do you feel the program is or is not doing for your boy? How do you think it might be improved or changed for the better? Table 22 shows the responses.

Table 22. PARENTAL ATTITUDES TOWARD THE WORK-STUDY PROGRAM

Attitude Toward Work-Study Program	Total Group (N = 155)	Negro Parents (N = 88)	White Parents (N = 67)
	Per Cent		
Negative—not in favor of program	16	15	20
Indifferent—do not know much about the program, appear disinterested	32	38	24
Ambivalent—critical of program but see some positive aspects	25	25	25
Positive and discriminating —have knowledge of the program and the way it has helped their boy	27	22	31

Slightly more than one-fourth of all experimental parents expressed clearly positive attitudes toward the Work-Study Program. Another one-fourth probably had support for the program, although they were somewhat ambivalent. Responses ranged from a few marked and hostile rejections of the program to very high praise for both the program and the staff. The ratings in between were based on somewhat vague parental responses to interview inquiry. As had been true with respect to attitudes toward school, many parents' responses to inquiry concerning the Work-Study Program were brief, with little elaboration and minimal expression of personal feelings and opinions. When further exploration failed to clarify the parents' attitudes and their level of awareness of the Work-Study Program, these responses tended to be rated as indicating indifference. However, we do not know to what extent responses so rated indicated inability to articulate or organize feelings or opinions into thought nor to what extent they were simply guarded and cautious response in the interview situation.

Negro and white parents of experimental boys differed somewhat in the distribution of ratings. About one in five white, in contrast to about one in seven Negro parents, expressed negative feelings toward the Work-Study Program. Almost one in three white parents expressed favorable attitudes, in contrast to about one in five Negro parents. Among the Negro parents the most frequent rating was indifference—the category which represented a somewhat unclear identification of attitudes. It should be noted, however, that the more frequent ratings of positive attitudes toward the Work-Study Program among white parents parallel the earlier reported finding that white youths benefited more significantly from the project than did Negro boys. Whether positive parental attitudes toward the Work-Study Program simply reflected parental satisfaction with their son's success or represent more basic parental support contributing to a boy's success can only be conjectured. We will look at these associations shortly when we compare the five late adolescent adjustment subgroups on these midadolescent variables.

Tied closely to parental attitudes toward school and the Work-Study Program were parents' assessments of their boys' progress in high school and their views concerning the probability of their staying in school. Parents were asked how they felt their sons were progressing in high school and what they felt the chances were that they would complete school. Responses were identified and categorized into four rating categories of school progress and probability of staying in school. Slightly more than one in five of all parents interviewed indicated their sons were doing fairly well in school. There were relatively more white parents (one in four) than Negro parents (one in five) who saw their sons' progress in this way. The larger percentage of both Negro and white parents, however, indicated that their boys were not doing well in school, and most of them did not expect their sons to stay in school. Only two parents expressed certainty that their boys would complete high school, although over two-thirds of parents indicated that getting an education was very important. Negro parents particularly emphasized this as essential to success in life. Yet Negro parents also expressed considerably less anticipation than white parents that their boys would be able to continue in school. Although relatively more white parents did express some optimism that their sons would stay in school, the larger percentage of them also expressed doubt that this would occur.

The belief of most parents interviewed that their sons would probably not complete high school and that without education life would be difficult for them is reflected in what parents said when asked about their aspirations and hopes for their sons. These responses were rated on a five-point parental aspirations scale and are summarized in Table 23. The high percentage of indifferent ratings suggests that the

Table 23. PARENTAL ASPIRATIONS FOR THEIR SONS

Parents' Aspirations	Total Group (N = 316)	Negro Parents (N = 178)	White Parents (N = 138)
	Per Cent		
Have no ideas, appear indifferent.	42	50	33
Express vague, unrealistic goals but expect only minimal adjustment.	7	7	6
Express aspirations for highly socially acceptable, but unrealistic, goals.	2	2	1
Express realistic and acceptable goals but expect only marginal adjustment.	21	24	17
Express positive realistic aspirations and anticipate achievement.	28	17	43

responses of many parents were grounded in a kind of pervasive expectation that their sons' lives would not be much different from their own. This seemed particularly true of Negro parents, half of whom indicated little thought concerning their boys' future and were either unwilling or unable to project themselves or their boys into an abstract future time. About one-third of white parents showed this kind of response. Rather than expressing aspirations for their boys, most of these parents, both Negro and white, simply voiced hope that their sons would be able to find jobs and stay out of trouble, that is, make at least a minimal adjustment to society. At the other end of the scale, relatively more white parents (43 per cent) than Negro parents (17 per cent) expressed both positive and realistic aspirations for their sons' future careers. Relatively few parents (9 per cent) expressed unrealistic aspirations such as for their son to be a lawyer, a doctor, or an architect, and most of those who voiced such hopes doubted that such careers would be achieved.

About one in five parents emphasized family relationships and the social maladjustment of family members as problems creating tensions and conflicts during the midadolescent years of study group boys. (See Table 20.) Less than one in five parents, however, identified the study group boy as a significant contributor to difficulties in family relationships. Nonetheless, as parents expressed their views on the school, assessed their son's school progress, and talked about their aspirations for him, they also revealed in various ways their affection or lack of it for the boy and the nature of their relationship with him, and this information was incorporated into attitude ratings. Additional information was gained through inquiry into specific parent-child relationships such as how parents coped with discipline and supervisory problems and how aware parents were of their boys' heterosexual and social adjustment.

Parental attitudes toward boys were rated on a four-point scale. Mothers' attitudes are presented in Table 24. Most parents expressed positive attitudes toward their sons even though parents generally felt their boys were not succeeding in school and were limited in what they would do or become. Only one-third of Negro and about one-fifth of white parents were hostile, indifferent, and rejecting toward their sons. These responses were easily identifiable in the interviews, and rater agreement was consistently high at this end of the scale. About one-third of parents' responses at the positive end of the attitude scale were also clearly identified by raters as expressions of affection and acceptance. Other ratings at this level tended to be less reliable and were based more on inference than on direct expression of parents' feelings, that is, parents would describe certain activities on their parts which suggested positive, supportive attitudes toward their boys.

Table 24. ATTITUDES OF MOTHERS' TOWARD
THEIR STUDY GROUP SONS

Attitude	Total Mothers (N = 318)	Negro (N = 175)	White (N = 143)
	Per Cent		
Hostile or indifferent	28	33	22
Generally indifferent, but tends to support or defend son when in trouble	4	3	6
Indulgent—spoils son, expresses indiscriminate affection	13	13	11
Positive but discriminating affection—indicates acceptance of boy, his strengths, and his limitations	55	51	61

ᵃ Mothers were usually the ones providing information directly.
Therefore, their attitudes were used in constructing this table.

To what extent expressions of positive feelings toward their sons were influenced by the parents' needs for social approbation is not clear. However, some parents who expressed positive feelings toward their sons also indicated that they were having difficulty in supervising and disciplining them and that some of them were getting into trouble. Slightly over one-third of Negro parents in contrast to half of white parents indicated that they were able to supervise and discipline their sons adequately and that there were no serious problems of parental control. Only one-tenth of parents indicated that they had in a sense given up attempting to exert guidance or supervision, while the remaining parents, almost half the total group, acknowledged that, although they continued their efforts, their attempts to supervise and guide their sons were not very effective.

In this context, interviewers asked parents about their sons' out of school activities and whether their boys had been in trouble with the police in the past or were currently in trouble. The large percentage of both Negro and white parents indicated that their sons had had no problems with the police. However, as we shall see in Chapter Nine, many of the boys from these families had been in trouble during this period, some of them frequently. Negro parents appeared less reluctant to reveal the delinquency of their sons; over one-fourth indicating that their boys had been and continued to be in trouble with the police. Several of these parents revealed that study group boys were currently out of the home and in institutions because they had refused to listen to their parents.

A number of parents emphasized that the social maladjustment of certain family members (other than study group boys) had created or currently was creating family problems. One of the most frequent problems mentioned was "trouble with the police." To identify the extent and chronicity of such problems among study group families, a survey was made of the police arrests of siblings during a three-year period. Additionally, the police records of parents were obtained. The findings from this survey, using only local police data, revealed that either one or both parents in slightly less than one-third of the families had been arrested on charges ranging from homicide to public disturbance. This does not include eighty-nine fathers and forty-four mothers who had arrests only for traffic violations. About one-third of these were for extensive violations. An additional eighty-five fathers and eight mothers had traffic violations in addition to other arrests. Most arrests were for public disturbance, with fighting in public, common assault, and drunk and disorderly conduct occurring most frequently. However, about half the male parents arrested were charged with felonies. Only about 10 per cent of all parents seemed to have been in serious or chronic difficulty with the police. The following brief sketches of arrest records are typical.

E's father was forty-nine years old. By the time he was thirty-nine he had been arrested twenty-five times on such charges as disturbing the peace, frequenting gambling games, drunkenness, investigation for assault, and nonsupport. Since this time he had had several similar arrests and recently was charged with shooting a man to death; he claimed self-defense.

C's father was fifty-four years old. He had had fifteen different arrests on charges including larceny, attempted strong-arm robbery, and rape, as well as drunkenness, disturbing the peace, careless driving, vagrancy, and nonsupport. He had spent a number of nights in jail for safekeeping.

G's mother was forty-three years old. By the time she was thirty she had a history of arrests for prostitution. She was found to have a venereal disease and was treated. Her recent arrest record included arrests for disturbing the peace and she had occasionally been hospitalized because she had periods of mental disturbance.

The survey of arrest records of siblings during the time most study group boys were between fifteen and seventeen years old revealed that one out of five work-study boys in midadolescence lived in homes where brothers and sisters were in trouble with the police. A large percentage of these siblings had been arrested on serious charges of delinquency, and over a fourth of them had more than three arrests for such delinquency during this period. Many of these siblings appeared to be in chronic difficulty. In a survey of a subsample of one hundred study group families in which all police records of siblings were examined, it was found that in 63 per cent of families there were siblings who had arrest records. Of the 656 children in this subsample, one out of five had arrest records.

We have seen that for most boys terminating school was really not a question. Everything from parents' appraisals of their boys' progress in school to the parents' own limited (but perhaps realistic) aspirations for their sons seemed to focus on when rather than if they would drop out of school. Some boys did not leave school; others continued school into the eleventh and twelfth grades before terminating. Still others left as soon as they could. Did differences in family life in midadolescence have any relevance to these patterns of adjustment? Table 25 compares the five late adolescent adjustment subgroups on a series of midadolescent family variables. Where our measures permitted, we divided our data into negative and positive attributes or characteristics; Table 25 shows the percentage of youths in each adjustment subgroup who fell at the negative end of the scale on each measure of family variables.

SUMMARY

Examining the family life of these boys during their midadolescence, we find that the principal factor appears to be family cohesiveness. There is a striking contrast in the degree of mutual support

Table 25. LATE ADOLESCENT ADJUSTMENT AND FAMILY VARIABLES IN MIDADOLESCENCE

Family Variables in Midadolescence	All Boys					Negro Boys		White Boys	
	Ser. Malad.	Marginal	Erratic	Wk. Adapt.	Sch. Adapt.	Maladap.	Adaptive	Maladap.	Adaptive
					Per Cent				
Broken home	64	65	46	55	53	65	53	40	46
Inadequate physical environment	31	33	27	22	8	35	10	22	20
Noncohesive family	61	46	23	24	14	49	18	32	17
Two or more major problems	60	37	31	23	14	49	16	36	19
Parents hostile or indifferent toward school	40	54	8	15	11	34	18	32	8
Generally negative attitudes toward Work-Study	50	53	48	35	44	51	39	57	34
Little progress in school	67	47	35	26	5	88	68	87	49
Little or no chance of staying in school	94	83	73	62	42	89	54	75	47
Indifferent or minimal parental aspirations for boy	63	46	51	37	23	64	36	63	30
Very limited parental ability to control boy	66	44	31	7	21	55	29	39	27
Boy has police record	76	43	41	14	16	58	21	52	9
Parent has police record	55	44	48	28	55	52	50	46	34
Sibling has police record	35	17	25	18	15	39	15	13	8

and affection in the family between the maladaptive and the adaptive groups of boys. This quality rather than the presence or absence of two parents in the home seems to be important. Whether a boy was living in a "broken" or "complete" home in midadolescence appeared to have relatively slight association with his late adolescent adjustment.

An outstanding set of family variables in association with late adolescent adjustment appears to be parental attitudes toward school, their son's school progress, and their aspirations for him, as well as their perceived ability to supervise and control him. Parents of boys who in late adolescence showed maladaptive adjustment expressed significantly often negative attitudes in these areas. This was true of parents of both Negro and white boys.

The World They Live In

The social space of an adolescent boy consists of three major areas—family, neighborhood, and school. The neighborhood as the boy perceives it and experiences it consists of several blocks around his home and the streets and alleys leading to school. This area has emotional importance; it is not a neutral, impersonal space. There are danger spots and safe spots in it and places where one's own group or gang has complete control. There are enemies to be watched for. Some of the enemies are older or stronger boys who bully younger boys. They are everywhere in the neighborhood, and one must learn to live in the same space with them. Other enemies are groups or gangs who dominate a turf which abuts on the turf of the local group.

　　Even though Kansas City does not have well-organized gangs, such as are characteristic of very large cities, there are quasi gangs, and boys either belong to them or work out informal arrangements which recognize them and their territorial claims. The quasi gang generally has an ethnic basis. On the West Side is a Mexican group, in the North End an Italian group. There are several Negro groups. Such conflict as takes place is more generally focused on ethnicity than on vicinity, although in certain neighborhoods both are important. For example, a white boy of Italian background spoke of relations between his group and a Negro group just south of his neighborhood. It was not safe for members of either group to go alone or in small numbers into alien territory after dark.

141

Me and Bill were watching a fire one night about nine-thirty when some guy threw some stones at our car. Well, we chased him and gave him a good beating, but then we saw some of his guys coming arunning. Well I hadn't noticed it, but we had run into their territory, and boy did we ever make tracks out of there. The leader over there got word to me that I had crossed into their territory and that I was going to get oiled. So now when I'm out in the evening I keep some tight friends with me. I wouldn't mind a fight with one guy, but I don't want the whole gang on my back at the same time.

For some boys of the same race and ethnic background, the territory in which they live defines their group loyalties. Josh, an eighteen-year-old Negro youth, explained to the interviewer, "We have what we call the ups and the valleys. The ups live up here on this hill where I do, and the valley lives under the hill. We don't allow the valley up on the hill, and the valley don't allow the hill down there. When we want to have a good fight we go down there or they come up here."

"Josh, how come you got in with the hill boys, since I know you were once with the valley?"

"That ain't hard to do. You see when you move—like I did up here to the hill—well that changes things. You just belong, that's all. You belong where you live."

The peer group is the chief social influence on the lives of most adolescent boys. It is a loosely constituted, unorganized group. Mainly, it is the group of boys living in the neighborhood, although the group in school also constitutes a peer group. Expressive values dominate the peer group. There is no preparation for the future; the group lives in the present. The boys do not organize, even for warfare with other groups. They live by the moment and for the moment. Their goal is excitement—doing something active, such as stealing a car for a joyride or going in a group of three or four to the army-surplus store and stealing a jacket or a pair of shoes.

A typical episode of peer group life occurred when Malcolm and James, both fifteen, met one morning as they came out of their homes. They had a problem. The preceding day they had been late to school and had been told by the principal to stay after school as a penalty, but they had not obeyed. Now they had to face a stronger penalty if they reported to school. As they wondered what to do, they came to the railroad and saw a slow-moving freight train. They climbed on, thinking to ride for a couple of blocks, but the train picked up speed and did not slow down enough for them to drop off safely until it reached the outskirts of the city.

Here they looked around for transportation back and spied an automobile with the keys in the ignition. Since no one was in sight, they got in the car and headed home. They had gone only a few miles when the car stopped, out of gasoline. They were near a used car lot with no salesman around. They found a car with keys in the ignition and drove off. By now it was midmorning, and going to school could only cause them more trouble, so they decided to go for a ride. It was a warm day in early spring. They crossed the Missouri River and sped north. After a while they became hungry. With a few cents in their pockets, they stopped at a food store. One boy slipped some sliced salami into his shirt while the other picked up a loaf of bread and paid for it.

Proceeding north through the countryside, they crossed into Iowa. They stopped by the roadside, ate some lunch, went walking in the woods nearby, and came back to the automobile as the afternoon was drawing to a close. They decided to start back home and headed south. They got off the paved road onto a graveled road, and then the car slid off the road into a muddy ditch. They could not extricate the car, so they slept in it until morning, when the sheriff's car appeared and the sheriff questioned the boys. They did not have papers for the car, and they had no drivers' licenses. The sheriff took the boys into town. Frightened, they gave him the names of their parents, and he telephoned Malcolm's home. Malcolm's mother left word with a neighbor to look after the other children and took a bus to the Iowa town. There she told the police that she would take the boys home and see that they were punished. She turned James over to his mother and took Malcolm home and sent him to bed.

Back in school, the principal warned them that any more absences would mean they would be suspended from school. They attended regularly a few days and then fell in with Ronald, a sixteen-year-old who had a reputation for stealing cars. He took them to a suburb where they found a car with keys in the ignition in a used car lot. They drove around a while and were accosted by police, who arrested them and took them to juvenile court. Previous car thefts were on file against Ronald. Malcolm and James were sent to a county home for wayward boys for several months. Although the routine in the county home was an orderly one and tended to teach the boys orderly habits, it had very little influence on Malcolm and James or on other members of the peer group. The boys told each other of their exploits and were just as ready for the excitement of stealing and fighting as before.

The neighborhood is anything but a safe place for a boy who has not established himself in the pecking order of a group. It is a jungle in which the strongest, boldest, and cleverest dominate the others. What is known locally as the con game starts in the experience of young boys when they are sent to the local store to buy a loaf of bread or a six-pack of soda pop. An older boy will stop a young boy and take his money. If the younger boy refuses to give up his money, the older boy beats him up and then runs off. The younger boy does not tell his mother for fear she will complain to the older boy's mother. If the older boy is punished, he will lie in wait for the younger boy and beat him more severely. In most cases the younger boy manufactures an excuse to his parents for "losing" the money, and he is likely to hear nothing further from the older boy, who appears to forget the incident.

As boys get older they come together for protection in street-corner groups or quasi gangs. Out of such a group emerges the leader, called the key man. Usually he is older and a good fighter. He is also one of the more fluent speakers. Boys join the group for security and status. The key man directs two or three of his subjects to get him some money so that he can take his girl out. Anyone is a potential victim—an old man unable to defend himself or a woman with a purse to snatch. Any person on the street alone is a likely target.

The boys who operate on behalf of the key man also serve themselves. Often, if they get a great deal of loot, they can keep some of it. The boys get a sense of accomplishment, which they cannot get in school or at work. Michael said, "You see it is like this. I ain't got no job, and money is hard to come by. So I figures if I helps the key man I gets him and myself some loot, and we both are happy. You see, I goes out with these guys, and we gets us a pigeon, and we takes his money, so we figure the key man needs just so much, and we kick in that amount and keeps the rest for us. After the key man gets off my back, I keeps the pigeons going, and I have enough loot that I don't need to work."

The interviewer asked, "What would happen if a pigeon squeals on you?"

"I would have to wipe him out, that is all. He ain't goin' to squeal if he knows what's healthy."

"Have you ever had one squeal?"

"Yeah, once, and he forgot everything after he was taken to the hospital."

For younger boys, who are victims of older boys not under directions from the key man, the experience is not so serious. One or two older boys, meeting a younger boy, say "Hey, punk, got a cigarette?" The boy answers, "No." "Got any money I can borrow?" Again the boy answers, "No." "Let me see." The older boys search the younger boy. If they find money on him they take it and push him around for telling a lie. If he resists the search, he is attacked by one of the group and the others hit him while he is defending himself. In most cases the victim attempts to get away by running. Boys who have been victims say something like, "I don't want to go down [fall to the ground] or they will oil me up good, so I try to run away from them any way that I can." Boys said that when a boy goes down that indicates he has no guts and the older boys punish him once he is down more severely than they do if he runs away. Tony said, "I don't want them to polish their shoes on me, so I get out of there some way even if I have to crawl."

"What does it take to keep these guys from bothering you when you are on the street?" asked the interviewer. The answer most often given was "fight." "When anyone tries to take something from you it has to mean fight or he'll try it again. If you fight and they know you will, regardless of whether you win or lose, the guys will leave you alone. Sure, some guys like to show off when they're with their friends, and so they pick on you, but they know that if you will fight, you'll find them by themselves some day, and they're afraid you might work them over, so they leave you alone."

The demand for nice clothing produces another operation of the con game. Gang members who spot a boy with expensive clothing will attempt to borrow a jacket or sweater or hat on the pretext that they are attending a big affair that night and need it badly. If the boy refuses to lend them the clothing, they pick a fight with him and ruin his clothing. If he makes the loan, it is seldom returned. If he attempts to get it back, he is usually roughed up, and the articles of clothing are returned soiled and in need of repair.

Fifty-three per cent of Negro boys in our study said they knew of the con game but denied having been victims. In each case they knew of someone else who had been a victim. Active participation as aggressor was admitted by 23 per cent of the Negroes. Only 6 per cent of the white boys and 10 per cent of the Mexican boys admitted knowing about the game. Some boys disavowed the con role because they felt it was wrong or stupid or because, as one boy said, "So you find a guy you can con and that's okay; but then he's got some friends and they find you alone some night and oil you up good, maybe even kill you, so what's the point to that?" Other youths, however, seemed to see the con game as one way of getting what they wanted and at the same time gaining a sense of power and control. It was seen as a means of building a reputation. For such boys, the danger of retaliation appeared to enhance the excitement and challenge. Many of these youths acknowledged that they enjoy a "good fight." A few indicated that they deliberately sought out victims just to test themselves or to impress friends with their physical powers. Often the potential victim was studied and then subjected to a kind of psychological warfare in which he was manipulated into a situation suitable to the aggressor's purposes. Jack, age eighteen, told how this worked.

> Sometimes a guy will be walking down the street and will see another guy, and for some reason he will think in his mind "I don't like that boy." Sometimes he don't even know his name, so then he will start looking and asking other people about this guy, wanting to know some of the things about him and who he runs with, the girls he dates, and so on. Then he will try to find fault with him in order to pick a fight with him. He will use all the information he's been able to dig up, and he'll needle him with it and then pick a fight. Like he will tell that boy he don't like his looks, his girl, or his friends, and this will usually start a fight. Every time he does this he's usually got somebody around that he wants to impress with what a tough cookie he is and how well he can handle himself. Lots of guys do this. Not only boys but a lot of men live that way today. I used to be that way, but I'm not anymore.

In such a world many boys become involved unintentionally. Alfred said,

I was going to work at this place, and I didn't have to get there until noon, so I stopped by to see my girlfriend. You see, she is going to have a baby. I talks to her for a while, then I gets ready to leave, and I see these cats on the street. I know them, so I go out, and we talk a few minutes until this other cat comes up the street trying to borrow some money from us. You see, he wanted this money to get his girl and his baby out of the hospital. Well, we didn't have anything for him, so he leaves. Why, man, you know what he did? He went down the street and robs this man on the street, then he beats him up. Well, we were in the street, and when people came out of the houses they done said we did it. I lost my job over that, and I was thrown in jail. I may serve time over this yet. I have to go to court in another week. So you see, man, when a guy tries to go straight he is just caught sometimes and people won't believe him, so he takes a rap. Sometimes I wonder if it pays to go straight.

For some boys, weakness is an open invitation to harassment and physical brutality; young children and old people are likely targets. For example, four boys in the study group left their ninth grade classroom and were walking home together. A small boy approached from the opposite direction. The four fanned out to block his way, and then one of them saw his wrist watch. They encircled the younger boy, and one of them threw a bottle which broke around his feet. Frightened, he dove through an opening and ran into a house nearby. The four boys went on and soon came to a park area. They found an old man asleep on the grass. Nearby he had a sack of greens. One of the boys tore the sack open and scattered the greens about. The old man stirred and then sat up, startled. One of the boys hit him in the jaw a couple of times, and another hit him three times. The old man got up on his knees and pulled out his billfold. A quarter fell out of it and one of the boys grabbed it. They ran off.

This atmosphere of terror encourages weaker boys to stay home from school. James said, "I might as well stay at home. When I do go to school I sit there and don't learn anything because I am thinking, 'I wonder if I will get beaten up this afternoon as I go home.'"

Adults in these neighborhoods are also affected by the atmosphere of fear. One mother said, "I wouldn't walk from my house to the store up the street after dark. I couldn't make it five times without being attacked." She also said her son was attacked as he sat in the family car. "We know some of the boys," she said, "but we are afraid they will cause us more trouble, so we keep quiet in hopes they will leave us alone." Boys in these neighborhoods say that social life is curtailed by troublemakers. Taking a girl to a local movie in the evening is risky, because "there is always some guys making cracks and trying to start something by meddling with your girl, so then you have to fight him and the guys he's with." Boys with cars now take their girls to drive-in movies. Boys say that they once had invitations to parties to take their dates to in the evenings, but there are few of these now because of partycrashers who "turn the party out," that is, start fights, break things, and break up the party. Social club meetings and dances in certain neighborhoods are also infrequent because of the drinking, fighting, knifings, and shootings which have occurred.

> There was a man in our neighborhood, and he had a little extra money, so he fixed up his basement so me and my friends could practice a little combo—we had a couple of guitars, and I was playing the drums. So we'd go down and practice, and we'd invite our girls down there once in awhile and play records and dance and booze a little bit. Well other cats got to finding out about this, and they started coming down there, and first thing you know one night we had our girls there and a bunch of these guys came in and started messing around. They started meddling with our girls and wanted to take them away from us. Well this man told them there was nothing for them around there and told them to go on. He was talking real nice to those boys when all of a sudden one of them hit him. Well, we had to step in and take care of that man—after all, we were using his basement. We got those guys outside, and they start shooting and banging around, and the neighbors called the cops, and they take us all down and kept us in the police station until five in the morning.

Many boys have a fatalistic concept of life. It really makes no difference who you are. If you happen to be by yourself and just happen to meet boys out for trouble, you have had it, unless you are prepared to use a gun or knife or can outrun your enemies, who may actually be unknown to you. In such a world, there is no safety or security. You can be completely innocent but still be picked up by police and thrown in jail on suspicion. You mind your own business and still get killed. Ned was standing on a street corner waiting for a bus. Some boys came by, and one had a gun. He started shooting at Ned's feet and one bullet hit Ned in the foot. The boys ran past, laughing, leaving Ned on the ground wounded. Ned claims he had never seen any of the boys before.

Newspaper reports like the following, in which one of the victims was a boy in our study, are numerous: A youth attending a party was wounded early yesterday when two bullets were fired through a front window. The victim, age sixteen, was treated at the general hospital for wounds in the upper back. Witnesses said a group of youths had been asked to leave the party about midnight after they became disorderly. Immediately after the shooting these witnesses reported seeing a car disappearing from sight. Police said witnesses were unable to explain an earlier shooting at the party in which a youth suffered a small caliber bullet wound in the left thigh. This youth, age seventeen, was taken to the general hospital. He was listed in fair condition. Police said they were unable to learn how the shooting happened.

Sudden and violent death was no stranger to the boys and their families. One of the boys in the experimental group was killed at a party. Another was found slumped over the wheel of his parked car with a bullet in his head. His wallet and wristwatch were both missing, and police believed robbery was the motive. This boy had been discharged from the Marines a month previously after serving two years in Viet Nam. He had lived on the West Side all his youth, had never been in serious difficulty, and had gotten a job as an apprentice machinist when he arrived home from the Marines. His wallet had contained money from his first paycheck.

Life in an atmosphere of such arbitrary violence seems to produce impulsive physical reactions to threat or perceived threat. Two boys in our study population were riding in a car. The boy driving was speeding dangerously and his companion objected. The car was brought to a screeching halt, and both boys jumped out ready to fight. The driver was suddenly stabbed in the stomach by his companion. He was taken to the hospital where blood transfusions were given. The victim's mother declined to prosecute. In another instance, a boy was playing pool early one Saturday morning. A man walked by and accidentally bumped him. Profanities were exchanged. The boy pulled a gun and fired, hitting a man in the head. The victim, who died the next day in the hospital, had not been the intended victim. Someone had bumped the boy's arm as he fired, and he shot the wrong man. The boy had fired twice.

Youth workers in the inner city talked about the apparent increase in such events. Increased use of drugs was suspected. One experienced West Side worker talked about the problem.

"Some of the boys that used to come in here [settlement
house] have drifted away recently. They've gotten on dope and
then get involved in burglary and other things, and we just
lose them. You know dope isn't hard to get."

"Is there much of that going on now?" asked the interviewer.

"Yes. We're getting a lot more of it since last year.
Many of our guys are high much of the time. It isn't mari-
juana or heroin. In fact most of it is pep pills, which I think
are just as dangerous or maybe more so than heroin or main-
liners. Our guys melt these pills down and are using it in the
veins. It stimulates them to where they don't seem to have a
conscience. They're able to do things that they wouldn't ordi-
narily think of doing. I feel this is the reason for the sudden
increase in all these bad knifings, fights, drunks getting rolled,
robberies, and things we've been getting over here. These guys
are using very potent stuff, especially the way they take it.
Some of them will take several pills with beer, then take a
sedative like phenobarbitol, and this has quite a reaction on
them. For seventy-five cents they can get a pretty good jag."

"Where do they get it?"

"Well, there are many rear-rank characters in the area
doing the peddling. I don't know if it's a syndicate involved
here, but I'm sure it's regulated from higher up. This is getting
to be a much bigger problem than alcohol, which you know
was the chief thing in the past. The boys could always get
booze—they could tip a wino and he'd go in and get them a
bottle, or they could always go over across the river when they
got to be eighteen and drink beer."

The worker was asked why he thought so many boys were involved in drinking and drugs.

"Well, it's just that there's nothing to do, and they
really don't feel there's much to be looked forward to. That's
my impression. Drinking or getting high on drugs is one way
of getting out of reality. After they stand around on the street
corner night after night with nothing constructive to do, and
most everything else in their lives being negative—school,
employment, family life—well, this is just one way to escape
it. Getting high is the excitement of the area. Kids get caught
up in this, girls as well as boys. Some get hooked very early.

I know of a thirteen-year-old girl who is already shot on dope. She runs the streets, is having sex relations, and looks and dresses a lot older than she is. She's out of school and when you ask her mother where she is she says she's sick, or she'll sometimes tell you she's at school even when you know she isn't. Why don't the school check on kids out like this? I know in suburbia they'd be out checking the second or third day a kid was absent from school."

A teacher of West Side youth echoed these impressions:

"Many boys see the drabness of their lives and that of their parents, the alcoholism, the crime, the prostitution. They see brothers and sisters go off into other worlds only to return because they can't hack it on the outside. They see themselves not fit to do much and not educated up to the standards of other kids. So they feel depressed, and they try not to think about how they live or the future. They don't think about to-morrow, just today, and how to get some excitement out of today."

This quest for excitement and its consequences leads to impulsive and often fatal choices of action. This is particularly apparent when escape from police is the immediate concern. Mike, age sixteen, and several other youths stole a car and headed out to the turnpike. Driving at a high rate of speed, Mike suddenly decided to turn the car around and return to the city. He attempted to make a U-turn across the green strip between the two double lanes. He caused a three-way crash. Five people were injured. Mike was killed. In another instance, Jack, age seventeen, stole a car and ran a stop sign. The police began chasing him. At the end the boy had twenty-five police cars after him and was driving a hundred miles an hour as he tried to lose his pursuers. He finally hit an abutment, wrecking the car. Bruised and shaken he attempted to escape on foot but was quickly captured.

In interviews many boys agreed that having nothing to do was a major problem and one of the reasons some boys got into trouble. Some youths were highly critical of the "troublemakers," describing them as "thugs," "punks," and "hoods." Gary, a seventeen-year-old Negro boy, complained to the interviewer, "Most guys around here are nothing but thugs roaming the street and causing trouble. They are always trying to borrow something from me, and of course any guy around here who is working is always getting the bead put on him 'cause they know he might have a little extra change on him. I don't

like it, and it's always happening to me. But the main thing is that
I'm put down by other people 'cause I live in the same neighborhood.
I'm judged by what these guys do."

Other youths, admittedly among those who crashed parties,
drank heavily, chased women, and fought, talked candidly about such
exploits. These youths emphasized the pursuit of excitement rather
than the dangers or the consequences. They described their world as
a place where you had to make things happen. Some boys attributed
their involvement to "just going along with guys in their neighborhood." Bill said, "I just got to going with these guys for something to
do and started boozing with them, and the first thing I knew I was
out chasing women and fighting and it was fun."

Youths in such neighborhoods cope with their world in various
ways. Some drift into neighborhood associations which provide some
excitement and a sense of security, but which often lead to trouble
with the police and sometimes to physical injury or even death. Other
boys are involved in the con game and other extralegal pursuits and
actively seek offensive and defensive security by associating with older
experienced youths and by building reputations as toughs. Some youths
in these neighborhoods are oriented toward other values and must
work out different solutions. Some do not describe harassment or physical violence of themselves, but agree that many boys they know are
victims. Most acknowledge that fighting is an acceptable way of handling most troublemakers. One youth said, "they don't bother me, and
they better not bother my friends. Mostly they pick on younger fellows
who can't help themselves. But I've told them, and I know them all,
that they better not bother my friends. And they haven't, because they
know I'll fight, and I can, too."

Other boys said they kept out of trouble by not associating with
troublemakers. As one boy put it, "I just mind my own business and
don't get out here and steal or try to act tough like some guys do."
Most boys did not seek help from the police or school personnel. One
who was badly injured by a gang attack said, "I didn't know the guys,
but I'd probably recognize them if I saw them. . . . But I wouldn't
say nothin' about it. You just don't do that around here. I wouldn't
even tell my friends, because if I did they'd try to get them, and then
those guys would try to get me again."

Some boys indicated that they tried to find other outlets and
thus avoid roaming the streets looking for excitement. One said, "Most

of the guys I run around with I chose because they try to keep out of trouble. We like to work on cars, and we pool our money to have some way of driving and keep from messing around where trouble is." Some boys indicated that they let it be known that they would fight to kill if anybody bothered them. Many acknowledged that they sometimes carried weapons just to equalize things if their attackers could not be handled with fists. A few youths indicated that they coped with what they acknowledged was a bad environment by avoiding it as completely as possible. "Just because we live here is no sign that we have to do like some people here do. You know, this is the heart of the poverty area, the center of it, and it will probably all be torn down someday. But this is our home now, and we are trying to take care of it and avoid any trouble. Before we had television we had to put puzzles together and sit and talk about the past and other things like that in the evenings. But now we have television, and we spend a lot of time watching it. We get our homework, do things around here to entertain ourselves, but we don't go out at night in this neighborhood."

The amount and nature of violence, threat, and intimidation occurring among these boys as they moved through adolescence, both as victims and as aggressors, is difficult to estimate. Among the 422 study group boys, there were seven arrests for homicide, sixty for aggressive assault, twenty-three for rape, and 115 for robbery including armed robbery. There were 272 arrests for somewhat less serious delinquent behavior, but nevertheless physically aggressive acts were involved such as disorderly conduct (198 arrests), fighting in public and common assault (twenty-two arrests), and destruction of property (fifty-two arrests). However, such official data considerably underestimate the situation as revealed in what boys told us in interviews. Of the 422 boys (experimental and control) who had entered the eighth grade six years earlier, ten were dead by violence, thirty others had been knifed or shot, sixty-four were in prison, and 238 had felony arrest records.

9

Delinquency

When study group boys were identified as school and social misfits in the seventh grade, it was predicted that without special help relevant to their special needs most of them would be early high school dropouts and a large proportion of them would be legally designated juvenile delinquents during adolescence. Chapter Five indicated that the majority of them did drop out of school. Chapter Six indicated that many boys enrolled in the experimental program apparently did not profit from it. In this chapter we attempt to determine whether delinquency emerged as a significant adolescent problem for the study group as had been predicted in the seventh grade. To do this we examine the extent and nature of officially recorded arrests for activities defined by juvenile statutes as delinquent activities. We begin with police and juvenile court data which we systematically collected from the start of the study in 1961. Much of what we have described about the families, neighborhoods, opportunities, and so forth among study group boys relates to various theories of delinquency. However, in this chapter we are not concerned with theories as such. Our intent is to provide a factual account of the extent of involvement of study group boys with the police and juvenile court as well as the nature of this involvement. We also present several case studies which attempt to relate our empirical findings to contemporary theories.

By the seventh grade, 30 per cent of the study group had police records. Eleven (3 per cent) had been confined for delinquency. Six years later, when most boys were between seventeen and nineteen years old, 68 per cent (289) had police records, amounting to 1,597 arrests. This did not include 448 moving traffic violations. The average number of arrests for delinquency among the 289 boys was 5.6, the median was three, and the range was one to thirty-one arrests. Twenty-five per cent of the arrest group had accumulated eight or more charges of delinquency. Twenty-five per cent had only one arrest.

Sixty-eight per cent of all adolescent arrests were for serious delinquency, that is, for behavior which would constitute a felony if committed by an adult. Twenty-two per cent of arrests were for behavior loosely defined as public nuisance, including drinking in public, loitering, trespassing, disorderly conduct, and the like. The remaining 10 per cent were arrests for investigation (2 per cent), home and school referrals (4 per cent), and response to arrest, confinement, and parole (4 per cent). The more serious charges of delinquent behavior were not confined to youths with long records of arrests, although the more arrests a boy experienced the greater was the ratio of serious to less serious charges. Among the 25 per cent of boys with only one police arrest recorded during adolescence, 60 per cent of arrests were for seriously delinquent acts. For youths with three or more arrests, police records were heavily weighted with charges of serious delinquency. Sixty-five per cent of these boys had two-thirds of their arrests at this level.

When delinquency of the study group was assessed at different ages during adolescence and when arrest data were compared with local youth norms for the same time period (1962–67), the delinquent character of the study group clearly emerged. Arrests on serious delinquency charges were four or five times greater for the study group than for the whole Kansas City youth population of the same age. To determine to what extent the research group differed in frequency of arrests from other youths in the inner city, a study was undertaken of the arrests of fifteen- and sixteen-year-old inner-city boys during the school year 1963–64, the year when most study group youths were fifteen or sixteen years old. Seven per cent of all inner-city boys of this age enrolled in school had been arrested one or more times during the year, in contrast to 20 per cent of study group youth. One in eight of all inner-city boys arrested had repeated police contacts in contrast to one in four of study group boys arrested. It is clear that our research groups were composed of boys who contributed disproportionately to the number of juvenile arrests in inner-city communities.

Most arrests for serious delinquency fell into two categories—aggressive acts against persons and things and acts of delinquency not directly involving physical aggression against others. The former category involved direct physical contacts with victims, and the use of force or intimidation was the major characteristic of such contacts. Arrests in the other category were for illegal behavior where direct contacts with the victim were usually avoided. Both categories included arrests for planned and deliberately executed acts of delinquency as well as arrests for what appeared to be spontaneous or impulsive, but nevertheless serious, delinquent behavior, that is, for both true delinquency and situational delinquency. (True delinquency consists of planned and deliberate acts which would be felonies if committed by adults. Situational delinquency may or may not involve serious breach of the law; it appears to emerge out of situations or conditions without deliberation or planning.)

Arrests in the third general class, public nuisances, were for behavior considered to be less serious breaches of the law and recognized as relatively typical expression of adolescent frustration, boredom, and search for excitement. This may account for the relatively fewer arrests in this category than in the others. For some youths, however, the repeated pattern of such arrests suggests that these behaviors represented expression more of life-style indigenous to the boys' social cultural subgroup than of their adolescent stage of development. Table 26 summarizes arrests of study group boys during adolescence. It is clear that arrests for serious delinquency occurred much more frequently than did public nuisance arrests. Arrests for nonphysically aggressive acts were more frequent than for physically aggressive acts, although the occurrence of arrests for aggressive acts was significantly higher than among the total Kansas City youth population. It also seems likely that the incidence of true delinquency was significantly higher than that of spontaneous delinquency. Arrest for auto theft, which frequently involved a spontaneous impulse to take a ride or to impress one's friends, was frequent compared to other arrest types, yet such arrests were considerably fewer than the combined arrests for larceny, burglary, and shoplifting, activities which usually require some kind of planning.

Within the aggressive delinquency category, the high numbers

Table 26. ARRESTS OF WORK-STUDY YOUTH DURING ADOLESCENCE

Seriousness and Type of Arrests[a]	Number of All Arrests	Percentage of All Arrests	Number of Boys with One or More Arrests
Serious delinquency	*1079*	68.0	
Physically aggressive behavior toward persons or things	*288*	18.0	
Homicide	7		7
Robbery	115		73
Rape	23		21
Aggravated assault (includes assault with intent to kill)	60		46
Extortion	3		3
Purse snatching	14		11
Destruction of property (includes arson and vandalism)	52		49
Common assault	14		9
Behavior not aggressive toward others	*749*	46.0	
Larceny	237		132
Shoplifting	52		46
Burglary	242		119
Auto theft—includes riding in stolen car (18) and driving car without permission (8)	200		111
Petty theft (till tapping)	5		3
Forgery	5		5
Possession of stolen property	8		8

[a] Seriousness ratings are based in part on Cambridge Sommerville rating criteria and in part on consultation with the Kansas City Police Department.

Table 26.   ARRESTS OF WORK-STUDY YOUTH DURING
ADOLESCENCE (cont.)

Seriousness and Type of Arrests[a]	Number of All Arrests	Percentage of All Arrests	Number of Boys with One or More Arrests
Other serious delinquent behavior	*42*	4.0	
Carrying concealed weapons	27		26
Exhibitionism	4		4
Crimes against nature (includes sodomy and other homo-sexual acts)	7		3
Possession of narcotics	2		2
Glue sniffing	2		2
Less serious delinquency[b]			
Public nuisances	356	22.0	
Drinking or intoxicated in public	55		42
Disturbance, disorderly, fighting in public	203		122
Loitering or vagrancy	28		25
Contributing to delinquency of minor	10		8
Trespassing	15		15
Prowling	21		15
Other—includes frequenting disorderly house (3), procuring (1), gambling (10), discharging firearms (3), false fire alarm (2), false report to police (5)	24		22

[a] Seriousness ratings are based in part on Cambridge Sommerville rating criteria and in part on consultation with the Kansas City Police Department.

Table 26. ARRESTS OF WORK-STUDY YOUTH DURING
ADOLESCENCE (cont.)

Seriousness and Type of Arrests[a]	Number of All Arrests	Percentage of All Arrests	Number of Boys with One or More Arrests
Other arrests (seriousness relative to other factors present)	162	10.0	
Investigation, interrogation	33		29
Truancy	26		22
Runaway from home	28	4.0	19
Beyond parental control	15		14
Response to arrest, confinement, and parole—includes runaway from institution (18), escape from police (7), resisting arrest (18), and parole violation (17)	60		55

[a] Seriousness ratings are based in part on Cambridge Sommerville rating criteria and in part on consultation with the Kansas City Police Department.

[b] Less serious as individual acts; in a pattern of arrests may represent serious maladjustment.

of arrests for strong-arm robbery and aggravated assault reflect the strong aggressive orientation of a segment of the study group in adolescence. Table 27 compares the study group and the total Kansas City population of the same age on arrests for offenses which would be felonies if committed by adults.

The extent and seriousness of delinquent activity among the study group during adolescence are reflected in the fact that one-fourth of the four hundred boys had one or more institutional confinements for delinquency during adolescence. This amounted to more than one-

Table 27. ARRESTS OF STUDY GROUP BOYS AND
TOTAL KANSAS CITY YOUTH POPULATION

| | Arrests from Age Thirteen through Age Eighteen | | | |
| | Study Group (N = 400) | | Kansas City Youth (N = 19,649) | |
Offense	Number Arrests	Percentage of Sample	Number Arrests	Percentage of Population
Homicide	7	1.7	53	0.3
Robbery	115	28.0	953	5.0
Rape	3	5.5	178	0.9
Aggravated assault	60	15.0	423	2.0
Burglary	242	61.0	3,128	16.0
Larceny	237	59.0	4,304	22.0
Auto theft	200	50.0	2,449	12.0

third (35 per cent) of the 289 youth with arrest records. Almost half these institutionalized youth were committed two or more times, and a number of them spent over half their adolescent years in institutional environments. The median number of weeks in institutions for the hundred boys committed was fifty-two; twenty-five boys, including most of those with four or more commitments, spent two years or more in institutions. Four boys were committed five different times. One boy had seven commitments by the time he was seventeen. Many of these multiple commitments were continuous, that is, there was little or no free time between them. Such extended institutional experience was usually a consequence of a boy's seriously disruptive adjustment to confinement in one institution which resulted in new court hearings, recommitment, and transfer to another institution considered better equipped to handle the problem the boy presented. Several youths during relatively continuous confinement moved through county and state training schools into more closely supervised correctional settings intermediate between juvenile institutions and prisons. These youths, for the most part, remained in confinement because of their inability to earn good behavior time because of failure to adapt to institutional life.

Other youths were in and out of confinement; they were capable of conforming while institutionalized and earning good behavior time, yet once outside they soon returned to former norm-violating behavior and subsequent arrest, conviction, and recommitment. In late adolescence several of these youths were convicted in criminal court of felonies and sentenced to prison for lengths of time ranging from one to thirty years. Of the total one hundred boys with commitment histories, 38 per cent were committed to juvenile institutions only. Another 36 per cent were committed first to juvenile institutions and later to adult correction facilities. Twenty-six per cent were not confined until their late teens and were then committed to adult correction institutions.

In addition to youths committed to institutions for delinquency, more than one-fourth (29 per cent) of study group boys experienced one or more temporary confinements in the juvenile court's parental home or, after age seventeen, in the city jail. These confinements were usually while the boys awaited court hearings or the outcome of investigations. A few boys over age seventeen were detained when they could not post bonds.

The generally serious nature of the study group's delinquency as perceived by the police was evidenced by their referral of the bulk of arrests (65 per cent) to the juvenile court for adjudication. The police department's youth bureau handled about 28 per cent of all arrests with a warning to the child and his parents of consequences of future misbehavior and release of the boy into his parents' custody. In only 7 per cent of all arrests during adolescence were youths released as cleared of suspicion. After age seventeen over half the charges were dismissed.

Youths who were committed to institutions during adolescence were for the most part quite visible as "bad actors" prior to commitment. Other boys appeared in many respects to be just as visible yet were able somehow to avoid institutional commitment during early and middle adolescence. Another subgroup of boys, although showing only minimal signs of delinquency during adolescence, had frequent contacts with police for traffic violations. The frequency of such arrests and the response to summonses for court appearances varied among these boys from one or two citations for minor infractions to as many as ten citations over a one- or two-year period. Failure to appear and the issuance of "wanted" bulletins on such charges were frequent. Of the 154 youths with such traffic arrests, 42 per cent failed to appear in court to face charges.

Of the 289 youths who had one or more police contacts by late adolescence, twenty-six had already established police records by ten years of age. An additional eighty-six boys had become involved with the police by age thirteen. Thus 112 youths (30 per cent of sample) had been arrested and had official police records before entering junior high school. Thirty-one per cent of this early arrest group had three or more arrests for serious delinquency.

After study group youths entered early adolescence, the number of boys coming into contact with the police accelerated rapidly. By age sixteen, 73 per cent of the 289 boys had police records. By age seventeen, the number had increased to 86 per cent. The remaining sixteen per cent of boys with police records showed no official record until they were eighteen or nineteen years old. By late adolescence 71 per cent of Negro boys and 60 per cent of white boys had police records. The average number of arrests for activities defined as legally delinquent (excluding traffic violations) was 5.3 for Negro youths and 3.6 for white boys. A higher percentage of white youths (41 per cent) than Negro boys (33 per cent) had traffic arrests for moving violations.

The average age of first police contacts for Negro boys was 13.7 years, for white boys 14.3. Thirty-five per cent of Negro youths with police records were first arrested before entering the eighth grade. Twenty-four per cent of white boys with records were known to the police before this time. Ten of the eleven youths who had been institutionalized during childhood were Negro.

There was about the same relative percentage of arrests for serious charges of delinquency and for less serious charges of public nuisance behavior among Negro and white boys arrested during adolescence. The Negro group, however, averaged almost five arrests for serious delinquency in contrast to three arrests for the white arrest group. One-fourth of the Negro group had eight or more arrests on charges of serious delinquency by late adolescence. One-fourth of the white arrest group had four or more such arrests. However, within this one-fourth of white boys was a subgroup with extensive arrests during adolescence. Among Negro and white study group youths aged thirteen to eighteen, the percentages of arrests which were for serious delinquency were similar—75 per cent for Negro boys and 72 per cent for white boys. Eighty-three per cent of Negro boys with arrest records and 84 per cent of white boys were arrested for serious delinquency. Twenty-five per cent of arrests of Negro boys and 28 per cent of arrests of white boys were for public nuisance behavior; 56 per cent of Negro boys and 48 per cent of white boys with arrest records were arrested for public nuisance behavior.

Among arrests for serious delinquency were the subgroup of arrests for physically aggressive, destructive acts against persons or things. Such arrests are considered most serious by the police and the courts, and they resulted in institutional commitments more frequently than any other type of delinquency. Twenty-five per cent of arrests of Negro boys and 15 per cent of arrests of white boys were for such acts. Forty-six per cent of Negro boys with arrest records were arrested for aggressive, destructive acts, as were 23 per cent of white boys arrested.

It is evident that Negro boys with police records in our sample were more often arrested and charged by the police with aggressive acts of serious delinquency than were white boys with police records. The relatively larger number of Negro boys in trouble with the police was reflected in their higher rate of institutional commitments. However, it should be noted that, within the Negro and white arrest groups themselves, the ratio of noncommitment to commitment was only slightly higher in the white group. Twenty-nine per cent of Negro study group boys (39 per cent of Negro boys arrested) were committed to institutions; only 17 per cent of white boys (33 per cent of those arrested) were committed. (This does not include detention in jail.) Fifty-two per cent of Negro boys committed and 50 per cent of white boys committed were committed only once; three per cent of Negro boys and 6 per cent of white boys were committed five or more times. The type of institutional confinement differed only slightly for Negro and white boys. During the adolescent period up to age eighteen, almost half the white boys committed had been confined only in juvenile institutions in contrast to slightly more than one-third of institutionalized Negro boys. Sixty-five per cent of Negro and 55 per cent of white institutionalized boys by eighteen had already been confined in adult or intermediary institutions. The amount of time spent in confinement was similar for both Negro and white groups; half of each group spent a year or more of their adolescence in institutions. Several boys were confined for four or more years in several different institutions.

Over half the institutional group had experienced confinement in adult institutions by the time they reached age eighteen. Most of these youths fell into our seriously maladaptive late adolescent adjustment subgroup, since a major criterion for inclusion in this group was institutional confinement for delinquency during late adolescence. The association of early and middle adolescent police and court experience to the five types of adjustment appears in Table 28. Seriously maladaptive boys had extensive police records during adolescence; a large percentage of these began before the eighth grade. Furthermore, this group contributed disproportionately to the high rate of delinquency, especially of serious delinquency, characterizing the study group as a whole. Most arrests for serious delinquency, that is, for acts which would have been felonies if committed by adults, were of boys in this subgroup. Some work adaptive boys had also been involved in serious delinquency during adolescence, as had a few school adaptive youths. Marginal and erratic boys had arrest records significantly less serious than those of the seriously maladaptive group but more serious than those of the adaptive groups.

Two different behavior patterns were evident among seriously maladaptive boys in our sample. As a starting point we employed the socialized-unsocialized classification system, proposed by Reckless[1] and others, which postulates two different types of delinquents at opposite ends of a socialized-unsocialized continuum, with many variations along the continuum. At one end are the socialized delinquents who include most of the delinquent population. They appear normal in personality, and their major apparent deviancy from so-called nondelinquents is their adolescent history of repeated arrests for delinquency, usually of a nonviolent kind such as shoplifting, burglary, or auto theft. In some studies the socialized delinquent is described as often a loyal gang member, a good comrade with a likeable personality. At the other end of the continuum are the unsocialized delinquents described by Jenkins, Hewitt, and others.[2] These boys are ex-

[1] W. Reckless, "The Etiology of Delinquent and Criminal Behavior," in W. L. Monroe (Ed.), *Encyclopedia of Educational Research* (New York: Macmillan, 1950).

[2] R. L. Jenkins, "Motivation and Frustration in Delinquency," *American Journal of Orthopsychiatry*, 1957, 27.

Table 28. Late Adolescent Adjustment and Arrest Records

	Serious Maladap. (N = 73)	Marginal (N = 56)	Erratic (N = 65)	Work Adaptive (N = 64)	School Adaptive (N = 77)
Boys arrested	90%	73%	57%	46%	26%
Boys arrested before 8th grade	67%	20%	33%	24%	13%
Median age at first arrest	13.5	14.5	14.0	14.5	15.5
Total number of arrests of all types	469	76	115	69	29
Percentage of all arrests	63%	10%	15%	9%	3%
Average number of arrests	7.1	2.5	2.9	2.3	1.5
Range of arrests	(9 to 17)	(3 to 8)	(5 to 10)	(3 to 11)	(2 to 3)
Boys with one or more arrests for serious delinquency	90%	31%	46%	28%	11%
Average number of arrests for serious delinquency	4.7	2.2	2.7	1.6	2.2
Total number of arrests for serious delinquency	310	37	80	33	20
Percentage of all arrests for serious delinquency	64%	8%	17%	7%	4%

tremely hostile and aggressive and they express bitter and hardened attitudes. They differ from socialized delinquents in their very marked lack of self-control and they express their hostility in fairly raw aggression. These youths contribute heavily to the arrest rate for aggressive assault, destruction of property, resisting arrest, and rape.

This classification seems applicable in some degree to our seriously maladaptive youths, most of whom, as we have seen, shared an adolescent world in which police, courts, jails, and institutional confinements were common features. We were able to identify the socialized delinquents in our group, but we found that although some of these youths appeared to be changing toward more socially adaptive styles with diminished delinquency, others moved more toward the unsocialized end of the continuum as they entered late adolescence. Most of our seriously maladjusted boys fell at the unsocialized end of the scale; as we have seen, their records of arrests and commitments began in childhood or early adolescence. About one-fourth of these boys approached the prototype of the unsocialized delinquent.

Jed Brown was an unsocialized delinquent. He was twelve years old when first apprehended by the police. He had stolen an air rifle one afternoon and by midnight had shot out eight street lights. The same evening he visited the school grounds and put holes in several classroom windows. Taken to the juvenile bureau of the police station, Jed was firmly lectured by the captain in the presence of the boy's parents, who agreed to pay for the damage. The captain had some misgivings about Jed. He appeared indifferent and sullen as the captain spelled out the seriousness of his behavior and the consequences for him if it happened again. However, since the boy had no previous police contacts and was only twelve, he was released to his parents. As they left the captain's office, Jed's father paused, commenting, "Now Jed isn't a bad boy. You know how it is—boys will be boys." However, in a home interview later, this father berated his boy, and Jed indicated intense dislike for his father and mother, calling them "sons of bitches and hicks who don't know for nothin'."

At the time of this first incident, Jed's school principal was informed but was not surprised. Although this had been the first time the boy had been taken to the police station, it was not the first time he had been in serious difficulty at school. His elementary school teachers had consistently reported that his aggressiveness was a serious problem. His third grade teacher's comment was typical. "Jed is very aggressive toward other children in class and seems determined to disrupt our group activities. He usually succeeds until he is physically removed from the group." Jed's aggressiveness did not abate, and his sixth grade teacher reported that Jed was "a real troublemaker. He poses a real threat to the other children. I heard him threaten a younger boy with a beating unless he handed over his lunch money. The younger boy was just about to submit to the threat when I interceded."

Jed's reputation as an aggressive, hostile fighter grew, and his peers left him alone because he fought viciously and at the slightest provocation regardless of consequences. Even boys who could fight avoided fighting with him when they could. By the seventh grade Jed was using his reputation as a tough guy to threaten younger or smaller children and get their lunch money or force them to trade personal articles for valueless junk. His victims talked reluctantly about their difficulties with Jed. In parent-teacher conferences Jed's parents stoutly defended him. They criticized the principal and school personnel, in the boy's presence, for never listening to Jed's side of a story. Jed's father became very profane at such times, cursing the school and the principal for not giving Jed protection against a "bunch of hoodlums" who, he said, attacked Jed frequently on his way home from school. The father added that he had taught Jed to defend himself, since the school was not protecting him. The parents heatedly denied that Jed used strong-arm tactics or threatened anyone at school because they gave him money for lunch and for other things and he "sure didn't have no extra money in his pockets."

One day the principal saw Jed jump from a bush onto the back of a fellow student, knocking him to the ground and kicking him viciously when he was down. The principal half dragged Jed, who was cursing and kicking violently, into his office and called the boy's mother. Both parents arrived soon and began cursing and berating the principal for manhandling their son. The principal waited until the invective had subsided and then stated that he had personally witnessed a vicious attack on another pupil by Jed and that he was prepared to go to court to testify about what he had seen unless Jed was referred to the psychiatric unit for a complete evaluation. Jed's parents reluctantly consented. The psychiatric report indicated that there was no gross psychopathology but that Jed was acting out many aggressive and hostile feelings toward his parents, particularly his father. Neither

Jed nor his parents were considered amenable to psychotherapy. It was advised that efforts be made to work with the boy in school through placement in classrooms taught by firm but understanding male teachers and that Jed's school program be kept flexible. Emphasis on shop work activities was suggested, since this would permit more physical activity during the day for this hyperactive, action-oriented boy.

Jed was readmitted to school after he and his parents had been informed emphatically that any additional difficulty with Jed would lead to referral to the juvenile court. Shortly after his return to school he was identified for the Work-Study Program to begin in the following term. It was felt that this program approximated the conditions Jed's psychiatric evaluation had suggested might be beneficial. However, before Jed could be enrolled, he was arrested for the shooting incident. Because he had not experienced his new program, the school did not press for referral to the juvenile court at this time. Jed's difficulties continued in junior high school, however. The special program appeared to be of little help to him. He soon became known as one of several toughs on the West Side—boys most people felt would end up in prison.

Jed's father continued to angrily denounce the school and specific teachers whom he accused of being unfair to his son. One day in class Jed cursed the Work-Study teacher, who then sent the boy to the office where he was suspended. Stomping out of the principal's office, Jed spun around and screamed, "You old bald-headed bastard, I hate your guts." He returned shortly with his father, who stated that he was taking his boy out of "this goddamn place" and enrolling him in a parochial school, which he said he should have done long before. From then on Jed's school career consisted of shifts from one school to another. There were many program changes and many stormy conferences between school personnel, Jed, and his parents. Jed continued to get into fights, but now these were mainly off the school grounds. Most students avoided trouble with him. He was a loner at school, but he began associating with several older out-of-school toughs in his neighborhood.

This group was not apprehended for about two years, but during this period they made several vicious attacks on youths who happened to venture alone at night into areas where Jed and his friends happened to be. These boys were also involved in very destructive vandalism. They broke into homes of vacationing families, took what they could sell or use, and then destroyed or disfigured the contents, leaving the message, scrawled in lipstick on mirrors, walls, and other surfaces, that "The Vultures was here." Jed was picked up several times for questioning during his fourteenth and fifteenth years but was released for lack of evidence. However, on one occasion, at age sixteen, he and three other youths broke up an East Side neighborhood party, and in the melee Jed drew a revolver, screaming he was going to kill all the sons of bitches there. After upsetting tables and chairs and spilling pop, he and his companions left but were quickly apprehended by the police who were cruising nearby. One of the boys confessed to some of the group's activities during the past several months.

In court Jed's father blamed Jed's companions for the trouble the boy was in, but the judge ordered Jed committed to the state training school. The father rose menacingly from his seat when the judge ordered the commitment. The boy's lawyer grabbed him and pulled him back into his chair, audibly warning him of a contempt of court charge if he argued with or threatened the judge. Jed spent two years at the training school; the second year was added for bad conduct. A training school counselor described the boy as "a real hard kid. You can't reach him. He came down here hostile and aggressive and I'm afraid he's going back that way."

Jed had no promise of a job or plans for the future when he left the institution. His parole officer attempted to place him in a job, but Jed showed little interest and he lost the one job as busboy after a week because he was always late and could not get along with his coworkers. Now eighteen, Jed began spending time in pool halls, and he and some friends, who also had served time in the training school, began going into a neighboring state where they could buy beer at age eighteen. About three months after his release from the juvenile institution, Jed stabbed and killed a man in a tavern brawl. Witnesses agreed that the fight was instigated by Jed and his friends. Before he was nineteen, Jed began a five- to ten-year sentence in the state penitentiary.

Some boys in our sample who fell toward the socialized end of the delinquency scale were also in jail or prison by late adolescence. Several in this group avoided commitment during adolescence in spite of repeated arrests and court hearings on charges of serious delinquency, although usually of the physically nonaggressive variety. Ron

Bowers was a socialized delinquent. Early in adolescence he expressed real reluctance to accept the fact that someday he must go to work. The first day of the Work-Study Program he scoffed at the whole idea of working, saying, "Why work? We get everything we need anyway, and what we can't get we can always steal." Ron's past and subsequent actions in the program seemed to confirm this basic orientation toward work and toward life in general.

By age fourteen, Ron had had more than fifteen police arrests; he had another five or six by age sixteen. He had committed several other acts of delinquency which had gone undetected, but which he acknowledged to his teacher and work supervisor. During adolescence Ron's work history was impressive for the number of jobs he held and either quit or lost. He could do satisfactory work, but he was irresponsible about being punctual and about informing his employer when he would be late or absent. His attitudes toward his job indicated to his employer that he would leave whenever the notion struck him. He was fired from several jobs because of his attitudes, and he quit several simply because his work interfered with his other activities. For example, he refused to work Saturday mornings because Friday night was his big night out and he slept all day Saturday. He refused the work in spite of the fact that the job was one of the first obtained for Work-Study boys and his quitting would probably end the availability of this job for other boys in the program. However, Ron had no difficulty getting work. He could put on a very respectful front and he had an easy manner. He could talk to anyone and had the faculty of talking at any level the situation required.

Ron had worked out a fairly adequate status for himself in his peer group. He early established a reputation for being able to take care of himself. He was from the West Side and he learned to use his fists when it was necessary. However, he was not essentially a fighter, that is he did not go around challenging others and looking for a fight. He gained respect from his peer group in the school and the community. He earned a reputation as a "cool cat," a designation he also applied to himself. In a school composition titled "The Person I Want to be Like," Ron wrote: "[He] is Ron Bowers. He is so handsome and charming. He has an outstanding personality and is the coolest of all males. He really has a way with the girls and young women. It is so exciting to see him walk down the street the girls tell me. So as you can see he is cool. He is the best singer and lover and even the talk he talks will knock you out."

Although Ron showed much egocentricity, he also showed himself fairly adept at handling adults. He had developed techniques which permitted him to get along with minimum discomfort with the representatives of the larger society—teachers, principals, judges, probation officers, and volunteers of a men's club who were working with West Side boys. Ron could adapt quickly when it served his purpose; he could be charming and display a wide-eyed innocence. He was a master at disarming, with his grin and manner, an adult about to reprimand him. There were also hostility and aggressiveness in Ron's approach to adults who represented barriers to his freedom in the classroom and school setting or whom he saw as trying to change him. However, this expression was controlled and took the form of verbal aggression which came out as teasing or as mimicking the adults when they were not looking. At times he seemed to ridicule the world outside his own. He often attempted to shock representatives of this larger world with his comments or behavior. In the first semester of the Work-Study Program, Ron's teacher reported an interview with him.

> I talked with Ron about school and his likes and dislikes. He answered very bluntly. For example, he said that school was all right except for all the other "shits," the other races, because "they think they are the big shits and run the place!" When I asked him what he was interested in he breezily replied, "playing the pinball machines, going to shows, buying cigarettes and gambling." He then began talking about his girls, stating that what he liked and looked for in a girl was a good body and large teats. He volunteered that he had a girl friend and he takes her up to his room at home. I asked him if he thought that was the thing to do, and he said, "Hell yes—no sense to have a girl just to look at her."

For a talk with the director of the Work-Study project, Ron strolled into the central office, propped himself in a chair with his feet on the desk, and puffed a huge cigar. Yet, he usually could sense when he had gone far enough and could then win over the authority figure before he got into serious difficulty. Although Ron's values were definitely delinquent, he did show loyalty to a few close friends and would not steal from them. Others were fair game, however. During the second year of the program he developed a liking for his female teacher and would not use profanity or vulgar language in her presence. During the evenings Ron was picking up some "easy money" from "queers" at the bus station, and he was arrested on several occasions for burglary. In the classroom that year Ron's behavior was excellent, and he was frequently the catalyst for getting discussions going. His teacher relied on him a great deal and felt he was making real progress. It must be noted that Ron was of average and perhaps greater ability and that his major difficulty in school came from failure to conform to school rules and regulations, not from inability to do the work. However, Ron was selective, and he applied himself only to those classroom assignments which interested him, except in the class of the teacher he liked. Ron definitely did not find the work experience part of his school day to his liking. His work supervisor reported that "Ron is always complaining and shirking work as much as he can." Thus, while Ron could show socially adaptable behavior in certain settings and in certain relationships, he expressed delinquent values in behavior in other settings and relationships.

Many study group boys were similar. Some youths not as bright as Ron came into more open conflict with legal authority early in adolescence and were less adept at swaying adults. These boys were committed for their delinquency. Others made surface attempts to conform to rules and regulations but broke them whenever they thought they could get away with it. As these youths grew older, their attempts to combat any encroachment on their values and lives became obvious. In early adolescence some of these youths seemed amenable to change. Those who did not show signs of changing by middle adolescence tended toward increasingly serious delinquency.

10

Sexual Experience

Sexual activity was another area of experience for study group boys through which strivings for masculine identity might be expected to find expression. As in the case of most adolescent boys, interest in girls and in maintaining a virile, "cool cat" masculine image was a dominant feature of our study sample. Sexual activity, as one expression of this image, was expected to be significantly heightened for our group because of their limited access to other adolescent experiences where they could be successful and masculine. In studying this area of experience two sets of interviews with the boys were employed, one when they were in midadolescence, the other when most were between seventeen and eighteen years of age. Interview inquiry was directed toward determining the relative extent and nature of sexual intercourse and other heterosexual pursuits and the significance and meaning of these experiences to the boys. The relative extent of sexual activity reported by boys was rated on a four-point scale including active and ongoing sexual experience, frequent sexual experience, occasional sexual experience, and denial of sexual experience.

Another scale described the boys' involvement or interest in girls as exploitation of girls, maintenance of a casual relationship with several girls, maintenance of a responsible and involved relationship with one girl, or denial of interest in girls or relationship with girls.

A number of study group boys responded openly to inquiry concerning sexual experience and many provided rich descriptions of

173

their sex lives. Other youths, however, responded to inquiry about sexual experience cautiously and noncommittally. Interviewers reported that in a few instances rapport seemed affected when the topic was raised. Interviewers were urged to explore this area whenever possible, but they were instructed that their own judgment should determine when such inquiry should be modified or omitted. Of 385 boys interviewed, about three in ten either were not asked about their sexual experience or responded to inquiry in such vague terms that their responses could not be rated. For the remaining 70 per cent of boys interviewed, the quality of interview data in this area permitted reliable ratings (84 per cent complete agreement) between two raters working independently.

In this chapter we provide examples of the kinds of sexual activity and the extent of such experiences represented in the different ratings assigned to boys. While our basic source of data was what the boys reported in interviews, we supplemented these data with information provided by adults who were in close and relatively constant contact with many of these youths for several adolescent years. Teachers and work supervisors, through anecdotes and taped interviews, provided particularly valuable information. These people were frequently with the boys in situations which facilitated informal discussion and expression of feeling and attitudes concerning personal experiences and problems. For example, on buses or in cars enroute to work sites or on field trips, spontaneous bull sessions, conversations, and discussions occurred and were rich sources of descriptive data concerning the sexual attitudes and concerns of the boys. These sources suggested that our interview-based estimates of sexual activities were conservative. However, these external data were supplementary and were not employed in rating the boys.

Jack, at age seventeen, was a six-foot, 180-pound youth who appeared to see regular and frequent sexual experience as a natural and necessary part of his everyday life. He was typical of boys rated as having active and ongoing sexual experience. When he was sixteen and still in school, he talked with the research interviewer about school problems. At that time he was pondering whether he should stay in school, which he admittedly did not like. He was not getting along with his teachers, was doing below average work in all subjects, and had little interest in school activities. However, he did like his associations with girls at school because they were his best contacts and for that reason he thought he might try to stick it out. When interviewed a year later, however, he had dropped out of school, explaining to the interviewer that, "I just couldn't take all that jive in the classroom, and besides I was always getting sent home anyway, so I just decided to quit."

Jack seemed to be continuing his active sex life. The interviewer reported firsthand observation of sex play among out-of-school adolescents when he visited Jack's home for a seventeen-year-old interview. As Jack and the interviewer began to talk in the living room, they were interrupted by a girl about fifteen or sixteen years old who, dressed in a bathrobe, had come down the stairs to the landing. "Are you going to come up here and take care of me, Jack?" she said. Jack responded that he would be up shortly, and after the girl had spun around on her heels and stomped back up the stairs, he turned to the interviewer. "She wants me to give her fifty cents for it."

Jack and the school visitor were not alone in the darkened living room. In one corner, a teen-age couple were engaged in intense sex play. Another couple were sprawled on a divan next to the interviewer's chair. Unmindful of the visitor, except for a momentary pause as he came into the room, the couple twisted and gyrated their bodies. The interviewer was somewhat startled when the boy, continuing to caress the upper thigh of his partner, turned to the visitor and asked if he was really "a school board man." To the affirmative reply, he said, "Well, man, do you think you could get me back in school?" The visitor briefly explained what steps the boy would have to take. "Well, thanks, I might just try to get back in." With that he turned back to his partner.

The girl from upstairs again stomped down the steps, still dressed in the bathrobe. She did not stop at the landing this time, but appeared angry and headed for the front door. Jack watched, making no move to stop her. An older man, perhaps forty years old, suggested that she was not dressed properly for the street and should remain in the house. He assured her that "Jack will take care of you in a minute." The girl stopped and looked hard at Jack as though waiting for some sign from him. The uncomfortable school visitor turned to Jack and asked if he should leave. "Well, yeah, I guess I had better take care of her." As the school visitor took his leave, Jack was following the girl up the stairs. In his report, the interviewer said in part,

I got the definite impression that this kind of thing was
so accepted that my being a stranger and from the school
made no difference at all. Jack's mother works during the day.
Jack works occasionally and earns a little money, but he still
has a great deal of free time. My visit, of course, was unan-
nounced, but I don't think it would have made any difference. It seems that much of Jack's free time is spent at home
and that sexual play and experiences fill much of this time.
The complete openness with which sexual activity was carried
on is pointed up by the fact that several young preschool children were playing in the dining room. Two older children,
probably about seven or eight, were in the kitchen doing the
dishes. I am not sure who the older man was. He appeared to
watch what was going on, but sat quietly by the door.

Parents of some boys who had active sex lives in adolescence
seemed to accept it as a natural adolescent outlet and simply advised
and warned their children to "be careful." Norman, sixteen and one-
half years old, was interviewed in his home in the presence of his
mother. Therefore, the interviewer did not ask Norman directly about
his sexual experience, but instead posed a general question about adolescent sexual experience. Without hesitation, Norman's mother acknowledged that she was aware that Norman was "satisfying himself"
and then she expressed her views on this with respect to Norman, his
eighteen-year-old sister and several younger children. "I've told my
kids that if they are going to have relations then they must be careful.
I know kids are going to do it. You know if you like somebody—well,
you can just expect that this will happen, so I accept this, but I teach
them to be careful." Norman stated that he was careful and that he
had not gotten himself or a girl in trouble yet.

Martin, who was leading an active sex life by age thirteen,
was not as fortunate as Norman, and by age fourteen he had contracted a venereal disease. However, with advice from his father and
somewhat more discrimination in selecting sexual partners, he was
continuing to lead a fairly active sex life without apparent worry when
he was interviewed at age sixteen. He told the interviewer about his
sexual exploits, his getting "burned," and his views of females.

"They all want it, man. But it's the easy ones that'll
burn you if you ain't careful. Man, they'll fix you up so that
after a few days you'll burn."
"Were you burned bad, Martin?"

"Man, you said that right [laughed with chagrin], I was just fourteen when I got burnt from one of them easy ones. I had to get me twenty-one shots of penicillin to get rid of it. They told my Mom it was some kind of kidney infection, but my Dad, he knew what it was."

"What about the girl?"

"Why, I had no idea who gave it to me. I was taking on anything then, but I don't worry no more about that. See, my Dad, he gave me a box of rubbers, and he tells me not to go barefoot again."

This interview took place in the interviewer's car parked in front of Martin's house. A teen-age girl, walking down the street, became the focus of Martin's attention as he continued talking without urging.

"See that girl. Well, she's like all the rest. She likes it, but some of them just play hard to get. I goes over to her house almost every night. You know, man, you gotta take care of these women. We go down to the basement and play records, dance, and love it up, and before long I gets it. At first, she tried to make me think she's hard to get, but all I got to do now is push her over and does she ever like it. 'Course I had to work on her before she'd give the first time, and that's the kind that ain't likely to burn you."

Jay, at age seventeen, was also actively engaged in sexual experience with the knowledge of his father who laughingly told the interviewer that his boy was "really making out with the girls." However, the father was somewhat concerned and told the interviewer why.

"Jay has been going out with lots of different girls. Well, he went with one that wasn't more than about fourteen, and she got pregnant and claimed Jay was the father. Jay told me there's several other guys making her so he didn't want to be responsible. Anyway, I saw a lawyer just in case her father made some trouble. But everything worked out okay. She and her family moved out of state, and according to the lawyer they can't do a thing now, so we are in the clear. I sure sighed with relief when I heard they had left."

"How did Jay feel when he found out the girl was going to have a baby?"

"Well, he didn't know if it was his, and he didn't want to be responsible."

Jay's father said he had always advised his boy to use condoms. Jay's father seemed to feel the boy was probably "running around too much now."

"I would like to see him begin to settle down some and be more careful but you know he's pretty stubborn and independent, a lot like me I guess and he won't listen or take advice. He's really begun to think he's a man and of course all the telephone calls from girls shows he's popular."

Vic, seventeen years old, was an extreme example of a parent's involvement in the adolescent sexual life of a boy. Vic's parents were separated when he was twelve and were divorced a year later. Vic talked about his sexual experiences and his parents, particularly his father, relating some of the activities they engaged in together and some of the experiences they shared.

"I have a lot of respect for my dad. He and I always get along great. But my mother and dad they didn't get along 'cause she was awful jealous of him. Even though she loved him, she didn't give him what he wanted. Dad just took off 'cause he wasn't getting satisfied at home, you know, he wasn't getting enough sex."

"After your dad left did you see much of him?"

"Sure, dad began chasing women, and I was about thirteen then and he'd take me along, and I began chasing them, too. Dad and I used to shack up together. We'd rent a motel room and get a couple gals and stay there two or three days. I remember once taking a girl on five times during the day. That's the best I ever done. Sometimes when we didn't want to spend any money we'd take the gals out in the car. He'd walk his down the road while I used the car, then when I got through I'd walk mine down the road and he'd use the car. Dad ain't here now. He got a job out of the city."

"Do you still chase the girls?"

"Sure. Now me and my friends sometimes take 'em to Forest Park because it ain't patrolled no more. Sometimes we take 'em to a drive-in theater and park in the back where we don't have too much difficulty with people bothering us. But the best place is at my house. We go there quite a lot now 'cause my mom is usually out at some tavern in the evening. We take the girls upstairs and we have more room and don't have to worry as much as we do when we are parked somewhere."

"Vic, suppose your mother would come and find you in bed with a girl at your home?"

"Oh, Mom knows what goes on. She'd just as soon we

would be doing it at the house than doing it somewhere else and getting caught at it."

Several boys indicated that the parents of their girl friends also knew they were having sexual relations with their daughters but ignored it or at least showed no signs of disapproval. Art, age sixteen and one-half, reported regular and frequent sexual experience with a fifteen-year-old girl living in an apartment house in his neighborhood.

> "I get it whenever I wants it. I'm over at her place about every night and when I gets ready I takes her out in the hall. It's dark out there and we just do it." Art did not appear to be boasting but simply describing a fairly common but satisfying experience.
>
> "How about her parents?"
>
> "Well, she lives with her mom. I don't know where her dad is. It's kind of funny, 'cause her mom says it's all right unless she catches us, but if she does all hell will pop. We been doin' it for about a year now, and she ain't caught us yet."
>
> "Do you worry about anybody seeing you out there?"
>
> "Naw, see her apartment is in the back, and it's dark back there in the hall. 'Course her nine-year-old brother sees us once in a while, but that's all. He don't bother us, and he don't say nothin'."

During high school many boys leading active sex lives showed poor attendance, and by age seventeen many of them had dropped out. Art was among this group, having left school six weeks prior to the interview. He was asked why he had missed so much school. Quite candidly, he explained,

> "Well, school sometimes got to be such a bore, so then we would just decide to skip out and have a sex party. A bunch of us get together and do it instead of going to school."
>
> "Where would you go?"
>
> "We would go to somebody's house where nobody would be home during the day. Somebody in the bunch usually has a house where no adults were around."
>
> "Did you take your girl friend?"
>
> "Well, I did. Some of the guys picked up gals. Usually about three or four couples went along."
>
> "Did each of you go to a bedroom?"
>
> "Hell no! We just did it when we wanted to. Everyone was doing it, and they don't pay attention to nobody else."

Another boy, Kermit, aged sixteen and one-half, told the interviewer about a clubhouse he and several friends used for "hooky parties." "We found this old house nobody lived in and we fixed it up. We made some furniture and got some cots and put in there and that's where we go for our parties. We decide to play hooky and the gals meet us there, and sometimes we just lay up with 'em all day until school is out. We ain't been raided yet."

A number of boys acknowledged some experience with prostitutes. A few boys indicated personal acquaintance with prostitutes and procurers. Matt, age seventeen, told the interviewer about his sexual experiences.

> "My gal is at Cliff View [institution for delinquent girls] and I'm waiting for her to get out, but 'course I got to take care of myself."
>
> "How do you do this?"
>
> "Well, I don't run with too many girls on the West Side or mess with whores too much unless I know them. See, I kind of hang around a shoeshine parlor on Third Street. It's kind of a shoeshine parlor and an employment office—you know. Several whores hang around this corner, and some of the guys that hang around the parlor are seeing this bunch of girls pretty regularly. Now I run with some of them whores, but I'm careful and take only the clean ones. Some of my friends run around with some of the pigs. These gals have got venereal disease and I stay away from that kind."
>
> "What goes on at the shoeshine parlor? What kind of employment office is it?"
>
> "Well, there's a fellow named Doc and he gets jobs for guys. It costs five dollars when he gets a job for a guy."
>
> "What do you mean by job?"
>
> "Oh, just a job—you know."
>
> Matt was asked if there was usually much action around the parlor. "Yeah, they run both black and white around that corner, and some of the girls dress like boys, they wear trousers and short haircuts, and then they act like the boys and take on other girls that like to have sex that way— you know, with other girls. Anybody can get just about anything he wants on that corner."
>
> Matt was asked what he did around the parlor during the day. "Well, I see my friends there and we spend a lot of time drinking and playing cards in the back room. Once in a while a fellow comes in wanting a shoeshine, and so I get to earn a little money."

In spite of a kind of street sophistication about sex, many of the boys with active sex lives indicated laxness in taking precautions to prevent having babies. Twenty boys in our experimental groups fathered children before they were seventeen years old. The boys and their families reacted in different ways to this situation. Some boys married the girls but appeared to continue active sex lives outside marriage. Bob, at age fifteen, was a father, an early school dropout, and married to the fourteen-year-old mother of his child. When the research interviewer first visited Bob and his wife in their apartment shortly after their marriage, the response to his knock was, "We're in bed. Who are you?" The apartment was in a shabby apartment hotel in a downtown section of Kansas City. It was half-past one in the afternoon. "I'm from the school. I'd like to talk with you about school," said the visitor. There was a long pause, then, "Okay, just a minute, I'll get my pants on."

A moment later the door was opened by Bob, a six-foot, physically well-developed boy of fifteen who appeared to be at least eighteen years old. His manner, while polite, was somewhat guarded and cautious. Bob's wife remained in the iron bed during the visitor's stay. A brown, army-type blanket loosely covered her body. As she attempted to adjust this blanket by tucking the ends in along one side of the bed, it became obvious that she was nude. Bob explained why they were in bed at this hour. "I don't have any work and we don't have enough money to go places so we spend our time in bed." When asked, he said his parents paid for the apartment.

Bob explained that they had been married about two months before, which was about two weeks after his wife had given birth to their child. Bob's parents had felt it would be best for them to get married. The interviewer asked where the baby was. "Well, my folks didn't think Irma could take care of it, so they took him and told me and Irma to grow up and be more responsible. They got this apartment for us and are paying the rent and groceries for a little while." The one-room apartment was meagerly furnished. The iron bed and a sagging, soiled divan were the main pieces of furniture. The bed had no sheets or pillows, only the small brown blanket which covered the girl. There were no clothes hanging in the apartment and the one closet was bare. There were a few clothes strewn on the broken divan, obviously those removed before going to bed. Bob was asked about his schooling, his plans for the future. "Well, I would like to go back but I guess I will have to find a job someday."

A year and a half later, the research interviewer again talked with Bob, who was now almost seventeen years old. By this time Bob and his wife had two children. They were living with the wife's parents because Bob was presently unemployed, although he had held numerous jobs during the past year and a half. He admitted that he had walked out on most of them because he just got the urge to do something else after a few weeks. Bob talked with the interviewer about his marital and extramarital life and some of the problems he was experiencing.

> "Me and my wife don't jell too good now. We fight and fuss all the time. I left her several times and just traveled around. You know, since the last time I saw you I've been in New York, Chicago, Los Angeles, and a lot of other places. I just get the urge to go, and me and some buddies go. We get jobs and stay for a while. I got me a job in New York as a cook, but I didn't like the way people treat you in that town, and so I came back to Kansas City. Then I went to Chicago to meet my real dad. He left me when I was three, and I never had seen him since. I stayed with him a few weeks, but then my wife charged me with child abandonment. They picked me up and took me to court, and well, we went back together again, but we ain't happy."
>
> "What seems to be the problem now?"
>
> "Well, I like to party and she doesn't. That's the main trouble. I was running around a lot with different girls before I got married. My wife was running around, too, but now she just don't want to do nothin'."
>
> "Do you plan on staying with your in-laws?"
>
> "Oh, it ain't too bad right now. When they start buggin' me I just breeze out of there."
>
> "How does your wife feel about this?"
>
> "Ah, she fusses and nags at me all the time. She wants me to do this and do that but I don't let her bug me too much."

Jimmy was another boy who married the girl who was going to have his baby. Like Bob, Jimmy, with almost two years of marital life behind him at age eighteen, appeared to have a promiscuous sex life outside marriage. This pattern was somewhat new for Jimmy, whose premarital sexual experience was somewhat infrequent and confined mainly to the girl he married. This may have been in part due to the fact that from age fourteen to almost sixteen he was confined in the county institution for delinquents, and so opportunity for heterosexual experience was limited. In a visit to the home of Jimmy's parents where Jimmy and his wife were living, the research interviewer found Jimmy's wife, sixteen years old and a school dropout, by herself caring for several young children. She expressed her feelings about her marriage to Jimmy and its impact on her life.

"Jimmy and I were married when I found I was going to have a baby. My folks disowned me for marrying him. I've got six brothers and sisters, and all but one told me they wanted nothing to do with me since I married him. They said he was no good but I use' to get him to go to church with me, and I thought he loved me. But I guess they were right. I shouldn't have married him."

"Why?"

"Well, he runs around on me all the time, and he has contracted a social disease now. He really has no respect for me. He runs with a bunch of boys who have long police records, and now he's got the sister of one of these boys pregnant. He won't go to work and support me. They tell me that I could made him go to work and support my child, but if he did he would probably just support this other girl's child. Besides, I don't have the money to bring it into court anyway. I'm taking in washing and ironing to try and make it, and Jimmy's mother and stepfather are good to me, but they have their own kids to take care of, and now Jimmy's mother is going to have another baby. They are letting me stay here and help out because I have no place to go. My folks won't take me back, and I'm just trapped."

"Was it always this way from the time you got married?"

"Well, just a couple of weeks after we got married he went to jail for a year for burglary. I was carrying the baby then, but I went up to visit him on every visitor's day until I got so big I couldn't get around. Then when he got out I thought things might work out for us, but then he began playing around and wouldn't get a job. He gets drunk sometimes and comes home and knocks me around. He busted my hi-fi set one night when he was drunk and then some of my dolls I had since I was a little girl. Then he goes away for a while and I don't hear anything from him. This time he has been gone three days."

"Do you ever have a chance to get away from these problems for a little while?"

"Not very much. Once in a while a few friends come over and I go out with them to a movie, but I don't date or anything like that. You know the hardest thing for me is at night when I'm lying there in bed by myself. I know Jimmy's out with other girls, some of them are whores and some of them are girls right here in this neighborhood. I think I'd just go crazy if it wasn't for my baby. When I get to thinking about my baby I know I have to take care of her, and that keeps me from losing my mind."

"Do you think there is any chance for making things work out right?"

"Well, I know Jimmy doesn't love me. When he's here I sleep upstairs and he sleeps downstairs because I don't want him to touch me now. He has come upstairs a few times when he comes in drunk, but so far I've been lucky and I haven't gotten anything. When he came home after he first got the social disease, he told his mother that it hurt him to make water, and she sent him to the doctor who gave him some penicillin so maybe he is cured. I hope so. Jimmy's mother is very understanding. She says he is acting just like his own father. He ran around, got drunk, and wouldn't support her, and then when Jimmy was about two years old he took off and she hasn't heard a thing from him since. She has tried to get Jimmy to go into service, and he made application some time ago but hasn't heard nothing, so I guess it's his police record. If he could have gotten in he would have had to support my baby, but now I really don't know what the future holds for us."

In contrast to youths like Jimmy and Bob, some boys with promiscuous sexual experience in adolescence seemed to be showing, initially at least, some indication of developing a stable and monogamous marital life. Jody, for example, had a busy sex life beginning in childhood and continuing through adolescence until he met the girl who became his wife. In an interview when he was fifteen Jody recalled his first sex experience. "I was about six or seven and my mother use to work and leave me with a ten-year-old girl who lived up the street. Well, one day she took me into the bedroom, took my clothes off, and told me what to do. Well, I did and I liked it. She went right over and told her girl friend who lived across the street, and she came up and I did it to her, and then she told her sister and she came up. So you can see I got broke in right. We moved not long after that, but I used to see this girl every once in a while up until she went to college. Now she runs with an older bunch."

Of his adolescent sex life Jody simply commented that he was getting his "share" and was "playing the field." Jody's stepfather in an interview about the same time described Jody as a "lady's man," and revealed that Jody was also "hanging out" at what the boys in the neighborhood called the "Play House." He described this to the interviewer.

> "It is a two story house owned by two old ladies. They've fixed it up, and a lot of boys go there to dance, play records and other things. You got to have a key to get in. There are girls there, and they have a big time with the girls. I've tried to get Jody to take me over there, but he always makes excuses saying the boys ain't there, he don't have a key to the place, or something like that."
>
> "What do you think they do there?"
>
> "Well, frankly, I know Jody is having a lot of sex there. I'll tell you that this place is actually nothin' but a whorehouse. He's up there every evening after school, and now I found out that lots of times he's playing hooky and that's where he goes. Sometimes he don't get home till early in the morning."
>
> "How does he get his money?"
>
> "Well, both his mother and I give him money every day for lunch and for spending. See, we both work and we figure he's got to have a little money or he'll get it some way, so we just give it to him. Now we find he's not going to school every day, and this has been a problem ever since second grade, but we still give him money so he won't have to steal to get it."

A year and a half later, when Jody was almost seventeen years old, the interviewer again visited Jody's home. There he found Jody's sixteen-year-old wife, Mary, caring for her four-month-old baby. It was late afternoon and Jody, who had dropped out of school a year before, had not arrived home from his job as busboy. The interviewer talked with Mary while he waited for the boy.

> "Well, we've been married three months now, but we went together almost a year. I met him at a party, and I had several dates with him. Well, he had lots of sweet talk, and I just fell in love with him. We wanted to get married right away when we found out I was pregnant, and my mother was willing but my father wouldn't hear of it. So I had my baby at a place for unwed mothers, but after she was born Dad said okay, and Jody and I got married."
>
> "Are you working?"

"No. I'm in school. I went back after having the baby.
There's a neighbor lady that looks after the baby when I'm
in school. You see, I want to finish high school. I'm a junior
now, and I want to go on to junior college and if I can to the
university. That's what my Mom and Dad wanted me to do,
and I know they were disappointed when I married Jody because he didn't finish high school. They feel we're going to
have a rough time. But Jody wants me to finish high school.
We both want some of the little extras that we can get with a
better education. I've urged Jody to go back too, but he had
a lot of trouble in school and he just can't bring himself to do
it. But he is thinking of getting some training to better himself."

Mary was asked how married life appealed to her after
three months. "Well, I love Jody, and he is working hard to
support me and the baby. We don't have anything yet, and so
it is kind of hard at times. But we don't want to do like a lot
of kids that get married. They aren't interested in the future
at all. They are only interested in themselves, and they live
from day to day. But that isn't the way Jody and I want to
live. We want to plan so we can have some of the extras, and
that's why I'm trying to go on with my schooling, and that's
why Jody wants to get some kind of training."

Jody arrived and greeted the interviewer warmly. He talked
frankly of what had happened to him during the past year and reiter-
ated much of what his wife had said concerning their plans for the
future. He was asked how he liked being a married man.

"Well, I want to take care of my family. You know I
was running with a bunch of pretty rough guys before I met
Mary. I use to be out every night drinking and chasing women,
but I don't want to do that anymore. Usually we stay home
during the week and go out on Friday to a party, or we have
a few friends in, but this is none of the rough bunch. My wife
ain't like that, and I'm not like that anymore either."

The interviewer was impressed with Jody's apparent growth in
maturity since he last had talked with him over a year ago. Changes
in orientation and outlook seemed particularly evident as Jody talked
about one of his major present concerns.

"My kid sister is just sixteen years old, but she is running wild like I did. I keep telling her she's headed for trouble, and I tell her everything I know about what's going on,

but she won't listen. I tell her she's got to stay in school. I even dragged her back to school when I found she wasn't going, but she's not going to listen to nobody. And she's going to be in serious trouble. I know some of those guys she's running with. They're a bunch of crumbs, but nobody can talk any sense to her.

"I was just like her, but I spent a few months in the institution and that gave me time to think. When I got out I saw the light. It hit me real sudden. I was at this party and two gals were fighting each other, and so I stepped in to break it up, and they pushed me back and one bit me. Well, I just looked at them, and they looked so silly fighting. I said to myself, I must look like that too. I must really look silly when I'm out there fighting over nothin' and getting myself all bloody and scarred.

"Well, then I just began playing it cool. Before that I had been in lots of fights over something somebody said just as a joke but which I took as an insult. I remember getting in a fight over something like that and almost got beat to death. Then I thought about it later and realized it just started out as a joke. Well, I decided from then on I was going to begin pulling away from that rough bunch. Well, I did gradually 'cause you can't break something like that sudden, and well, Mary helped me. I just spent more and more time with her and we made different friends."

Jody was asked if any of his old buddies ever come around. "Yeah, [laugh] they can't understand why I don't want to get drunk or chase women anymore. Some of these guys are married too but it just seems they got to keep trying."

The significance of sexual experience for boys with active sex lives in adolescence is clear from interviews with boys committed to state institutions for delinquency. Sam, age sixteen, voiced the problem succinctly. "The one thing I miss more than anything is my girl. I was getting it about three times a week and now I'm not gettin' nothin'." This was Sam's major complaint to the interviewer visiting at the state training school. "I don't mind the work and school so much here, but I sure miss my girl." Sam had a history of running away from home when he was still in elementary school, and by the time he was thirteen he had also had several police contacts for delinquency. During adolescence he continued to run "pretty wild." Sam's mother died when he was four years old, and his father began drinking heavily. A series of different young women moved in and out of their lives. Three of these his father married, only to divorce them after a few months.

Sam grew up with very little supervision or guidance. As he developed into adolescence he was quite handsome and physically mature for his age. At age sixteen, he was having sexual intercourse with his father's nineteen-year-old wife during his father's frequent absences from the home. After his father divorced this third wife, Sam became increasingly hard to handle. He ran away and stole a car, some groceries, and money to sustain him and his girl with whom he lived for a while. When he was arrested and brought into juvenile court, the father came, pleading that the boy be given one more chance and that he would see he stayed out of trouble. However, the judge decided that Sam should have a more adequate home, and the boy went to live with relatives in a middle-class residential neighborhood in the southern part of the city. After a few weeks, Sam ran away, stole a car and some money, and was headed out of the city when apprehended by the police. He did not want to return to live with his relatives because they were "too strict," so Sam was committed to the county home for delinquents. However, he soon ran away and was then committed to the state training school.

In the interview Sam acknowledged that he had gotten started on sex "pretty early," and that this was the first time he had gone so long without it.

"Do you feel other boys here find this as big a problem?"

"Sure. Some of 'em get so hard up they punk sometimes."

"How do you mean?"

"You know, they use a guy."

"Do the guys object?"

"At first some do."

"Why do they let themselves be used this way?"

"Well, usually they are the weak ones, you know, won't put up no fight and they ain't got nobody here they know. If they do try to put up a fight they get the shit beat out of 'em."

"Do you ever do this?"

"You mean, get punked? Hell, they know better than try that on me. Naw, I don't bother with punking either."

In a series of interviews with boys in the state institution, a number of others acknowledged that lack of sex was the big problem they had to face while in the institution.

Jerry, sixteen and one-half years old, was typical of boys who had occasional sexual activity. He did not have a girl friend and he did not date, but he knew a girl who was occasionally available for sex. "Me and this girl who is in my block and who is my age got started playing with each other when we were kids. Then when we were about ten we started doing it, and we been doing it off and on ever since when we get the chance. We don't do it too often because there is usually somebody home, but once in a while she's by herself, and then she calls me up and I go over and we have the bedroom to ourselves." Jerry stated he had never been on a date with this girl, or any girl, because he had neither income nor transportation for that.

Tim, also sixteen, reported a similar arrangement with a girl he knew, although Tim had a steady girl friend. He explained that his steady was a nice girl and that he had never had sex with her and never intended to. When he wanted sex he went to his other girl's house, and they went to the basement. Her mother drank a lot and her father was a salesman and away a lot, so they did not worry about being observed.

Ron, age seventeen, said that he did not date because he could not afford it. He relied for his sexual gratification on an occasional party where there were girls who wanted sex.

Mike, sixteen and one-half years old, acknowledged that a year previously he had dated and had sex fairly often, but now he had laid off that sort of thing because he was busy at school. He was on the swimming team, played basketball, and also played the drums in the school band. Like Ron, Mike occasionally went to a party where he got some sexual gratification.

Ken, age seventeen, reported that he was going with a nice girl now. While he had been "to bed with a girl every weekend last year" he had not been doing this nearly as much. He explained that since he had met his current girl friend, he had not been nearly as interested in partying as some other guys. He added that his coach had also advised him to avoid getting messed up with a girl.

Will, age sixteen, reported that he had sex with a girl about two years before, but he really felt she pushed him. He did not use any precaution because he just did not think of it. It was usually only when she kept pushing him that he would have sex with her. Will expressed his opinion that girls were the cause of a lot of the trouble because they would push a guy until there was nothing else he could do. Will had not had any sex since he stopped going with that girl over six months before. He was now going with a girl he liked very well, and he had not done anything with her. He was not sure he was going to try. A year later, when Will was seventeen, he again talked with the interviewer. At this time he was engaged to be married to the girl he had been dating. He and this girl were occasionally having sexual intercourse, but Will emphasized that they were being very careful because, "We just got too many things to do before we get a bunch of kids running around." He explained that he and his fiancee had talked it over and decided that since they could not get married right away, they would have sex, but not very often, and when they did they would always be very careful.

Will was asked if it bothered him to have had sex before he met the girl he wanted to marry. He answered candidly, "Why should it? Girls around here know the score. They know that girls in our part of town have this happen to them quite a bit, and that most guys have had some sex before they get married."

Pete, age sixteen and in the tenth grade when interviewed, asserted his intention of getting a high school diploma. Pete was doing much better in high school than he did in the elementary grades. He was doing at least average classwork, was active in sports and in the school band, and was well liked by both students and faculty. Pete acknowledged that he liked girls, enjoyed dating, and had sexual experience occasionally. He explained some of the obstacles which limited his sexual experience.

> "I'm not ready to get serious with a girl, so I don't have a special girl, but I do go with one more than the others. I date sometimes, once or twice a week, because—well, it depends. You see my mom has got to know the girl, and I have to get permission from the girl's parents. Then Mom has got to know where I'm going and when I'll get home."
> "Does this kind of slow you down, Pete?"
> "Well, yeah, in a way [smile]. I would like to be able to date a girl without taking her home first, and I'd like to have a little more freedom to come home when I wanted to. But you see, my Mom wants me to be careful. She doesn't want me to get a girl in trouble—you know, pregnant—and boy, I sure don't want that to happen, and it hasn't either."
> "How do you manage?"
> "Well, I've had it a few times, and of course, I always take precautions. But it depends. One problem is I don't have a car, so usually I take my date by bus, or if it's something in

the neighborhood like a football game or something like that, we just walk. Once in a while I can borrow a neighbor's car, and that's when I do it. It's usually the girl I go with more than the others. She's a nice girl, and we enjoy doing it, but as I said, we don't have the opportunity very often. Anyway, I don't do it very much. I just don't want to get a girl in trouble. My Mom would be terribly upset. She works awfully hard and is trying to see we stay in school, so I wouldn't do anything to worry her."

Pete's parents were divorced, and his mother worked as a waitress during the day to provide for her five children.

Gregg, age sixteen, reported that he liked to date and had a special friend, but that he has had only one sexual experience.

"Me and Jack heard about a party, and so we got our girls and went. When we got there some woman opened the door, and she didn't have much clothes on. There was a lot of music inside, and we saw people running around with hardly nothing on. Our two girls were nice girls and didn't want to go in, so they left. Me and Jack, we went in just to get something to eat. They had a table loaded with stuff. I looked in a bedroom and saw them doing it, and then this girl comes out and she lays all over me, so I do it too. I didn't feel very good about it afterwards so I went home. I ain't never done that again."

Vern, age seventeen, described his first and only sex experience to the research interviewer.

"I've never had a girl or dated because I'm kind of shy around girls, but I did entertain a girl about a week ago. See, my roommate Dave, he's a salesman about twenty-five years old, has a lot of girl friends, and he said I ought to have a woman take care of me and he was going to fix me up. Well, over came this girl, a twenty-year-old beatnik, and Dave and some of his buddies was having some drinks and they was going to go out and leave me with the gal. Well, me and this girl went upstairs in the bedroom and well, she just tore me all up. We was in there, I don't know how long, but when I came out the door I almost fell down the stairs. It was my first time, and she really tore me up. But the worst thing was that I thought all those other fellows that were there had left, but they were all sitting downstairs laughing as I almost fell down the stairs. They made me come down and tell 'em actual step by step about everything that went on. I think that beatnik gal was one of Dave's girl friends, 'cause all the guys knew everything she did up there."

Vern was asked if he felt bad about this experience. "Well, I was embarrassed, but I guess I liked it. In fact I'll probably be getting me some more before long. I know an airman, and he's supposed to fix me up with some girl. She ain't no beatnik though."

Vern had recently left home because, "My ol' man gets drunk all the time and my ol' lady is running around with other men, and I just couldn't take it no more." His employer was letting him stay in a house he owned in return for Vern's doing some repair work, painting, and upkeep on it. Dave, the salesman, worked at the same company as did Vern and had just recently moved in with him.

Bill, a handsome sixteen-year-old boy, reported that he had had no sexual experience because girls were likely to get you into trouble. He explained that "they are apt to burn you, or they get pregnant." Bill's mother said he was very popular with the girls at school, but that he seldom dated. She complained that girls were always calling the house asking for Bill, and that although he was polite to them he just did not seem to want to get involved with any of them yet. Bill was on the football team; sports, particularly football, seemed to fill most of his time outside class. His seventeen-year-old sister worried about him and tried to fix him up with a date occasionally, but he just was not interested.

Frank, age seventeen and still in school, denied sexual experience or any real interest in girls. He said he did not have time for them. He liked girls but was not dating now and did not want to even think about that because "the only thing I'm trying to do right now is to make my grades and stay on the football team and make the track team this spring." The interviewer commented in his report that Frank's interest in sports seemed to dominate the boy's life at the time.

Micky, age sixteen and one-half, reported he had had no sexual experience, but admitted it was not because he was not interested in girls.

"I'm interested in girls all right, but I never had one myself. I like a lot of 'em at school, but I never had the courage to ask one to go out with me. In fact, I've never had a date with one yet."

"Why is that, Micky?"

> "Well, I don't know, except I guess I just don't know how to act around them yet."

The boys presented as examples in this chapter represent the variety and extent of sexual activity reported by boys in interviews. The examples also include various conditions and circumstances which appeared associated with different patterns of sexual experience. Over two-thirds of boys reported sexual experience during adolescence; about one-fourth described a fairly active adolescent sex life, including eleven boys who were married. Thirteen per cent of the 385 boys interviewed reported active and ongoing sexual experience, that is, regular and frequent intercourse. Sixteen per cent reported frequent sexual experience, that is, intercourse several times a month, depending on circumstances. Thirty-seven per cent reported occasional or infrequent sexual experience, and 2 per cent denied sexual experience. Thirty-two per cent of boys either were not asked about sexual behavior or responded so vaguely their experience could not be rated.

The significance or uniqueness to the study group of these self-reported patterns of sexual activity is difficult to determine in the absence of normative data on adolescent sexual experience. Additionally, self-reports of sex lives can be expected to be unreliable and to under- or overestimate or distort the picture of such experience. However, during the study there were several external indicators that extramarital sexual activity in the community where many study group boys lived was high in comparison with other areas of the city. Rates of illegitimate births were higher than in other communities and were increasing. The numbers of girls dropping out of school because of pregnancies were the highest in the city. Public health records showed higher incidence of venereal disease in these areas. That study group boys did not exaggerate their sexual behavior is suggested by the anecdotal reports from Work-Study staff and by the observations and experiences they related in taped interviews with research associates.

Mrs. B., age twenty-six, a teacher of an eighth and ninth grade class of experimental boys, was interviewed at the end of her first year in the Work-Study project.

> I try to grope for words. It's awfully hard to know what to say. I try to direct their comments and questions into some kind of constructive discussion. At the beginning of the year, when I was first involved with these youth, I must admit

I was really shook up at some of the things they brought up. I learned a whole new vocabulary, words like "fags" and things like that.

Anyway, I talked with the boys about premarital sex relations at the beginning of school. I told them that it wasn't the thing to do, that they should wait and share this experience in marriage with someone they love. I try to get them to see this is more than what they seem to see it as being.

Some of these boys, well, all they have on their minds is girls, girls, girls. They talk openly about having sexual experience. They don't seem to feel any shame about it at all. Now the eighth graders don't talk so much about it, but when they do they are kind of boasting. Most of the ninth graders talk about sex like it's just a part of their everyday lives.

They are still curious about it. They'll come to class with some idea they hear about or something they've seen on TV. For example, yesterday one boy came to class and immediately began talking about the TV show, "The Nurses." He had seen this show the night before. It was about syphilis and he wanted to know about it. Well, of course I want them to discuss things, and they feel free to do this so we talked about it. When we got to the point when I was trying to show that sex outside marriage could lead to diseases like this, and that it was better to taboo sex until marriage, this boy really shook me up.

He asked me what you are supposed to do when a girl throws herself on you? He then proceeded to give a particular instance where he couldn't get around it. He showed no shame in bringing this out in class and giving details. He asked me, "Now, what are you supposed to do about that?" He had me where I didn't know what to say, because the example he gave certainly indicated that the girl was throwing herself at him. I thought a moment, and then I suggested that he not put himself in that position, but he said there was nothing he could do to avoid it because there she was. I then suggested that the next time he just try to embarrass her, and maybe that would stop her. But he didn't feel too well about doing this. He seemed to feel he was kind of obligated to go ahead because he sees this as kind of what makes him a man.

When we were talking about syphilis all the boys indicated they knew what this word meant. However, I saw several boys seeking explanations from other boys. The boys want to act worldly and knowledgeable about sex. Most of them are, where the sex act itself is involved, but they are sometimes very limited in knowledge about changes in their own bodies and often are quite misinformed about conception. For example, one boy asked me if you didn't have to be eighteen before you could father a baby. When I told him differently, he started shaking his head and muttering, "Oh, oh, maybe she's right," explaining that a girl he knew said he had her pregnant, and up until now he didn't believe it could have been him since he wasn't eighteen.

Mrs. C., in her middle forties, was the tenth grade classroom teacher of an experimental group.

Girls, girls, girls is what these boys have on their minds most of the time, it seems like. Every time a girl comes in here with a message from the office there is an uproar. Some of the boys are really brazen, saying things like "how about it, babe" and even worse. There are several that I think must be oversexed. One boy openly masturbates by twisting his legs together. I tell him to stop it and he says it's just a habit with him and he can't. Sometimes he comes into class moving his body in a very suggestive way. I tell him to stop it, that this isn't the place to dance. Then there is G who sees all women and girls in only one way. The first day I came in here he made some very suggestive remarks to me. [This was also reported by G's teacher of the previous year, who said that G had offered to take care of her in bed if her husband was not doing the job.]

Mr. D., age twenty-eight and single, was an employment coordinator for experimental boys.

One thing my working with these boys has convinced me of is that most of them have had a tremendous amount of sex experience by the time they are seventeen. The most striking thing is that some of them talk about their sex life very candidly. Like that's the way it is. There are others, though, who just don't talk about it directly with an adult, and so if you ask them about girl friends they will usually say that they have one or several but give you ambiguous answers like "Oh you know, man, we have fun," when asked about sex experience. However, I have heard these same boys talking with their buddies about their sex experiences in the bus or car enroute to a work placement. They aren't talking to me or answering questions I put to them but are just sharing some of their experiences with their friends, and my being there in the bus or car and overhearing doesn't seem important. Most of the time boys who talk a lot about sex like this don't seem to be boasting but just talk about it in a kind of matter-of-fact way. One boy I talked with about his relationships with girls mentioned something about taking a girl to a hotel. When I asked why, he stopped and looked at me for a moment and then said, "Man, you know why, don't you?" Then he added, "You ain't no square, are you?"

Mr. A., age forty-five and married, was on the central staff of the Work-Study Program for four years.

> From my observations of these boys, sex experience for many of them seems to be an acceptable and very pleasurable way to spend time. This seems so natural to them that they don't even think about deceiving anyone about it. For example, D, a boy in an experimental group, dropped by my office one day just to say hello and to shoot the breeze. He also wanted to tell me that he had gotten a job in a parking lot nearby. In the course of our conversation I asked him how he and his girl friend were getting along. He said they had parted company and he was now playing the field. At that point he reached for his wallet, pulled out a picture of him and a girl both nude and in coital position. I told him to put that picture back in his wallet and keep it there. He laughed and said, "You know, that's what a cop friend of mine said when I showed him the picture." He said the picture was taken by a friend of his over in The Hut, a clubhouse that he and some friends had started in his neighborhood. The girl was one of several living in the neighborhood that the boys had available. D said the girl was only thirteen, [D himself was seventeen at the time] but added, "She's really built for being only thirteen, and she really knows how."

Mr. J., aged thirty-five and married, was a teacher half day and a work supervisor half day; he had four years' experience in the Work-Study Program.

> One of the things about these boys that really got to me was their attitude toward sex. This bugged me the most. They had no respect for it. The word *respect* never entered their vocabulary. It wasn't just talk that got me, it was the fact that they were actually doing what they talked about. I'll give you a clear-cut example of what I mean. There was this girl, N, a local girl. I'll never forget the day they asked me why she didn't get pregnant. I asked them why they asked. Several started to tell me, and then one of them said, "Well, we hit her every night, and don't use any rubbers or such." What really got me was that they didn't show any feeling of responsibility or concern about the consequences—they were just curious why she didn't get pregnant. I asked them how they

would feel if she did get pregnant, and they agreed that it was her hard luck and had nothing to do with them. There were about five or six boys in the room [out of fifteen] who said they hadn't had sex with this girl, but the other boys said that several of them would take her on at the same time. They told about how five of them had taken her on just the other evening. I just couldn't believe it. Of course all the boys in this group get around and they get different girls, but this girl is one that they use this way and she is the butt of their jokes. They tease each other about her all the time.

Mrs. Y., in her midforties, was classroom teacher of a tenth grade experimental group; she had six months' experience in the program.

I went into this class after it had been going for about two years. The first thing I did was try to establish rapport by telling the boys about myself, my qualifications, and why I was interested in being their teacher. I feel I was successful, and I think that's because I listen to them. I even listen to the boys talk about some of their sex problems. Things like this don't bother me. I talked to them and we had a few lessons on sex. Of course, some of the boys wanted to talk about sex indefinitely. But you have to be broadminded and understanding. . . . In my afternoon class I have two girls who look like angels, but both are being treated for syphilis. One is pregnant. But these girls talk to me about their sexual problem just like the boys do. They talk very openly. One thing they talk to me about is oral sex, which is going on in the schools today. There is a lot more of that going on than used to, and the boys tell me it's because that way they won't get a girl pregnant. But it's gotten now so that boys will pair up with boys and girls with girls, and this is not normal. I think this is happening because these kids just aren't getting the right kinds of education about sex. Yet people who are teaching these kids never get the kids to talk about these kinds of things— the kinds of things that are actually going on."

Mr. P., thirty-seven and married, was a work supervisor with three years' experience in the Work-Study Program.

The group of boys I've been working with have been exposed to sex at an early age. They begin to talk about it in the seventh and eighth grades and by the ninth grade, well, most have experienced sex by then. There were a few in my ninth grade group who probably hadn't. But they all talked as if they had, because to still be a virgin by age fifteen or six-

teen is something they don't want anybody to know about. I
think there is definitely more sex among these boys, as well as
other kids, than there has ever been before. For one thing,
there are more such kids now than five or ten years ago. I
think the group grows larger all the time and has more freedom, or maybe less supervision. For many of these boys it's
their background—it's almost a way of life.

We have seen that sexual experience is a relatively accessible
and pleasurable experience for many study group boys. Is it more than
this? Do some boys use these experiences in their strivings toward masculine identity, and are such adolescent experiences associated with
social and work role adaptations in late adolescence? Or are such adolescent experiences and associated attitudes simply a reflection of the
adequacy of the developing masculine identity? Did opportunity and
the use of sexual activity differ among white and Negro boys in our
sample? We compared the five late adolescent adjustment types on two
sets of ratings, one identifying boys who reported sexual experience
and the other indicating the boys' relationships and attitudes toward
girls, as indicated in interviews. In an exploitive relationship with girls,
the boy stated he wanted girls for sexual purposes only and indicated
no responsibility or concern for consequences. In a casual relationship,
the boy indicated he had one or several girl friends, enjoyed their
company as well as sex, but did not want to get seriously involved. In
a responsible relationship, the boy indicated he had a girl friend, spent
much time with her, enjoyed being with her, knew her parents, and
acknowledged that he might marry her someday. Table 29 summarizes
the data for boys who reported sexual experience. These data indicate
that boys showing maladaptive adjustment in late adolescence tended
more frequently to report sex experience. They also more frequently
indicated exploitive relationship with girls.

Table 30 compares the self-reports on sexual experience and
relationships with girls of Negro and white youths. Negro boys more
frequently reported sexual experience than did white boys. Whether
this was simply because they were more willing to describe this aspect
of their adolescent experience can only be conjectured. However, in
both groups, significantly more maladaptive boys reported sexual experience, and the seriously maladjusted described more exploitive relationships. For the most part, however, in both Negro and white
groups, boys in all adjustment subgroups expressed a casual attitude

Table 29. Sex Experience and Relationship with Girls and Late Adolescent Adjustment

Relationships with Girls	Total Group (N = 308)	Serious Maladap. (N = 70)	Marginal (N = 48)	Erratic (N = 58)	Work Adap. (N = 60)	School Adap. (N = 72)
Boys reporting sex experience	71%	85%	80%	76%	62%	52%
Exploitive	22%	33%	23%	19%	18%	6%
Casual	56%	49%	57%	57%	54%	66%
Responsible	22%	17%	20%	24%	28%	28%

Table 30. SEX EXPERIENCE AND RELATIONSHIPS WITH GIRLS

Sex Experience from Self-Reports in Interviews	Relationships with Girls	1 Serious Maladap.	2 Marginal	3 Erratic	4 Work Adap.	5 School Adap.	Total
Negro boys		n = 52	n = 30	n = 33	n = 38	n = 45	n = 188
				Per Cent			
Indicates sex experience		88	75	89	67	60	77
	Exploitive	35	14	23	21	7	22
	Casual	54	71	45	53	81	57
	Responsible	11	15	29	21	7	16
	Not indicated	0	0	3	5	5	5
		100	100	100	100	100	100
White boys		n = 18	n = 18	n = 25	n = 32	n = 27	n = 120
Indicates sex experience		76	73	61	43	36	55
	Exploitive	46	36	6	14	0	20
	Casual	23	28	47	36	33	35
	Responsible	31	36	6	50	23	28
	Not indicated	0	0	41	0	44	17
		100	100	100	100	100	100

toward girls. Many emphasized their reluctance to become involved seriously with any one girl. This was the major attitude of most boys regardless of their level of social adjustment in late adolescence. The exception was the white work adaptive group, 50 per cent of whom reported a responsible relationship with one girl.

11

Attitudes, Values, and Identity

In this chapter we focus on what the boys themselves told us about how they saw the world, their aspirations, their feelings about school, their concerns and problems. Several measures were administered to experimental boys during the first three years of the Work-Study Program, some of which attempted to elicit expressions concerning the boys' personal aspirations and feelings about being adult males.

Every individual has some concept of the kind of person he would like to become. This is the ideal self or ego ideal which emerges out of the individual's experience with people. The shape of the developing ideal self is dependent on the nature of these experiences. As the child's experiences with people become broader and as he finds new values in them, the ideal self changes and becomes more refined as he grows toward adulthood. Studies both national and cross-cultural have shown that certain ideal selves occur more frequently at different age levels and that as early as age six or seven children can fairly well describe the ideal self when asked such questions as, "Who would you like to be like when you grow up?"[1] For example, children

[1] R. J. Havighurst and others, *A Cross-National Study of Buenos Aires and Chicago Adolescents* (Basel, Switzerland: Sikargen, 1965).

under the age of ten usually name the parent of their own sex as the person they would like to be like, or the adult who has been parental surrogate. In the early teens, most adolescents mention glamorous adults, heroes, or saints, and in their later teens they name attractive adults known personally to them or composite or imaginary figures. Other less typical ideal selves are age-mates and occupational identities such as lawyer or carpenter. Another kind of response is not classifiable in the above categories and frequently takes the form of rejecting the whole idea of wanting to be like someone else and saying, "I want to be like myself." As Havighurst has pointed out this is an increasingly frequent phenomenon not seen in earlier studies of the ideal self.[2]

Early in the Work-Study Program, experimental boys were asked to describe their ideal self by answering the question, "Who would you like to be like?" The instructions were written on the black-boards in Work-Study classrooms and explained briefly by the teacher: "Write a paragraph about the person you would like to be like when you grow up. This can be a real person or an imaginary person, a live person or one who is no longer alive. If it is a real person, say so. You can name the person or not, as you please. Tell something about this person's appearance, his personality and character, what he does for a living, what he does for fun."

The essays were read and classified in the ideal self categories mentioned above. Boys were in the eighth grade when first asked to write these essays. They were asked to write them again in the ninth and tenth grades, so that changes in the ideal self measured in this way could be assessed. Since the attrition rate was rather high in exper-imental groups and attendance was frequently poor, complete coverage of experimental youths' descriptions of ideal selves was not possi-ble. This was particularly true by the tenth grade, when the experi-mental group was reduced to almost one-third of the original number. Response categories typical of children and young adolescents dimin-ished for experimental boys over the three years of adolescence. How-ever, categories typical of adolescent boys also diminished, and there was a shift toward the "self" response category. How different were these patterns from those of urban boys from families of comparable socioeconomic status? Table 31 compares the distribution of ideal self categories for experimental boys when in the three grades with the

[2] *Ibid.*

Table 31. THE IDEAL SELF

Age Levels	8th Grade (N = 113)	13-Year Chicago (N = 30)	9th Grade (N = 90)	10th Grade (N = 50)	16-Year Chicago (N = 32)
			Per Cent		
Ten years or younger					
Parent or parental surrogate	20	7	12	6	9
Early adolescence					
Glamorous persons, heroes	22	50	31	17	16
Adolescent midyears					
Attractive young adults known to person, composite or imaginary figures	44	36	34	28	53
Other[a]					
Age-mates	3	0	1	10	0
Occupational identities, e.g., doctor, lawyer	3	7	0	0	0
Nonclassifiable	2	0	6	2	0
Self					
"I want to be like myself"	6	0	16	37	22

[a] Other studies show no obvious relation to age after about age ten.

distribution of such categories for samples of thirteen- and sixteen-year-old boys from working-class families in Chicago. (Most boys in the eighth grade are thirteen years old and most boys in tenth grade are sixteen.) One important difference between groups is that the experimental sample represented longitudinal data while the Chicago sample was cross-sectional. Additionally, the socioeconomic level of the Chicago sample was probably somewhat higher than that of the experimental group.

The frequency of responses in the "self" category increased as boys grew older in both the experimental and Chicago samples. However, this category occurred less frequently in the Chicago sample, where the major shift with age was from categories representing immaturity to categories of ideal selves typical of adolescents. In the experimental group the major shift with age was toward the "self" category. Since this occurrence seemed atypical and also because we were interested in difficulties encountered in eliciting from some boys their feelings about themselves and their world, we studied these "self" responses carefully. We were interested in the possibility that the "self" response reflected a healthy kind of self-esteem which was being nurtured in experimental classrooms and work settings. Our survey indicated that the nonclassifiable and "self" responses could be divided into three subcategories. One group rejected the task. "Nobody" and "ain't been born yet" were typical responses to the question of whom such boys would like to be like. Boys in the second group gave direct statements without elaboration of wanting to be like themselves. Typical responses were "I want to be like myself" and "I want to be like nobody but me." The third group elaborated on their satisfaction with themselves. They responded,

> Me because I'm satisfied with myself. I like myself because I don't envy anybody. I want to go in the Navy, come back home, and get a job, get married, and raise a family.

> I am satisfied with myself because I am trying to straighten up. I like myself for trying to do something on my own.

> About the only person I would like to be like is myself. If God wanted me to be like somebody else he would have made me that way. But there are a couple of things I would like to change in myself. I would like to stop talking so much.

> I would like to be like [own name] 'cause he is a cool cat and

I would like to be like him 'cause he is a bad stud and don't take no jive from no one. When he walks down the street people go to the other side of the street. When he gets on a bus, people get off.

I would like to be like myself. Because I think that I'm just getting to know myself and I don't want to go through that shit again.

Some of these responses appear to reflect fairly healthy self-attitudes. However, some do not, and a few may simply express attitudes toward the inquiry. To what extent these responses were attempts to avoid dealing with an abstract, unknown future or perhaps with the boys' inability to project themselves into adult roles can only be conjectured. It appears that many of these "self" responses share with responses typical of early adolescence (glamorous person, heroes) the avoidance of such projection. We found this to be the case with many experimental boys in our interviews with them as well as in self-descriptions in other essays we asked them to write.

Why was it difficult for many of these boys to organize their futures around ideal selves projected into adulthood? Some clues are provided by a sentence completion measure administered in the eighth grade to 129 experimental boys, about 74 per cent of the total experimental group. This measure consisted of sixty incomplete sentences which elicited personal-attitudinal expression somewhat indirectly in areas believed relevant for identifying social development and adjustment. One item required that boys complete the sentence "To be grown up." The completions to this item fell into six response categories. One of these was similar to the nonclassifiable category previously described, with boys simply responding "is to be twenty-one" or "is to be an adult," that is, giving neutral nonpersonal responses. This category was one of the two most frequent categories. Four more categories involved gaining of privileges and benefits of adulthood, achievement of adult goals such as a job, a family, or independence, acceptance of certain responsibilities, and giving up adolescent ways. The sixth type of response stated that growing up was difficult and that the boy did not look forward to it.

Of all experimental boys responding, 76 per cent either focused their sentence completions on what they would have to give up and the difficulties and responsibilities involved in being grown up (50 per cent) or took a neutral stance (26 per cent). Only 24 per cent of experimental boys indicated that to be grown up had some rewarding and attractive features. Because normative data on the sentence completion measure were not available, the uniqueness of these responses for this group is not clear. It is possible that these adolescent boys responded to the sentence completion stems in much the same way as would adolescent boys in general. However, as we shall see, some differences in percentage distribution of these response categories were found among eighth grade experimental boys who in late adolescence showed differences in progress toward work-role identity.

In view of the experimental boys' generally negative or neutral stance concerning growing up, it might be expected that their views of the future would not be strongly optimistic. Responding to the stem "the future looks," over half the boys expressed positive orientation toward a future time. However, the larger percentage (62 per cent) of these responses were relatively mild and conventional expressions of optimism such as "fair," "okay," or "all right." Only about one in five experimental boys gave such clearly positive expressions of optimism about the future as "very good for me," "like it will be exciting," "wonderful," or "bright." A slightly higher percentage (one in four) expressed a clearly pessimistic outlook, such as "bad," "no good," "horrible," "like trouble," or "like the end of the world." One-fifth of the boys either did not respond to this item (13 per cent) or gave responses such as "like the present," "like the air force," or "on me," which did not express personal views of a future time (7 per cent).

Although only about one-fifth of experimental eighth grade boys expressed definitely positive views of the future, and most boys seemed to have reservations about being grown up, more than one-fourth (28 per cent) responded to the stem "After high school" that they expected to go on to college. This expectation ran in the face of their original seventh grade identification as school failures and potential early high school dropouts. Another 30 per cent of boys stated their intentions of getting jobs after high school; over one-fourth prefaced this statement with "I hope." Seventeen per cent of boys mentioned going into the service, and 6 per cent stated that their major goal after leaving high school was to get married. There were several unique responses, including one boy's assertion that he would rob banks, and another's plan to become "a bum." Six per cent of boys responded with such statements as, "I will get my car fixed," or "I will be out of school." Most of the 28 per cent of boys who expressed aspirations for college were among the 42 per cent who also expressed aspirations to positions of status, fame, glamor, and wealth in their completions to the stem "I would like to be." (Twenty-five per cent mentioned glamorous and exciting careers as professional athletes, rock-and-roll singers, actors, and race car drivers. Twelve per cent mentioned professional careers as doctors, lawyers, and military officers. Five per cent simply wanted to be rich.)

Only 23 per cent of experimental boys indicated they aspired to working-class careers. (Seventeen per cent mentioned skilled careers as mechanics, carpenters, electricians, mailmen, and policemen. One per cent mentioned unskilled construction work. Five per cent mentioned the military services.) Twelve per cent of boys responded with aspirations for personal physical characteristics, such as to be grown up, to be good, strong, tough, big, smart, or better readers. Twenty-three per cent of responses were in other categories. (Six per cent gave no response, 6 per cent were unintelligible or illegible, and 11 per cent were unique responses which seemed to reject the task, such as "nothing," "a dog," "a hobo," "I can't tell you," "home," "a car," "go to Mexico," and "in a play.") Although only a few boys expressed interest in military service, 17 per cent indicated that after high school they expected to enter the service.

These findings tend to correspond with ideal selves described by boys in the eighth grade. However, the stem "I would like to be" elicited a somewhat higher percentage of aspirations for status positions than did the essay. The relatively frequent sentence completions which emphasized glamorous and exciting careers appear typical of young adolescents. In contrasting the stems "After high school" and "I would like to be," it is clear that considerably more experimental boys expressed aspirations to status careers (42 per cent) than aspirations to college (28 per cent). Almost all the status careers aspired to were in professional sports and entertainment. Over half the thirty-four boys with responses in this category identified career athletics as their goal, and many of these youths did not indicate that college was anticipated. Thus, it was in those glamorous career areas where educational requirements were not perceived by eighth grade experimental boys as serious barriers to entry that many envisioned career opportunities.

Midadolescent interviews were conducted about two years after these measures were administered, when most boys were about sixteen years of age. Both experimental and control group boys were interviewed individually to determine how well the process of identity achievement was developing. Several major areas were explored in this interview, including boys' attitudes toward school and their vocational aspirations. Boys' responses in these areas were rated on four-point scales. Most study group boys doubted that they would continue in school much beyond the legal dropout age of sixteen. Ten per cent definitely did not intend to complete high school and saw little value in school. Another 16 per cent doubted that they would continue school and were uncertain of the value of school. Most boys (56 per cent) saw value in school and wanted to complete high school, but were uncertain they would be able to do so. Only 18 per cent expressed definite intentions of staying in school and believed they would be able to do so.

Many boys could not or would not express vocational aspirations. Twenty-six per cent expressed no aspirations. A typical response was "I've never given it much thought." Even when asked what they would like to do if they had the opportunity, many of them could not or would not project themselves into future adult work careers. Many of these boys focused on the present with almost complete exclusion of concerns about or commitments to the future. One boy said, "I ain't got no plans. I just want to get me a job and earn some money. I'll do any kind of work where I can make some money." Another said, "I don't know what I want to do to earn a living. I ain't given it much thought. Right now I want a job so I can make some good money. I want to buy me a car, have some dates, get me some sharp clothes and some smokes."

General indifference toward work in both the present and the future was expressed by a few boys. Said one, "I haven't really thought about the future. I know I don't want no part of the service. Right now I'm doing okay. I got me a job cleaning bricks once or twice a week, and I earn enough money to have a little fun with. This way I get to sleep most mornings, run around with some buddies, shoot some pool, so I'm not looking for a regular job. I can enjoy myself without working every day." When this boy was asked about the value of planning for a more permanent future, he responded, "Why a permanent job? What's the point? It ain't worth it."

A few youths were able to express rather directly the sense of futility in planning for the future which was strongly implied in the responses of many other boys. One boy said, "I actually have no plans for the future. I've found out that if you make plans, well they usually don't work out anyway, so I'm not making any at this time." He was asked what he would like to do in the future if he had the chance or opportunity. "Well I don't think about the future. You know, it don't do no good to think about it when you know you can't do it. I mean, I think about a lot of things that I would like to do, but I know I can't so why think about it? When I was young—maybe five or six— I always wanted to be a policeman or a fireman, but now I have grown older, and I have begun to think about life, and I often wonder what I will be. It is always best not to plan because it will never work out. I try to take life the way it is, but it is hard to do."

Twenty per cent of boys interviewed made some attempt to respond to inquiry about their vocational aspirations, but their responses indicated little thought concerning the future and their aspirations were vague and poorly defined. In some instances it is likely that they responded only because they felt it was required of them. A typical response was "Well I guess I want to be some kind of construction worker—something like that. Something that pays three or four dollars an hour. It don't have to be construction work but any kind of work out of doors where I can earn good money part of the time and loaf the rest of the year." Another said, "Well I just want to get into a job where I can earn good pay. I've been thinking I might like to be a fireman. I've got a friend who's a fireman, and he don't do much work most of the time, and in fact he's got it pretty easy."

Thirteen per cent of boys expressed unrealistic aspirations to careers which required years of special training or to probably unattainable income levels. This percentage of unrealistic aspirations was considerably less than had been indicated in the eighth grade ideal self essays and sentence completions two years previously. Unrealistic aspirations generally expressed desire to become professional persons, for example doctors or lawyers. In contrast to the relatively high frequency of boys expressing aspirations to careers in professional sports in the eighth grade, only a few indicated such aspirations in midadolescence. Although there was some evidence of athletic skill among these boys, the chances were considered slight that they could move into such vocations and so their aspirations were rated unrealistic. The professional occupations aspired to required college and graduate work and, in the context of the boys' acknowledged difficulties in reading and in study habits and their generally poor or failing work, were also considered unrealistic.

Forty-one per cent of boys expressed realistic aspirations based on knowledge of requirements for entry into the chosen career. In contrast to the emphasis on glamorous, exciting, and professional careers in eighth grade measures of aspiration, most vocational aspirations expressed in midadolescence were to manual skilled trades. A few youths expressed goals which involved college or technical training beyond high school, but because these aspirations appeared associated with some progress in school and an awareness of requirements necessary for achieving the ultimate goal, they were considered realistic. One boy said, "I plan on being a television and radio repairman— some kind of technician in that field. I'm taking an electrical course in school, and I like it a lot. I'm also getting a little bit of experience and learning about TV sets. The man on the corner has a TV shop, and he lets me go with him sometimes on service calls, and I've gotten to the place where I can do minor repair work—like I can locate if a TV tube burns out and then I can replace it." Another said, "I'm planning on finishing high school definitely, because I want to go on to college if at all possible. I'm not the best student now, but I'm making average grades, and I can do better once I improve on my reading and I'm working at that now. . . . I am athletic and I do good in sports, so I'd like very much to become a physical education teacher. I've already got my school picked out. It's a fairly small one, but I think it would be good for me, and it's got a good reputation."

In general, there were marked shifts away from the immature fantasy aspirations expressed in the eighth grade. The shifts were in two different directions. One was toward more realistic aspirations (41 per cent of the boys) and the other toward rejection of commitment to a future time (46 per cent). This latter trend parallels the increasing frequency of "self" responses of boys in the "Person I would like to be like" essays. This suggests that, for some youths in the study group, focusing on themselves and on the present was much easier or more meaningful than projecting themselves into an unknown future.

Boys who showed differences in social adjustment and work role development in late adolescence did not differ significantly in their responses to any of the personal aspiration measures administered in the eighth and ninth grades. At this early adolescent stage, both maladaptive and adaptive youths described personal aspirations and ideal selves generally characteristic of a younger age group. Some boys expressed personal aspirations fairly typical for their age level, but these boys did not appear to have any better chance of adaptive adjustment in late adolescence than did the others. By midadolescence, some differences in personal aspirations, although not statistically significant, began to appear.

In the midadolescent interview, 37 per cent of the maladaptive group, in contrast to 19 per cent of the work adaptive, expressed doubt they would stay in school and questioned the value of education. None of the school adaptive group questioned the value of education, and 43 per cent of these youths stated their intention of completing high school. A considerably smaller percentage of boys in other subgroups, including the work adaptive group, expressed such intentions. Most midadolescent study group boys, regardless of later adjustment, did express a desire to continue in school but indicated they felt little chance this would be possible. Even among school adaptive boys who did stay and complete four years of high school, over half had expressed doubt in midadolescence that they would graduate. School and vocational aspiration ratings are summarized in Table 32.

Work adaptive boys tended to be most realistic and work-oriented; slightly more than half (52 per cent) of them expressed aspirations to what appeared to be realistic and feasible vocational objectives. However, as Table 32 indicates, there was no clear differentiation of late adolescent adjustment subgroups in terms of expressed vocational aspirations. In all subgroups except the work adaptive, over half the boys indicated either no vocational aspirations or vague or unrealistic aspirations.

In our midadolescent interviews, we employed a simple semantic differential measure of self-attitudes which interviewers administered at the completion of the interviews. This measure was based on Osgood's[3] approach to the measurement of meaning in concepts, which requires the respondent to place an object toward which he has an attitude on a scale formed by a pair of opposite adjectives. The object in this series of interviews was "myself," and boys were instructed to rate themselves on seven six-point scales: strong-weak, hardworking-lazy, good-bad, happy-sad, smart-ignorant, big-small, and tough-soft. Since boys tended to rate themselves toward the positive end of each scale, the median score on each adjective pair was selected as the cutoff score for dividing the responses into positive and negative self-attitudes.

[3] C. E. Osgood, *The Measurement of Meaning* (Urbana, Illinois: University of Illinois Press, 1957).

Table 32. School Attitudes and Vocational Aspirations in Midadolescence

Rating Category	Serious Maladap. (N = 63)	Marginal (N = 48)	Erratic (N = 57)	Work Adap. (N = 68)	School Adap. (N = 72)
			Per Cent		
School attitudes					
Value of school questioned; most likely will drop out.	44	41	23	18	0
Values school, but uncertain he can complete high school	45	53	57	68	57
Values school; intends to complete high school.	11	6	20	14	43
Vocational aspirations					
None expressed or vaguely defined.	48	47	52	39	40
Unrealistic.	8	11	9	9	20
Realistic.	44	42	38	52	40

Chi-square analyses of differences in the distribution of positive and negative responses among adjustment subgroups were then made. The findings are summarized in Table 33; percentage distributions of choices are given only for those adjective pairs on which adjustment subgroups showed trends of differences.

Maladaptive boys tended to place themselves toward the negative ends of three of the seven scales significantly more frequently than did adaptive boys. In fact, the maladaptive group more frequently placed themselves toward the negative ends of all seven scales. That is, boys who were to have difficulties in late adolescence in social adjustment and work role development tended to describe themselves in midadolescence as lazy, bad, and sad more frequently than did boys who showed adaptive adjustment in late adolescence. Although it might have been anticipated that maladaptive boys would present positive, masculine pictures of themselves as tough, big, smart, and strong, the adaptive group consistently showed a higher frequency of such descriptions. The seriously maladaptive subgroup tended to describe themselves in somewhat more negative terms than did the other two maladaptive groups. When the total numbers of relatively negative self-descriptions on the semantic differential measure were tabulated for each boy and the adjustment subgroups were compared on these totals, the generally unfavorable self-description of seriously maladaptive boys became even more obvious.

At the time the semantic differential was administered, the boys were also asked to indicate with check marks on diagrams their feelings about how close or how distant the relationship was between school and their homes, school and their friends, and friends and their families. Each diagram, on a separate piece of paper, depicted a square and a circle in four different positions from half an inch apart to intersecting. For example, in one diagram the square was labeled "school" and the circle labeled "home." Boys generally responded without hesitation to the task and seemed to quickly grasp what was wanted. Since the responses tended to concentrate in the two intermediate categories of the diagrams, the four categories were combined into two, distant and close, for scoring purposes. Most study group boys indicated relatively close relationships between school, family, and friends; this pattern was particularly emphasized by the adaptive group. Sixty-seven per cent of adaptive boys, compared to 56 per cent of maladaptive boys, perceived the relationship between school and

Table 33. SELF-DESCRIPTIONS OF LATE ADOLESCENT ADJUSTMENT SUBGROUPS

Category	Total Maladap. (N = 151)	Serious Maladap. (N = 59)	Marginal and Erratic (N = 92)	School and Work Adaptive (N = 124)
		Per Cent		
Self-descriptions				
Lazy	53	61	48	37
Bad	52	64	51	39
Sad	45	57	27	27
Ignorant	48	53	44	41
Number of negative self-descriptions				
None—all positive descriptions	6	7	6	9
One to three negative descriptions	36	26	44	46
Four to seven negative descriptions	58	67	50	45

friends as close. Seventy-seven per cent of adaptive and 56 per cent of maladaptive boys perceived a close relationship between school and home. Seventy-two per cent of adaptive and 64 per cent of maladaptive boys perceived a close relationship between friends and family. Only one-fourth of maladaptive boys rated all three sets of depicted relationships as close, but almost half (47 per cent) the adaptive youth indicated this.

12

Social and Educational Implications

We have been describing a pathological group of boys and their families whose counterparts can be found in any large city in the United States. In a rich and democratic society, there is no reason a pathological group as large as this should exist. These youths constitute about 10 per cent of inner-city male youths and about 5 per cent of all male youths of the city, since a big city population is normally about 50 per cent low-income and 50 per cent middle- and high-income.

These boys looked like "losers" when we studied them at the age of thirteen or fourteen. They could be picked out by relatively simple screening methods, which could be applied at very low cost in any school system. The majority of them came through the next five years as could have been predicted. Ten were killed by violence or accident; thirty others were knifed or shot. Fifty-five per cent showed serious social maladjustment. Sixty-five per cent had been arrested on charges other than traffic violations. Sixteen per cent had accumulated eight or more charges of delinquency. Twenty-three per cent had been confined in juvenile institutions. The arrest rate for offenses which would have been felonies if they had been committed by adults was about 40 per cent per year for study group boys, compared with about 20 per cent for the total metropolitan area population of this

217

age. This does not tell us what per cent of boys were arrested, since it includes multiple arrests. But a study made in 1963–64 established that 20 per cent of the study group were arrested one or more times during that year, compared with 7 per cent of all inner-city boys of this age.

One-fifth of study group boys were placed in the seriously maladjusted category when they were evaluated at the age of eighteen. These youths showed a consistent pattern of disruptive behavior and poor adjustment both in and out of school. Seventy-five per cent of them were confined in institutions one or more times. The two other maladaptive subgroups, the marginal and erratic, comprising together slightly more than one-third of the total study group, appeared to be in less serious conflict with society than the severely maladjusted. However, the marginal group appeared seriously handicapped in making even a start toward achieving a work-role identity. The erratic group, although appearing capable of some adaptive adjustment, seemed generally unable to sustain efforts in this direction. In contrast, 43 per cent of the study group, equally divided between the work adaptive and school adaptive subgroups, showed reasonably good social adjustment by the age of eighteen.

The research design, with its control group, proved to be extremely valuable as a means of making an objective judgment concerning the values of a work-study experience for this type of boy. Our conclusions from the comparison of control and experimental groups are based on the data for Group Two, the second-year group, since the first year's sampling procedure favored the selection of seriously maladjusted boys for the experimental rather than the control group. There was little apparent difference between experimental and control Group Two boys in the frequency of various types of late adolescent adjustment. Somewhat more boys made adaptive adjustments in the experimental group than in the control group (31 per cent and 26 per cent, respectively). Experimental and control groups contributed the same relative numbers of school adaptive adjustments (18 per cent) and about the same proportion of maladaptive adjustments (45 per cent and 52 per cent).

The most striking differences were found between control nonconsent subgroup boys and experimental and control youth. (In evaluating the record of the experimental group, it is important to remember that it did not contain any nonconsent boys; the control group did contain such boys, since their parents were, of course, not asked to consent to the Work-Study Program.) The control nonconsent youths were oriented in work and deed toward completing high school. Sixty-two per cent of them, in contrast to 14 and 28 per cent of experimental and control boys, managed to finish high school. Only 31 per cent of control nonconsent boys, in contrast to 61 per cent experimental and 54 per cent control, showed signs of maladjustment in late adolescence.

The frequency of maladaptive late adolescent adjustments among Negro boys was significantly higher than among white boys. Sixty-two per cent of black youths in the sample, regardless of their research groupings, showed signs of maladaptive adjustment in late adolescence; 27 per cent of the black group showed serious maladjustment. In contrast, 46 per cent of all white boys showed maladaptive adjustment; 13 per cent were seriously maladjusted. A significantly higher number of white boys (32 per cent) than black boys (13 per cent) showed work adaptive adjustment in late adolescence. A slightly higher number of black youths (25 per cent) than white youths (22 per cent) showed school adaptive adjustments. The fact that the white boys seemed to profit more than the black boys from the work experience is at least partly attributable to the less attractive employment opportunities for black youths at the time of the experiment. Black boys tended to remain in school longer than white boys, because the alternative of employment was less open to them.

As we saw in Chapter Four, the amount of time spent in the Work-Study Program appeared positively associated with late adolescent adaptive adjustments among experimental youths. Many Negro boys in experimental groups, particularly in Group One, spent much less actual time in the program than their periods of enrollment indicate. They were in trouble with the authorities from the very beginning of the program. Many were in and out of the Work-Study Program due to suspensions and institutional commitments, so that their involvement in terms of amounts of time and experience in the program was minimal. The Work-Study Program remained flexible, permitting boys returning from institutional confinements to reenter work experience groups. (There was no other place for them.) These frequent changes in group structure and membership created problems in some groups, making a difficult learning and teaching situation.

Only about one-fourth of all boys enrolled in the Work-Study curriculum seemed to be making progress toward work-role identity in late adolescence. As we have indicated throughout this book, the boys screened as a relatively homogeneous group of school misfits in the seventh grade actually showed considerable heterogeneity in their responses to and progress in the work experience program and high school. We have attempted to look at these different patterns of responses and identify their sociopsychological correlates. What essentially did we learn about boys who seemed to be moving away from disruptive antisocial activities toward identity as responsible self-sufficient young adults? How did they differ in background characteristics from the others who continued to show maladaptive patterns?

The typical unsuccessful Work-Study boy had an early childhood police record. His parents and siblings also frequently had police records. He often came from a broken home, and broken home or not there was usually considerable tension, conflict, or indifference in family relationships. He often came from a large family (seven or eight people)', and his father was unskilled. During his childhood he and his family moved about from one neighborhood to another, and he attended several different schools. He usually came from the most delinquent neighborhoods in the inner city and the physical environment of his home was inadequate for his family's needs. He typically began showing signs of serious school maladjustment not later than the third grade, and his elementary teachers saw him as particularly limited in self-control and regard for school rules and regulations.

The typical successful Work-Study boy did not have an early childhood police record, nor did his parents or siblings. He usually did not come from an incomplete home, but broken home or not it was usually cohesive. His father was semiskilled. During childhood he moved once or twice with his family and attended only one or two elementary grade schools. In general, he had a much more stable family life than did the unsuccessful boy. The successful boy's neighborhood was usually less delinquency-prone and his family dwelling was somewhat more adequate. In the early elementary grades he generally did very poor schoolwork and was consistently rated poor on work habits and other traits important to organizing and doing his schoolwork. He typically was seen by his teachers as showing relatively good self-control and having a healthy attitude toward school rules and regulations. On other traits, including responsibility, initiative, work habits, and personal habits, he usually was rated low; in this respect he was much like the unsuccessful Work-Study boy.

The typical school adaptive boy did not have an early childhood police record although there was a good chance that his parents had been involved with the police. He most often came from a cohesive and relatively small family. His parents' education was slightly better than the average for study group parents, and his father's occupational level was semiskilled or skilled. His socioeconomic background was better than average for the total group. During childhood he had a fairly stable and relatively adequate physical environment. In fact, he and his family lived in the best physical environments found among the study group, and his neighborhood was less delinquency-prone than other inner-city areas. He and his family seldom moved, and usually he spent his elementary school days in one or two schools. In his early elementary school grades, he did generally below average work and was considered an underachiever. He had average intellectual potential, better than most of the other boys screened, yet had difficulty with classroom work. He was more likely to have had reading or speech therapy than other Work-Study boys. In spite of his slow progress in school, teachers consistently rated him higher on personal traits in elementary grades than other study group boys.

A fairly thorough examination of these boys as they moved through adolescence has helped us to understand the problems they faced in trying to grow up. There seemed to be five main aspects of the problem. The first was lack of opportunity to be a man. Most of these boys seemed to have been blocked in their efforts to grow up by lack of models of successful manhood. Many boys did not have fathers in their homes. The fathers who were at home were often examples of failure, as were many male adults in the neighborhoods where boys lived. Boys were also handicapped by inadequate basic reading and arithmetic skills to support a semiskilled job or to permit high school graduation and by lack of work opportunity.

The second aspect of the problem was inadequate family support. Some parents were indifferent and hostile toward school and did not insist that their children attend school regularly. Some parents changed homes so frequently that their children had to adjust to new schools continuously. Others were so involved in trying to provide for large families that they had insufficient time and energy to provide help and emotional support to children having difficulty in school.

The third aspect of the problem was neighborhood settings which exposed boys to trouble. Just happening to be at a place where there was trouble seemed to account for many of the episodes that got the boys into trouble, which resulted in additional problems of public police records, increasing sense of alienation, and forced association through confinement with severely maladjusted youths at an early age. Having to get along with tough boys singly and in gangs often meant adopting the behavior of these boys.

The fourth aspect of the problem was lack of a sense of control over the environment. Most of the boys saw the world around them as operating by chance or under the control of powerful people alien to them. This limited them in studying a situation, deciding how to act rationally and effectively, and then acting in the expectation that they would produce the desired effect.

The fifth aspect of the problem was the prevalence of delinquency in the lives of many of these boys. It must be stressed that their delinquency was different from the "normal" delinquency of adolescent boys. Many research studies have shown that the majority of boys commit delinquent acts during adolescence. But most boys do this very seldom. Many are caught and punished or warned by parents or police. Many come from families which have taught them to feel guilty about delinquency. To them, adolescence brings only a temporary disruption of their formerly docile and self-controlled behavior. The boys in our study had a very different experience with delinquency. They did not feel guilty over their delinquent behavior. They got rewards from it, and what little punishment they got was unsystematic and may have been seen by them as a source of prestige with their peers, as was the case with commitment to the county correctional institution in many instances.

These sources of the problem, particularly those limiting both work opportunity and adequate adult male models and those contributing to development of a pervasive sense of helplessness in controlling their destiny, seemed most evident among the Negro youths in our sample. Among white youths who were most seriously socially and economically disadvantaged, however, these sources of problems also appeared predominant. As we followed these youths through adolescence, it became increasingly clear that the study group was having difficulty with identity achievement for all of the reasons outlined here. It also became evident that progress and adjustment in school and work experience could not be understood and evaluated unless they were seen as segments of the total life space of individual boys.

A few conclusions from this study can be applied to the education of maladjusted boys, although they could hardly be guaranteed to solve the problem. One involves the importance of choosing the right kinds of persons to teach such boys. On the basis of our observations, as well as on theoretical grounds, we concluded that certain kinds of men and women were much better for these boys than just a random cross section of teachers. The teachers who worked best were patient but determined. They were flexible in teaching personality, able to adapt differently to different boys. Such teachers are not especially rare. We observed several who did work well with these boys.

The second conclusion involved the importance of male teachers. Almost all these boys lacked close relationships with stable men who led orderly lives. Their fathers either were absent or tended to be erratic, unstable men. If boys struck up relationships with men in the community, these men were also likely to be bad models. Yet it was clear that, in time, several of the male teachers developed good working relations with some of the boys. This development seemed to work best when there was ample time for the teacher or work supervisor to enter into spontaneous and natural relationships with boys, as in the summer work and the Rotary camp project. It was noteworthy that boys returned to school to see male teachers and work supervisors several years after leaving school, invited them to their weddings, and so forth.

The third conclusion was that work experience had a good effect on boys who found their employers to be friendly and helpful men. It was the man-boy relationship, as much as the work skills learned by the boy, that made this project useful for the minority of work adaptive boys.

The fourth conclusion was that most of these boys wanted to be part of the school group but did not know how to measure up to the expectations of the school. Two of the classroom teachers showed special ability to win the loyalty of the boys and to establish orderly situations in which boys could go to work with some assurance that what they learned in school would lead to a better life. One of these was a woman and one was a man. They were competent people, and they worked hard at the job of teaching, but there was nothing magic about their methods.

The fifth conclusion was that learning from failure is a valuable experience to some boys. A few boys were able to look at their inadequacies realistically and work systematically to reduce them. But most boys gave up easily when the way became difficult. Here too, the relationship between boy and teacher was crucial. A teacher can help a boy face his failure constructively or he can make a boy feel he cannot learn.

A more general proposal for educational improvement—one which would be more preventive than curative—is that the school system might assign a special kind of counselor to work with the families of such boys while the boys are still quite young, in the primary grades. It seems likely that at least half the families could have been identified by their sons' school problems as early as the third or fourth grade. The school-home coordinator might work out a relationship with the family and with the boy that might help the family do a better job of cooperating with the school in the boy's development. This role is somewhat different from the role of the school-community coordinator that usually exists, where this person, acting as a social worker, is brought in only after there has been a great deal of trouble, and tends to work intensively with the family and school only until the immediate trouble is past. The preventive role should be started before the trouble reaches an acute stage and should be maintained at a relatively low level of intensity throughout a boy's school career.

Society, and teachers and other surrogates for society, may have to find ways to tolerate some of the delinquent and antisocial behavior of boys. There is a good deal of evidence that many young men grow out of their adolescent maladjustment as they get married and settle down as workers and citizens. School personnel and others dealing with these boys may have to tolerate behavior in the early stages that they would not tolerate later when their influence with the boys has grown. While there must be limits on society's tolerance of violence and of irresponsible behavior by adolescent boys, possibly these limits should be extended somewhat. If this is done together with provision of more juvenile jobs and other ways of filling masculine roles, the combination may work well enough to allow us to claim that we have a workable social-educational program for maladjusted boys.

The experience of observing and studying the four hundred boys as they moved through adolescence has brought us to two conclusions of a very general nature concerning the provisions our society should make to prevent the trouble such boys make for society and for themselves. The first is aimed at strengthening the family as the group which gives the boy his basic moral training. This applies especially to the early school grades and to the preschool years. This means basic reform of welfare legislation and institution of procedures which will encourage low-income men to stay with wives and children, and it means some kind of floor under wages that guarantees a family an adequate income. Beyond that, such a policy could support a program of preschool education for children of the poor and would bring mothers into this program in ways that would teach them how to raise their children in a more orderly manner and also how to get their children ready to learn to read. This, coupled with the employment of a school-home coordinator, would probably reduce considerably the numbers of boys and girls who get to high school unready in motives and skills to do high school work.

The other policy proposal has been discussed in one way or another ever since William James wrote that youth need a "moral equivalent to war" to give them an opportunity to be of service to their society in ways that everyone considers essential and useful. With the decreasing need of the labor force for juvenile labor, it seems inevitable that the employment of young men and women between the ages of sixteen and twenty will decrease even further. This means that the socially satisfactory roles will be restricted more and more to the student role in high school and college and to marriage and homemaking for many young women. There will be steady jobs for a minority of youth under twenty, but not enough to meet the need for employment by young people who do not desire an academic program in school or college.

Some kind of public service employment program should be established, which provides young people with training in work attitudes and habits, basic vocational skills, and the opportunity to be useful to the local community or the state. This program should be administered by state and metropolitan youth authorities working closely with school systems. It should be supported with federal funds. This should be one of the options for young men and women between the ages of sixteen and twenty-one. Other acceptable alternatives would be full-time stable employment in the private economy, satisfactory work in high school or college, marriage and homemaking for girls, and military service. The public service employment would probably have to be provided for about 15 per cent of youth aged sixteen to twenty-one, two-thirds of them boys. Since a substantial number in this program would be boys and girls with histories of maladjustment in junior high school, it seems likely that a work-study program of the kind we have described in this book would be needed for boys, at least, in the age period from thirteen to fifteen. The problem of identity achievement for young people who are not successful in the common roles of high school or college student cannot be solved by the present arrangements in our society. We must create new roles for them.

APPENDIX A

Screening Measures

BEHAVIOR DESCRIPTION CHART (TEACHERS' RATINGS)

Directions: In each of the sets of descriptive statements below, pick out two statements. (1) Pick out that statement which you find fits the child most aptly—the one which the child is *most like*. (2) Then pick out the statement which the child is *least like*. Place the letters of these statements on the record sheet under the number corresponding to the set of statements. Do not be concerned if the statement does not apply exactly, and do not dwell too long upon your decision. Go through the entire chart for one child at a time. Experience shows that the ratings can be completed in just a few minutes per child.

1. A. Others come to him for help
   B. Causes disturbances
   C. Lacks confidence in himself
   D. Doesn't go along with those who break the rules
   E. Shows emotions, but in a restrained way

2. A. Other people find it hard to get along with him
   B. Is easily confused
   C. Other people are eager to be near him or on his side
   D. Is usually willing to go along with the group
   E. Interested in other people's opinions and activities

3. A. Sensitive, touchy, hurt by criticism
   B. Shows off, attention-getter
   C. Is self-confident

    D. Enjoys being a part of the group without taking the lead
    E. Dislikes criticism

4. A. Is extremely quiet and passive
    B. Is a natural leader
    C. Is boastful
    D. Does his share, but does not seek leadership
    E. Finds excuses when his work is not done

5. A. Frequently gets into fights or heated arguments
    B. Exerts a good influence on the class
    C. Seems anxious and fearful
    D. Is sometimes critical of other people
    E. Is generous when in the mood

6. A. Makes sensible, practical plans
    B. Breaks rules frequently
    C. Becomes discouraged easily
    D. Usually willing to share with others
    E. Doesn't rub people the wrong way

7. A. Takes an active part in group projects and other activities
    B. Is shy and retiring
    C. Others cannot work with him
    D. Polite
    E. Occasionally contributes to a discussion

8. A. Quarrelsome
    B. Is tense or ill at ease when reciting or appearing before a group
    C. Likes jobs which give him responsibility
    D. Is quiet and seems content with himself
    E. Enjoys a conversation

9. A. His presence or absence is not noticed by other children
    B. Figures out things for himself
    C. Is impulsive and easily excited
    D. Is a good follower
    E. Is usually courteous to other people

10. A. Tries to bully and domineer over others
    B. Is quick to see valuable things in other people's suggestions
    C. Is hard to get to know
    D. Is boisterous
    E. Pleasant to talk with, but seldom initiates a conversation

WHO ARE THEY (PEERS' RATINGS)

Here are some descriptions of different kinds of boys and girls.
Read each description and ask yourself: "Which boys and girls in the

seventh grade are like this?" Under each description write the names of as many boys and girls as you can think of who are like this. You may choose any boys or girls in the seventh grade. To help you think about the boys and girls in this class, a list of their names has been prepared for you. Be sure to use both first and last names. Do *not* write your own name under any of the descriptions.

1. Who are the leaders? They are leaders in several things.
2. Who are the ones who break the rules?
3. Who are the boys and girls who usually come and go alone and stay by themselves most of the time, even though they aren't troublemakers?
4. Who are the boys and girls who are troublemakers?
5. Who are the most popular boys and girls?
6. Who are the boys and girls who seem quiet and happy?
7. Who are the boys and girls who make good suggestions when an activity or project is being planned?
8. Which boys and girls quarrel and get mad easily?
9. Who are the ones who are too shy to make friends easily? It is hard to get to know them.
10. In a group discussion or in planning an activity, who are the boys and girls who can take the suggestions and ideas of *others* and build on them?
11. Who are the boys and girls who seem to be against everything that is suggested—the gripers?
12. Who are the ones who get bothered and upset if they are called on to talk or to recite?
13. Who are the ones who come up with good ideas of interesting things to do?
14. Who are the bullies—the boys and girls who try to push others around?
15. Who are the boys and girls you run around with? (Do not name more than five.)

APPENDIX B

Interview Schedules

INTERVIEW WITH PARENTS AT TIME OF SCREENING

Identifying data—name of person interviewed, relationship to boy, birthdate of boy, school attending, name and birthdate of parents, home address, telephone number.

Description of family dwelling—number of rooms in dwelling unit, number of persons living here, sleeping facilities (Does boy have own room? If not, with whom does he share sleeping quarters?), monthly rental or payments, house or dwelling type. (Describe the physical characteristics of this dwelling unit, both inside and outside.)

Years at present address; last previous address; number of years in metropolitan Kansas City; head of household (mother, father, other—specify).

Marital, racial, or ethnic identification of parents and family; date of marriage.

Religious activity (father, mother—active, average, slight, none).

Education—Last grade attended—mother and father.

Occupation—Kind of work and work record—begin with present job and account for past five years for father and mother.

Per annum family income—check (less than $3000, $3000–4999, $5000–6999, $7000–8999, $9000–10,999).

If there is no father in home, is there a father substitute? (relation to boy; race or ethnic identification).

If no mother in home, is there a mother substitute? (relation to boy; race or ethnic identification).

What language is spoken in the home?

Name all siblings, age, sex, relation to boy, what are they doing?

Who else lives in home? (name and relationship to boy).

If a one-parent or broken home, how old was boy when this occurred?

With whom has boy lived besides his parents (for any period over three months)? (relationship, city, date [from–to], reason).

Questions to parents about boy

In what kind of occupation do you expect your boy ——— to be working when he grows up?

Tell me about the troubles you have had with ——— since he was a baby.

In the next four or five years we hope to work closely with you in ———'s interest. I am going to ask you if you have noticed some little things about ———. This information is confidential. I will check any characteristics you have noticed. (Check once and double check the most outstanding characteristics parent indicates.)

Behavior Checklist [examples]

A. Blames others for his difficulties, resents criticism, makes excuses, is secretive, crafty, sly, is suspicious, distrustful, rude, impudent, disobeys.

B. Is extremely self critical, worries, is moody, is unsuspecting, is easily hurt, sullen, has fears, is jealous, restless, nervous.

C. Seeks attention, boasts, is a show off.

D. Is seclusive, is shy, modest, daydreams, lacks self-confidence, is apathetic, puts things off.

E. Swears, argues, bosses, teases, is leader of gang, quarrels, fights, stubborn, domineers, does not conform, lies, has undesirable companions.

F. Stutters, depends on constant direction, is picked on, has few friends, dominated by others, easily fooled, easily led.

G. Plays truant, steals, destroys property, gambles, smokes, talks obscenely.

H. Is dull, slow, retarded, has poor work habits, wets clothes, sucks thumbs, bites nails, is a poor sport, is untidy, is often tardy.

Are there any other things you have noticed about your boy?

Can you tell me about ———'s social life when he is not in school? (Inquire about friends, group, gang, or club activities, work activities, etc.)

How do you feel about the school which your son attends? (Inquire about his school experience as fully as you are able.)

CHILD REARING PRACTICES OF PARENTS

Questions pertaining to discipline

Father and/or mother: Inquire about methods used, i.e., physical punishment, deprivation of privileges, discipline left to other parent, etc.

'(Explore consistency-inconsistency of discipline, and whether the
parent sees the boy's understanding of his discipline important. Describe in detail parental handling of misbehavior.)

Supervision by mother: Describe extent to which mother keeps an eye on
boy during hours he is not in school. If mother works, how does boy
spend his leisure time? Does he play unsupervised in the street? Is
he in the care of a responsible person? Describe in detail.

Questions pertaining to parents' affectional relationship to boy

Father: How much time does the father spend with boy? What is attitude of father toward boy? Give evidence to show it can be considered kindly, warm, indifferent, hostile, etc. How does boy get approval from father? In what way does the boy identify with his
father? During what periods of the child's life has the father been in
the home? Have there been father substitutes? What has their relationship been with the boy?

Same kind of evidence of relationship between boy and his mother: Include some detail of child's upbringing that will indicate positive or
negative attitudes of mother toward child in early training, in dealing with misbehavior, etc. Give specific details to substantiate attitude of mother which may be hostile, rejecting, overprotective, warm,
positive, etc.

Cohesiveness of Family: To what extent does the home environment of
the boy provide a feeling of security for him? Do the members of
the family constitute a group with some cohesiveness, with positive
relationship existing between members? Is it a broken home with
friction between various members? Describe relationship between
parents, evidence of quarreling, attitude of parents toward siblings as
compared to their attitude toward this boy. Include boy's relationship to siblings. What activities do members of the family participate
in together? Do they attend church together? What meals are eaten
together? Describe weekend activities such as trips to the park in
which the whole family participates.

RATING SCALE FOR SIXTEEN-YEAR-OLD INTERVIEW

(Modified for eighteen-year-old interview)

Note: On rating any of the various categories, where applicable,
"a" following the number designating the rating indicates attitude
expressed is quite evident and/or strong;
"b" indicates attitude is specifically focused upon individuals rather
than the school in general.
It is feasible that both an "a" and "b" could be employed in one
rating.

I. Attitudes toward school
   1. Hostile: Feels people at school are unfair and out to make it as tough as they can for him.
   2. Critical of the teachers, administrators, and school policies: Feels teachers don't teach the way they should and school policies, rules and regulations are too restrictive. (Differs from hostile in that there is less personal, individual animosity expressed.)
   3. Indifferent, shaded toward the positive: Seems to see going to school as just something that one does; no clear attitude expressed toward school personnel or policies.
   4. A favorable attitude is expressed toward school: Feels school people are doing their best and have the interests of their students at heart.

II. Attitude toward his education
   1. Intends to drop out: Sees little value in remaining in school or is a dropout.
   2. Uncertain as to whether he will remain in school: Has no clear view of his educational future.
   3. Wants to stay in school and finish: Is uncertain as to his being able to do this.
   4. Intends to stay in school: Sees advantages to doing this, which he can discuss effectively.

III. Work attitudes
   1. No interest or desire indicated for getting a job.
   2. Somewhat interested in a job, but shows little inclination to implement this with actively seeking work.
   3. Is interested in working, but is unrealistic concerning the types of job and the money paid for unskilled workers.
   4. Expresses interest in working or is working: Sees a job as opening doors to get the things he wants and to get ahead.

IV. Future vocational aspirations
   1. No plans for the future expressed: "I've never given it much thought," is typical response.
   2. Vague and general: These aspirations are poorly defined, indicating that little thought had been given to the future.
   3. Has fairly definite ideas but unrealistic aspirations and/or expectations: States he wants to become a professional of some type requiring years of training and certain kinds of ability; or technical work also requiring extensive preparation. May also have realistic aspirations but unrealistic expectations concerning the wages he will earn and the hours he will work.

4. Realistic aspirations: May know what he wants and realizes how he can get it, i.e., realizes the requirements of his aspirations. He may not have definite plans but weighing realistic alternatives toward decision making.

V. Preparation for work career. Training sources perceived as important in preparing for adult work. 1. None indicated. 2. Armed services. 3. Trade schools. 4. Apprenticeship. 5. Work experience. 6. High school. 7. College.

VI. Broken home (Who is in the home?)

1. Parental surrogates (nonrelated, or aunts, uncles, sisters, grandparents, etc.).
2. Father only.
3. Mother only.
4. One natural parent and parental surrogate.
5. Doesn't apply. (Both natural parents in home at the time of sixteen-year-old interview)
6. Doesn't apply. (Boy living on own)

VII. Attitude toward parent or parental surrogate
"m" mother or mother surrogate.
"f" father or father surrogate.

1. Negative and/or hostile attitudes: Expresses resentment toward parent. Shows derogatory attitude and lack of respect. May express fear of parent, and in general feels that parent is not out to help him. May want to leave home because of his parent.
2. Indifference: Has little to say about parent. May express views that home is just a place to eat and sleep. May show indifference by knowing very little about parental activities. Very little involvement with parent. Parent not important in his everyday living or in planning for the future.
3. Ambivalent: Boy expresses both negative and positive feelings toward parent, i.e., mixed emotions. May appear hostile and resentful in attitudes concerning certain aspects of his relationship but in other aspects quite positive.
4. Positive attitude toward parent: Expresses positive feelings about parent. Indicates a firm positive relationship.

VIII. Heterosexual interests—interest in girls

1. No interest in girls: Denies dating or having an interest in doing so.
2. Expresses some interest: Likes girls, but other things are more important at present time. Expects to date within a year or two.
3. Considerable interest in girls: May express desire to date and to be involved with girls. May be dating frequently or for

various reasons not dating. May show considerable interest in girls but not dating because of money lack, shyness, fear, etc.

IX. Sexual experience

0. Not given.
1. Acknowledges sex experience.
   (a) Married.
2. Denies sex experience.

X. Relationships with girls

0. Not indicated.
1. Exploits girls without respect.
2. Casual relationship with girls.
3. Responsible relationship with one girl.

XI. Attitude of Work-Study boys toward the program

0. Doesn't apply.
1. Negative and/or hostile feelings toward program.
   "P" directed mainly toward instructional personnel.
   "G" directed mainly toward the program in general.
2. Essentially neutral. Very little to say for or against program.
3. Feels positive toward Work-Study Program.

XII. Delinquency

1. Acknowledges police contacts both in past and present.
   (a) Learned lesson—will not repeat.
2. Acknowledges current police contacts.
   (a) Learned lesson—will not repeat.
3. Acknowledges police contacts in past, but denies current or recent contacts.
   (a) Learned lesson—will not repeat.
4. Denies either past or present contacts with police.

XIII. Attitude toward police authority

0. Not covered.
1. Negative: May be hostile—feelings of being unjustly treated or being hounded; ridiculing police by telling how they can be outsmarted; telling of police brutality, etc. (may be fear); feeling of being under surveillance (of being limited in one's legitimate pursuits).
2. Indifferent: Has little to say about police when asked. Seems to see police contacts as a part of life, not a particular problem, just one to live with.
3. Ambivalent: Expresses both negative and positive feelings. May point up how police are needed to protect people but then criticizes the police for the way in which they treat teen-agers, etc. Both hostile feelings and positive attitudes are the identifying features.

4. Positive: Expresses respect for the police in general. If critical, this is directed toward an individual policeman, but the general attitude is one of healthy respect for police and the job they have to do.

APPENDIX C

Criteria for Identifying Late Adolescent Adjustment Subgroups

Each youth was assigned a quantitative value from 1 to 4 or 5 on several dimensions in each of three areas of adjustment. The three areas were delinquency and crime, school, and work. A value of 1 represented negative or unfavorable adjustment; values of 4 and in some cases 5 represented positive or favorable adjustment. Where the data permitted, median and quartile (Q) values for the group as a whole were used to establish the rating values assigned a given youth. The three areas rated and the dimensions rated were:

A. Delinquency and Crime
    I. Police arrests during late adolescence:
        1. Number of arrests—Q3 or above.
        2. Number of arrests—Between median and Q3.
        3. Number of arrests—Between Q1 and median.
        4. Number of arrests—Below Q1.
        5. Number of arrests—None.

    II. Types of arrests (seriousness of charges):
        1. All arrests were for charges involving acts legally defined as felonies.

      2. One-half or more were defined as felonies.

      3. Less than half were defined as felonies.

      4. None were felonies.

      5. No arrests of any type.

III. Institutional confinements or detentions:

      1. One or more court commitments to intermediary reformatory or prison.

      2. Commitment to jail or county farm.

      3. Jail detention only.

      4. No detention or commitment.

B. School Adjustment: By their seventeenth birthdays, research youths who remained in school were in their third or fourth year of high school and in their fourth or fifth year (eighth grade included) of the Work-Study Program. A number of youths had dropped out of school by age seventeen or dropped out during their seventeenth or eighteenth year.

I. School status during late adolescence:

      1. Early high school dropout—before age seventeen and before completing three years of high school.

      2. High school dropout during late adolescent period and before completing fourth year of high school.

      3. In school during late adolescent period, that is, during fourth year of high school, but did not graduate during this period.

      4. Graduated during the late adolescent period or received a high school certificate.

II. Grade point average during late adolescent school enrollment: (1.0 = failure; 3.0 = average; 5.0 = excellent)

      1. Failure (1.0–1.4).

      2. Inferior (1.5–2.4).

      3. Average (2.5–3.4).

      4. Above average (3.5+).

III. Ratings by teachers during late adolescence of three best and three poorest pupils in class: These ratings were based on a spring survey of all classrooms of the Kansas City school system in which research youth were involved. This included all control youths in school their seventeenth year as well as experimental youths who left the Work-Study Program and enrolled in the regular high school curriculum. It also included a few experimental youths who, after successful completion of Work-Study, enrolled in the regular high school curriculum, ostensibly to earn a high school diploma. In this survey, teachers were requested to identify the three poorest and the three best students in their classes using specific criteria. Teachers did not know who control youths in their classes were. While the chances were somewhat greater that experimental youths were known, this was considered of minimal importance, since this group was scattered in several Kansas City high schools, that is, most were in other than the original high school at time of survey.

1. Identified by three or more teachers as among three of poorest boys in class—by none as best.
2. Identified by two teachers as poorest—by none as best.
3. Identified by teachers both as poorest and as best.
4. Identified by teachers as best—by none as poorest.

IV. Absences from school during late adolescence (Percentages based on absences for school population.):
1. Days absent—Q3 and above.
2. Days absent—Between median and Q3.
3. Days absent—Between Q1 and median.
4. Days absent—Q1 and less.

V. Ratings by teachers of personal adjustment: Students were rated on work habits, responsibility, self-control, and getting along together. Ratings assigned (Teachers' ratings averaged.):
1. Unsatisfactory (1.0–1.4).
2. Below average (1.5–2.4).
3. Average (2.5–3.4).
4. Above average (3.5+).

C. Work Adjustment:

I. Employment coordinators' ratings of experimental youth's adjustment in paid work: Two sets of ratings covered the late adolescent period. One set was made when most experimental youth were between 17.3 and 17.6 years of age. The second set was obtained when boys were between 17.6 and 18.6 years of age. These ratings were based on employment coordinators' records on youths' employment, which included number and type of jobs held, total time and average amounts of time on each job, and reports from employers concerning punctuality, job responsibility and initiative, getting along with others and reasons for job terminations.

0. No employment during period covered.
1. Unsatisfactory progress.
2. Relatively satisfactory progress.
3. Satisfactory adjustment and progress.

II. Ratings based on late adolescent interviews: These interviews included obtaining a work history of the late adolescent period. At the time of these interviews most youth were between 17.6 and 18.6 years of age. For the control group these interview data were the primary source for ratings of work adjustment.

0. No employment.

1. Occasional part-time jobs briefly held—termination usually by being fired or quitting without notice. Little initiative or interest in obtaining work.

2. One or more full-time jobs held for several weeks or months. Job attitudes appear somewhat immature— quits without notice and without prospects for employment. Quits for apparently minor reasons and on sudden impulse. Somewhat unrealistic expectations about wages and wage increases. Youths rated in this category considered to be demonstrating fairly typical adolescent behavior.

3. Has a job and works steadily at it. Work record indicates that job terminations are usually by quitting with notice in order to move into a job better in pay, working conditions, or advancement possibilities; discusses work in mature and realistic way. Sees work as important and doing a good job as the way to get ahead.

In the actual assignment of youths to late adolescent adjustment categories, certain ratings were given priority since they were found to be significantly associated with rating values in other adjustment areas. For example, most youths with institutional records during late adolescence did not show favorable ratings in work or school adjustment. The exceptions to this finding were placed in the erratic adjustment type. The others were assigned to the seriously maladaptive subgroup. Likewise, most youths with favorable ratings in work adjustment did not have serious police records or records of being institutionalized, although a few in this group did; these few were also assigned to the erratic subgroup. Many youths with favorable work adjustment ratings had unfavorable ratings of school adjustment. Most of these youths were assigned to the work adaptive group. Youths who graduated or received high school certificates during late adolescence were assigned to the school adaptive category unless they had records of serious police offenses or institutional commitments. In that event they were placed in the erratic subgroup. If a youth was rated favorably in both work and school adjustment, he was assigned to the school adaptive subgroup if he graduated or received a high school certificate. If he had not completed high school during late adolescence but had remained in school, relative success in school and work was the basis for assignment to either the work adaptive or the school adaptive category.

Assignments to the marginal adjustment group were made where youths dropping out of high school before age seventeen had minimal work experience, and, when employed, had unfavorable work adjustment. Included in this group were youths with police records during late adolescence and in some cases with records of brief jail confinements. Youths with institutional commitments, however, were excluded. Within each late adolescent adjustment, of course, were individual patterns of ratings which varied in the extent to which they approximated the extreme form of the adjustment type to which they are assigned.

II. To what extent did youths in the research sample fit into the five types of late adolescent adjustment?

Of the total group of four hundred youth, 15 per cent were not assigned to adjustment categories because of inadequate information. Of the 341 youth who were assigned to adjustment subgroups, 63 per cent appeared to be identified reliably. The seriously maladaptive and school adaptive subgroups were easily identified among both control and experimental youths because indices of adjustment in these areas were available and relatively clear cut. Among experimental youths, work adaptive adjustment was also relatively easily identifiable. For control youths, however, information concerning work experience and work adjustment came from self-reports in the late adolescent interviews, and indices of work adjustment had to be derived primarily from this source. Therefore, these ratings and the assignment to an adjustment type were somewhat less reliable. However, many of these self-reports appeared to be fairly straightforward accounts of work experience and work attitudes, and so probably more than 68 per cent of all assignments were reliable. Identifying marginal and erratic adjustments was somewhat more difficult, although again with experimental youths the process was easier because of the greater amount of information available about them.

Index